PRAISE FOR C PEOPLE THRO... ORGANIZATIONAL CHANGE

'Every coaching client is a person undergoing change–even if they are not fully aware of how radical that change is. The role of coach is evolving from coaching individuals to coaching individuals within their systems, to coaching the systems themselves. A substantial change-related toolkit is essential for coaches and that's what this book provides.'
Professor David Clutterbuck, Practice Lead at Coaching and Mentoring International Ltd, and Practice Lead at David Clutterbuck Partnership

'If you care deeply about your organization and your people, then put this book on your reading list and get to it quickly! Amy and Sue hold your hand through the journey, planning for today and ensuring benefits tomorrow with this no-nonsense guide to delivering organizational change through coaching.'
Hina Shavdia, Head of Change, AXIS Capital

'Coaching generates engagement, puts responsibility and authority with others and enables high performance. It's fundamental to successful change. This comprehensive and profound book makes this case and gives the reader the practical directions to get on with the job. It will be a bible and handbook for anyone concerned with delivering large scale change.'
Myles Downey, leader, performance coach and author of *Effective Modern Coaching, Effective Coaching and Enabling Genius*

'Organizational Change is all about producing benefits and you can't do this without individual change. This book brings humanity, care and respect to those experiencing organizational change through the use of coaching in a way most organizational change books have not. It's about time change was made more humane in organizations and this is the book to start the journey.'
Ketan Patel, Founder, Change Reaction, and UK Co-lead, Change Management Institute

'The world needs more people that combine organizational, team and individual change. Sue Noble and Amy Tarrant, provide a very practical and informative book to help those facilitating organizational change understand how they can utilize coaching to support the process.'

Professor Peter Hawkins, Chairman, Renewal Associates

'This is it... a practical and thoughtful formula for organizational advancement and impact! It's the first business-related book that I have read during my 40-year career that is truly a page-turner. It seamlessly integrates two timely, timeless and must-master success topics–coaching people and change. Through relevant and global examples, strategies and use-them-now tools, the authors expanded my mindset and toolkit around change and continuous improvement today. By giving us the What? So what? and Now What? regarding the drivers, opportunities and challenges around change, it's a blueprint for engagement and action. It's an essential read for advancing companies that want to leverage their human capital technology and build for sustainable change.'

Robin Peppe Sterneck, President of Sterneck Capital Management and Co-Facilitator of the Emerging Leaders programme at Central Exchange

'*Coaching People Through Organizational Change* impressively uses the brain science of Emergenetics® as a vehicle to more effectively navigate change. This connection, lucidly explained, is the gap that this book fills in the workplace. It is clear, pragmatic and therefore powerful in helping people to be more effective at work.'

David Sales, Director, Emergenetics UK

Coaching People through Organizational Change

Practical tools to support employees
through business transformation

Sue Noble and Amy Tarrant

KoganPage

Publisher's note

Every possible effort has been made to ensure that the information contained in this book is accurate at the time of going to press, and the publishers and authors cannot accept responsibility for any errors or omissions, however caused. No responsibility for loss or damage occasioned to any person acting, or refraining from action, as a result of the material in this publication can be accepted by the editor, the publisher or the author.

First published in Great Britain and the United States in 2022 by Kogan Page Limited

2nd Floor, 45 Gee Street
London
EC1V 3RS
United Kingdom

8 W 38th Street, Suite 902
New York, NY 10018
USA

4737/23 Ansari Road
Daryaganj
New Delhi 110002
India

www.koganpage.com

Kogan Page books are printed on paper from sustainable forests.

ISBNs

Hardback   978 1 3986 0704 0
Paperback 978 1 3986 0702 6
Ebook   978 1 3986 0703 3

British Library Cataloguing-in-Publication Data

A CIP record for this book is available from the British Library.

Library of Congress Cataloging-in-Publication Data

Names: Noble, Sue, author. | Tarrant, Amy, author.
Title: Coaching people through organizational change : practical tools to
    support employees through business transformation / Sue Noble and Amy
    Tarrant.
Description: New York, NY : Kogan Page, 2022. | Includes bibliographical
    references and index.
Identifiers: LCCN 2022024165 (print) | LCCN 2022024166 (ebook) | ISBN
    9781398607040 (hardback) | ISBN 9781398607026 (paperback) | ISBN
    9781398607033 (ebook)
Subjects: LCSH: Organizational change. | Executive coaching.
Classification: LCC HD58.8 .N62 2022 (print) | LCC HD58.8 (ebook) | DDC
    658.4/06–dc23/eng/20220610
LC record available at https://lccn.loc.gov/2022024165
LC ebook record available at https://lccn.loc.gov/2022024166

Typeset by Integra Software Services, Pondicherry
Print production managed by Jellyfish
Printed and bound by CPI Group (UK) Ltd, Croydon CR0 4YY

CONTENTS

12   Techniques to coach people through change 212

FOREWORD

Change only happens if we change attitudes, which lead to changes in behaviour. For someone to change their attitude, they must see their situation in a new light, they have to step away from their current assumptions and be willing to explore alternatives. Coaching is not telling, it is not explaining, it is a process of listening as someone works through these new viewpoints. Talented coaches guide the process through questioning, playback of what they have heard, more listening, more questioning and playback until the other person has ordered their thoughts, had new insight and is ready to act.

Effective coaching conversations don't happen by accident. Without a framework of ideas, techniques and processes to follow, you will have a conversation, which might be informative, it might be interesting, and it might even lead to a solution. But a structured approach dramatically increases the chance that your coaching will make a worthwhile difference.

To write this foreword, I needed to step back and think what coaching means to me, and where it fits with all the skills we need for effective change. The phrase that I kept coming back to is "unconditional positive regard", which Carl Rogers identified as one of the three steps of personal growth, along with authenticity and empathy. Unconditional means not entering a conversation with conditions, it requires us to stay out of judgement even though our brains are screaming at us to emotionally label what we are hearing – "that is wrong", "that is stupid", "my idea is much better than that!"

In any coaching situation, we are battling this automatic response to judge. Turning it off is very difficult, but we can learn to feed our response with curiosity and interest in what the other person is saying to us. We can bring to mind phrases including "that's different!", "I hadn't thought of that", "that is a new perspective". The techniques in this book will help you find your way of listening without overlaying your values onto what is being said.

Positivity is a core foundation to effective coaching. We are more able to identify the negatives of a situation and to hold onto these negative thoughts more strongly than the positives. As a coach, you need to be able to share alternative views, and the most common alternative you will be called upon to share is a positive view of the situation. Looking at an issue for what it offers, not what it threatens. Being positive is not about ignoring the problems, it is about sharing a different view, where learning, improvements and opportunities can be found from what appears on the surface to be failure. This positivity is the foundation of resilience, which I believe is a key outcome of coaching. As a coach, you are helping your coachee to keep going despite the setbacks, to develop persistence in the face of obstacles.

This book will help you learn to coach, by debating a range of alternative actions, identifying and planning what happens next. You will find guidance on different ways to structure your coaching conversations, with examples that bring the ideas to life. If you are going to invest time in reading this (or any other business book), remember that on every page you must ask yourself "how would I do that?" and "what parts of this idea are relevant to my situation?" A successful outcome from reading the following pages is that you design and practise your approach to coaching. This is a worthwhile investment in yourself and your development, because coaching is part of life – work life and home life.

Melanie Franklin

PREFACE

The primary purpose of this book is to explore the ways in which a coaching toolkit can support and enable the delivery of organizational change. Many books have been written on the subject of organizational change and there is a similarly high number of coaching guides available. However, there are no books which specifically explore the benefits that applying the coach's skillset to organizational change challenges has to offer.

Given that many of the barriers to change delivery are behavioural, psychology and understanding human behaviour play a significant role in organizational change. Similarly, the coaches' toolkit harnesses a broad cross-section of psychological tools, techniques and frameworks, leading the two disciplines to overlap in a way that would add significant value to change practitioners everywhere.

Organizations and their employees face a continuous cycle of change. Businesses are re-structured; software is replaced and firms are reducing operating costs by investing in areas such as offshoring, digitalization and automation. When this book was conceived in late 2019, COVID-19 had not yet arrived in our lives. The virus has had a significant impact on the way many of us work, crucially, not being able to interact with people face-to-face has had a deep impact on the way organizational change is planned and delivered. In addition, the economic damage wrought by the virus will make organisational change more prevalent and more urgent than ever, with many small and medium-sized firms trying to survive and larger organisations seeking to become more efficient.

There are three target readerships for this book. As a primary audience, we want to share with change practitioners the ways in which many of their day-to-day challenges could be mitigated using skills traditionally linked to coaching. The secondary audience are coaches who wish to understand more about how their existing skills could be deployed in a change setting. However, the book is not aimed at qualified and experienced coaches wishing to learn more about coaching as it stands alone. The third target readerships are students of organizational change who wish to carry out wider reading on the topic and a more 'hands-on' guide than the traditional academic texts offer.

The book is organised into a series of commonplace change challenges, which have been selected based on research conducted with a cross-section of change practitioners. Each chapter addresses a new challenge, split into two sections. The first section identifies the nature of the challenge and outlines a number of traditional organizational change tools to overcome the challenge. The second section introduces coaching skills that could also be applied to the challenge.

In reality, we are not suggesting the user should choose either a traditional change tool, nor solely a coaching method. For optimum effect, we see the two approaches being blended and deployed simultaneously and interchangeably. This is where the true benefit of these complementary skill sets lies.

ACKNOWLEDGEMENTS

Amy

The idea for this book would never have got off the ground if I had not met Sue at an event in 2019. We both recognized the synergy between our respective professions and decided to write an exploratory article on ambiguity. I never could have predicted that two years later that would have resulted in an entire book!

I also have Sue to thank for introducing me to the multi-talented Suzie Grogan, author and editor extraordinaire. Not only did she edit the very early versions of the book, she also provided invaluable input to the submission process.

Similar thanks goes to Lara Morgenstern, who helped me edit later versions of the book when work commitments and editorial deadlines collided.

I am very grateful to Lucy Carter from Kogan Page for accepting our book proposal and Anne-Marie Heeney for guiding us through the editorial and publication process.

My special thanks will always go to Melanie Franklin and Ketan Patel who, through the Change Management Institute, have provided encouragement, information and suggestions.

On that note, many people kindly responded to the survey we conducted for this book, most of whom are members of the Change Management Institute and have been very generous with their time. In a similar vein, my thanks go to Timothy Galpin and Aubrey Mendelow, whose Change Pyramid and Stakeholder Matrix respectively I have reproduced in this book with their kind permission.

My thanks also go to Suneeta Padda of Padda Consulting for her input and advice on all things regulation and compliance.

I could not compile this list without mentioning my AXIS family, namely Hina Shavdia, Ben White, Stuart Taylor and Toby Ducker, for their encouragement and understanding as I came up against professional and book deadlines. Signed copies await!

Similarly, my friends deserve my thanks for always nodding and smiling in the right places when I talk about the book.

My family has always supported me in my many projects and plans – thank you Jacquie Tarrant, Lucy Tarrant and Tilly Storey for having my back.

Last and by far the most I want to thank my husband, Steve Clewer, whose steady supply of tea, patience and love have enabled me to achieve far more than I ever would have alone.

Sue

Lockdown gave me the impetus I needed to make a start on writing this book. The process has been enjoyable, challenging and also fulfilling. I have learnt so much from so many inspiring people. Those I have mentioned below have all made this amazing journey possible. My apologies for those I have inadvertently missed.

I would like to say a personal thank you to Sarah Boorman, who introduced me to Amy Tarrant and without this introduction, it is unlikely that this book would have been written.

Likewise, my sincere thanks goes out to my co-author, Amy, who also shared my belief that we had something to offer in writing. Our shared experiences evolved over time and together we have successfully managed to combine our ideas and our different writing styles. Thank you Amy for your patience and guidance and expertise on structure and writing style.

A special thank you goes to my friend of 30 years, Suzie Grogan, a successful author in her own right and who kindly offered to help us with editing and proof-reading. Suzie has providing me with sound advice on wording, grammar and the importance of crisp and succinct writing. I am eternally grateful for Suzie's support and guidance on how to write a winning proposal and get the attention of Kogan Page. Suzie has continued to be a great support and inspiration for me.

I would also like to thank Lucy Carter from Kogan Page for accepting our proposal and Anne-Marie Heeney for her patience, guidance and different perspectives on how to tweak and improve my work and providing useful and gentle feedback when I needed it.

Thanks also go out to David Sales and Kylie Seaman from Emergenetics® UK, who provided invaluable support and guidance on writing the chapters on how Emergenetics impacts on the world of change and coaching.

I have a wonderful network of associates who have become good friends over time and this includes my group coaching supervision network and my fellow associate coach and trainers. There are too many people to mention here but a special thanks goes to Julie Pelych, Stewart Beamont and Sarah Law, whose enthusiasm for what I was writing helped to inspire me even further and continue adapting my writing based on their own experience of working within global organizations experiencing change.

A big thank you goes out to Mary Cross, my friend and fellow coach and supervisor who gracefully and enthusiastically agreed to peer review one of my chapters when I had concerns about the content. Her valuable experience as a coach and sharing her ideas enabled me to refine my writing.

I would also like to acknowledge all of those who liked, commented and who lifted my spirits with their kind words of congratulations and support, sadly too many to personally mention here, when I shared the proposed Kogan Page front cover of our book on LinkedIn.

There have been many people, including learners, delegates, coaching clients, supervisees and organizational clients, who listened patiently to my ideas for this book over the course of my writing, I would like to thank you all for your kind words of enthusiasm and wonderment at the thought of actually writing a book which I hope has inspired them. My recommendation to you would be to just do it! Everyone has a book to write.

Finally, my love and thanks goes to David, my husband who has been with me all the way on my writing journey, encouraging and having confidence and pride in me. He has listened patiently to my ideas for each chapter, shared his thoughts and ideas, and generally been a supportive listening ear and sounding board on our regular morning walks along the beach where we live. The opportunity to talk, think, reflect and share ideas has now become part of our routine and therapy. His support and pride in me has helped me to continue and consider other ideas for writing. Thank you – always.

ABOUT THE AUTHORS

Amy Tarrant has been delivering organizational change for 15 years, primarily in the insurance sector. Most recently she led the project delivery team for a London Market insurer.

Although Amy's professional life has been heavily focussed on project and programme delivery, she has been drawn to the discipline of change management. She joined the Change Management Institute in 2015 and in 2017 founded its South East Chapter. Over time, she started to recognise the many synergies between coaching and change, leading her to found the Change Management Institute's Coaching Special Interest Group.

Amy holds a BA in Modern Languages from the University of Salford, an MBA from Durham University, and a Bachelor of Laws from the Open University. She is currently studying for a Master of Laws at Queen Mary University.

Amy is also a Trustee for the Brighton Yoga Foundation, taking the lead on fundraising to enable vital outreach work in the community.

Amy lives in Sussex with her husband, Steve, and dog, Molly.

Sue Noble is owner and Director of Noble Learning Ltd, a training and coaching organization specializing in all things coaching and mentoring and people-centred leadership development. Noble Learning is a recognized provider with Chartered Management Institute (CMI). She works with private and public sector organizations supporting them to embed a coaching and mentoring culture and supporting learners with supervision. Sue has membership with CMI, European Mentoring and Coaching Council (EMCC) and Henley Business School. Sue holds a Level 7 qualification in Executive Coaching, a diploma in Coaching Supervision and in April 2022 achieved her Senior Coach Practitioner and Coach Supervisor accreditation with EMCC.

Over the years, coaching and training has brought Sue into contact with a variety of people who are invested in self- and professional development and who have recognized that, in order to get to where they want to be, change is essential. Coaching only really works if the client is motivated, has the energy to change and is ready to move on in their journey.

Sue lives in Sussex with her husband, Dave, and Betty the dog. They have one daughter and two granddaughters.

Sue and Amy connected at a Change Management Institute event in 2018, quickly realizing the extent to which their skillset overlapped and the significant benefit there would be in blending these skillsets to deliver successful, long-term change. Amy subsequently invited Sue to talk at one of the Change Management Institute's events. This led to many conversations on the synergy between the two disciplines and the relevance coaching can have for change practitioners.

They recognized that, although there were plenty of books on Change and many books on the subject of Coaching, there seemed to be very few which attempted to fuse the two subjects. Sue and Amy wanted to write a book which was not aimed purely at experienced coaches, but which encouraged non-coaches and change practitioners to embrace the many coaching tools and techniques that can help deliver lasting change.

Organizational change in context 01

Change is inevitable – except from a vending machine.

ROBERT C GALLAGHER

Introduction

This book is about organizational change, its key causes, the primary challenges it creates and how they can be overcome. However, before doing so, it is important to appreciate the wider context for the volume and complexity of change that today's organizations are faced with.

In this chapter we will consider:

- Change on a global level and its key causes.
- Organizational change and its drivers.
- Why organizational change can be problematic.
- How organizational change is delivered.
- How a change team is organized.

Global trends and change

The world is changing faster than ever and to provide the context for organizational change, it is important to understand change more broadly. In his 2005 book, *The World Is Flat*, Thomas Friedman noted that even the rate of change we are experiencing is greater than ever before 'the speed and breadth with which it is taking hold… is happening at warp speed and directly or indirectly touching a lot more people on the planet at once.

The faster and broader this transition to a new era, the more likely is the potential of disruption.' This observation provides the ideal platform from which to survey the macro causes of change.

The environment

Natural disasters such as flooding, forest fires and drought are linked to climate change and are increasingly leading people to change their habits. Many travellers are rejecting high-polluting air travel, while train travel and 'staycations' are on the rise as people become more aware of their carbon footprint. For example, according to PolicyAdvice (Kopestinsky, 2021), a US-based insurance consultancy, global sales of electric vehicles increased by 64 per cent from 3.4 million in 2018 to 5.6 million in 2021, representing 3 per cent of global car sales. Electric vehicle adoption will continue to grow and by 2025 should reach 10 per cent of global passenger vehicle sales, growing to about 28 per cent in 2030 and 58 per cent by 2040.

Investment firms are also getting in on the act and according to J P Morgan (2020), Environmental, Social and Governance (ESG) funds increased by 10 per cent between December 2018 and May 2020 with two new ESG funds launched by an asset management firm every day. This is set to increase as a result of the Covid-19 pandemic.

Consumers have also made the link between climate change and the consumption of animal products. According to global marketing firm Mintel (2020), sales of meat-free foods in the UK went from £582 million to £816 million between 2014 and 2019 and major supermarkets have responded to this demand by increasing their range of meat-free products. For example, Tesco, the UK's largest supermarket by market share, introduced its Plant Chef range in 2019, which boosted their plant-based offering from 32 to 300, and a brand spokesperson has stated that it is this vegan range that will fuel the company's future growth. This desire to avoid animal products extends to other consumer goods such as clothing and cosmetics. Mintel reports that new cruelty-free and vegan cosmetics launches saw a 175 per cent increase between 2013 and 2019 and the industry has a projected growth rate of 6.5 per cent over the next four years. Unilever has set itself a target making the remaining 20 per cent of its products vegan by 2021 and a senior executive there reported that 'vegan' is the number one search term on its website, signalling the level of interest in the topic and underscoring the extent to which mass consumer behaviour and demand drive change in brands' behaviour.

Social justice

Global social justice movements such as Black Lives Matter and Me Too have led to significant social change in the last few years. Although the Black Lives Matter movement started in America in 2013 in protest at police brutality against the black population in general, it gained global traction following the murder of George Floyd by a police officer in Minneapolis in May 2020. These movements, among others, have created a groundswell of support for a fairer society, which in turn has forced many corporate brands to sharpen their ethical credentials. This has led to firms taking steps to reassure consumers and employees of their social responsibility, for example by developing and communicating Diversity and Inclusion (D&I) agendas.

Technology

Automation is nothing new: since the Industrial Revolution, workers have been 'replaced' by machines. The use of robots in vehicle manufacture to perform simple and repetitive tasks became increasingly common in the 1970s, leading to increased output and cost maintenance. In the 1980s, computers became sufficiently commonplace in the workplace that significant administrative work was eliminated. Since the eCommerce revolution, retailers and financial services organizations have moved services online, reducing the need for staffed high street branches and the costly overheads they bring. More recently, Artificial Intelligence and Robotic Process Automation (RPA) have brought fresh disruption to many industries, including manufacturing and financial services.

These are just some of the global trends that are driving change and the list is by no means exhaustive. Although the world around us is always changing, the pace of change is speeding up and organizations will be forced to transform at the same speed to guarantee they remain relevant to consumers. Change is changing, and organizations ignore this at their peril. We will return to these themes later in the chapter, as we discuss organizational change, what causes it and how firms can respond.

Organizational change

The most comprehensive definition of organizational change comes from Oreg, By and Michel (2013) as being 'any adjustment or alteration in an organization that has the potential to influence the organization's stakeholders' physical or psychological experience'. This is a far cry from the first documented explanation by Kurt Lewin's 1947 'Change as Three Steps' (CATS) model. Lewin was a German-American psychologist and is recognized as one of the modern pioneers of social, organizational and applied psychology in the US. His CATS model distils organizational change down to three components, which take place chronologically – unfreeze, change and refreeze:

- Unfreeze – refers to stopping existing behaviours, such as the use of a system or a process that is being followed.

- Change – relates to the transition period, in which facilitation activity such as communication and training take place to bring about change.

- Refreeze – the implementation and embedding of the new normal, such as the new system or process.

However, as the discipline of organizational change has evolved, the CATS model has been criticized for its over-simplified interpretation. Marshak and Heracleous (2004) point out what any seasoned change practitioner knows – that the model is inappropriate 'for the rapid pace of change at the beginning of the 21st century', which demands more flexibility and adaptation than Lewin could have predicted in 1947. The model also overlooks the fact that employees impacted by change are not inanimate objects to be frozen and unfrozen but instead are active participants to be engaged (Buchanan, 2003). Finally, the model's linear and chronological nature is not a realistic reflection of the complexities of modern organizational change.

Nonetheless, as an introductory explanation of change, Lewin's model has two key advantages:

1 Its simplicity provides a convenient illustration to less experienced practitioners.

2 As the 'original' change model, it provided a foundation from which many subsequent models and theories have evolved (see References).

A word about terminology

The terms organizational change and organizational transformation are often used interchangeably, which is incorrect. The clearest description is from Ron Ashkenas in his 2015 *Harvard Business Review* paper, 'We still don't know the difference between change and transformation':

- 'Change' refers to finite initiatives that are focussed on implementing a defined change to ways of working.
- 'Transformation' covers a portfolio of change initiatives aimed at reinventing the organization and its business or operating model. As a result, transformation is less predictable and more experimental than change.

Throughout this book we will refer to both organizational change and organizational transformation because both concepts can benefit equally from blending change and coaching skillsets in their delivery.

What causes organizational change?

In a 2021 study by the Human Capital Institute (HCI), 77 per cent of the 432 respondents reported that their organization was in a state of constant change. In this section we will consider the various causes and drivers of organizational change.

In truth, many firms are highly reactive, waiting for something to break down, become obsolete or fail before addressing the problem. Others are more proactive and strategic, scanning the horizon and pre-empting events and triggers for change. For the latter group of firms, there are tried and tested tools which provide a framework to brainstorm, define and prioritize potential drivers of change, the most common being PESTLE and SWOT. The objective here is not to unpack the efficacy of these strategic tools, which goes beyond the scope of this book, but to illustrate how they can be used to identify events or factors which may act as a catalyst for organizational change.

PESTLE

Sometimes known as PESTEL, this strategic tool provides six categories of external influences – Political, Economic, Social, Technological, Legal and Regulatory and Environmental. This framework helps to focus thinking and generate ideas in a structured way. It is most effective if carried out with a cross-functional team of managers and leaders to ensure a wide range of external factors are considered.

SWOT

An acronym for Strengths, Weaknesses, Opportunities and Threats, this tool can be used in tandem with PESTLE but differs as it is half internally focussed (Strengths and Weaknesses) and half externally (Opportunities and Threats).

The output from these exercises can be used to inform a 'pipeline' of change activity. Here are some examples of the change initiatives that a financial services organization might decide to initiate as a result of its SWOT and PESTLE findings.

PESTLE

Political

Example: The UK's decision to leave the European Union (EU) (implemented in January 2021) means the removal of 'passporting', which allowed companies to provide financial services, trade funds and open branches in the EU with minimal prior authorization.

Resulting change: Establish a new legal entity in an EU member state, for example Belgium or Luxembourg.

Economic

Example: Increases to corporation tax or Value Added Tax may cause a firm to move its headquarters to a country with a more benign tax regime.

Resulting change: Change legal entities and staff location.

Social

Example: Demographic trends such as a growing middle class in developing countries bring attractive growth opportunities.

Resulting change: Acquire in the target country or enter into a joint venture with a local firm (see Chapter 2).

Technological

Example: The digital revolution has resulted in faster, more flexible and more user-friendly systems (see Chapter 2). Cybercrime is becoming increasingly sophisticated.

Resulting change: Implement digital solutions to build competitive advantage over their peers.

Environmental

Example: Climate change is causing extreme weather such as floods and wildfires. Consumers expect companies to minimize their carbon footprint.

Resulting change: Introduce video-calling and collaboration tools to reduce the amount of business travel required.

Legal

Example: New legislation is designed to protect consumers from poor corporate conduct, for example Solvency II or BASEL III (see Chapter 2).

Resulting change: Re-design processes and produce additional reports to evidence compliance.

SWOT

Strength

Driver: The company has grown in recent years and is ready to expand.

Resulting change initiative: Open a new branch in the same country or enter a new market.

Weakness

Driver: There is an unprofitable product in the portfolio.

Resulting change initiative: Invest in product development or divest it.

Opportunity

Driver: Increased accuracy of Artificial Intelligence.

Resulting change initiative: Automate tasks carried out by employees in high-salary countries.

Threat

Driver: Start-up firms, for example 'challenger' banks, enter the market quickly and client switching costs are low.

Resulting change initiative: Invest in customer retention tools such as self-service portals or free financial advice.

This is an overview of the key drivers for organizational change and how companies can take steps to be better prepared for them.

Why can change be problematic?

Different people react to change in different ways, and it is a fallacy to state that all employees dislike change. However, looking at some of these examples of change activities, it is obvious why people might react negatively. For example, team members often dislike using a new system as it involves re-training and giving up specialist knowledge accumulated over many years. Similarly, it is understandable that an event as significant as an acquisition or company restructure leads to fear and anxiety, given the risk (or at least perceived risk) of job losses.

Figure 1.1   The 'iron triangle'

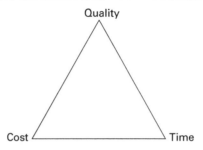

Fear of change has been the subject of significant research by psychologists, sociologists and neuroscientists. This fear is rooted in something far more complex than simple unwillingness or recalcitrance – human beings are hardwired to preserve existing social structures as a fundamental part of our survival instinct. This translates to the organizational setting and manifests as resistance. We will delve more deeply into this in Chapter 7 but for now, let us take a step back and consider why organizational change is so challenging.

In their 1993 paper 'Reengineering the corporation: A manifesto for business revolution', Hammer and Champy state that 70 per cent of organizational change projects fail. In 2009, McKinsey consultants Derwan and Keller carried out a global survey of 2,512 executives and reported that only 33 per cent of change initiatives succeeded. It seems that the ratio of success to failure is not improving.

Whether or not a change initiative is successful is widely measured against the 'iron triangle' (Figure 1.1) – if a change is delivered on time, on budget and to the agreed quality standard then it is successful.

While the triangle's derivation is undocumented, it has been in use since the 1950s and is accepted by most change practitioners. However, the tool has its limitations, which we will explore in 'Making change stick' (Chapter 10).

The failure rates noted by Hammer and Champy are unlikely to surprise change practitioners. Indeed, the difficulty of delivering successful change led John P Kotter, a Harvard academic and change expert, to carry out extensive research into the reasons why organizational change initiatives are so prone to failure. In his seminal 1995 article, 'Why transformation efforts fail' he sets out eight reasons:

- Allowing too much complacency.
- Failing to create a sufficiently powerful guiding coalition.

- Understanding the power of vision.
- Under-communicating the vision.
- Permitting obstacles to block the new vision.
- Failing to create short-term wins.
- Declaring victory too soon.
- Neglecting to anchor changes in the corporate culture.

The following year, Kotter published a change theory to counter his eight errors. This now famous 'Kotter's model' proposes eight steps to do this:

- Create a sense of urgency.
- Form a guiding coalition.
- Develop an inspired vision.
- Convey the new vision.
- Empower others to enact the vision.
- Generate short-term wins.
- Build on the change.
- Anchor the change in the corporate culture.

Making change happen

Returning briefly to the PESTLE and SWOT activities referenced earlier, let us consider what organizations can do with the insight they gain from these exercises. Senior leaders may know what activity is needed in response. Examples include:

- Upgrading technology.
- Developing a new product or service.
- Entering a new market.
- Restructuring teams, departments or functions.
- Re-engineering processes.
- Automating activities.
- Offshoring or centralizing tasks.

Whatever activity is deemed appropriate, it is going to lead to change for that organization and the change requires a method or mode of delivery.

Organizational change initiatives are delivered via projects and programmes. Often referred to interchangeably, projects and programmes are in fact different. According to APMG, issuers of the Managing Successful Programmes (MSP®) certification (Sowden 2011), a programme is a 'temporary, flexible organization created to coordinate, direct and oversee the implementation of a set of related projects and activities'. Temporary does not necessarily mean short term – many programmes take several years to deliver but as they do not form part of the organization's standard business activity (referred to as Business as Usual), hence they are considered temporary.

A project is also a temporary structure but differs from a programme as it is created to deliver business benefits according to a specific Business Case. Projects often have a shorter duration than programmes and while they are often part of a programme, as noted in the above MSP® definition, they often stand alone within the wider change portfolio as shown in Figure 1.2.

Roles and responsibilities

If a change activity is approved by senior leadership, it can be initiated as a programme or project and a delivery team can be assembled. This team typically consists of several individuals with different roles and responsibilities and the team dynamic will vary depending on the type of project being delivered. Table 1.1 explains these roles and their responsibilities:

Traditional change team structure

The roles and responsibilities described above are those typically involved in delivering a change initiative. However, this structure differs from the everyday structure of the change team, from which most of the resources are drawn.

Figure 1.2   Example of a change portfolio with a variety of projects and programmes

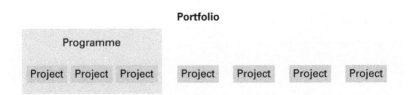

Table 1.1 Roles and responsibilities

Project or programme role	Project or programme responsibility
Steering Committee (often referred to as SteerCo)	Approves the Business Case. Acts as decision-making body. Escalation point for high impacts risks and issues.
Executive Sponsor	Accountable for successful delivery. Formulates and communicates the vision – the 'why'. Secures appropriate budget and resources.
Programme Manager	Responsible for programme budget, resources and overall delivery. Facilitates appointment and allocation of project team resources.
Project Manager	Day-to-day management of the project. Ensures project delivers to time, scope, quality, risk and benefits as agreed with Project Board/SteerCo.
Business Analyst (BA)	Ensures business requirements are correctly defined and documented with the end 'customer'. Defines and documents business processes impacted by the change.
Change Manager	See box
Project Management Office (PMO)	Designs project and programme governance framework and documentation. Provides ongoing assurance to enforce governance and maintain consistency of standards.
Project Support Officer	Supports Project and Programme Managers by undertaking administrative tasks such as updating plans, risk logs, status reports and other documentation.
Subject Matter Expert (SME)	Works within and represents the functions and departments impacted by the change. Supports the project team in understanding how the business currently works. Contributes to the definition of requirements and subsequent acceptance testing.
Change Agent	Champions and supports the new way of working, helping with the adoption of change.

The change team structure often depends on the maturity of the organization in question and most teams will have a slightly different design. There are also many organizations without a dedicated change function and they rely on untrained employees delivering projects in addition to their day jobs. The ideal approach is to establish a dedicated team of change professionals because:

- It provides a centralized change 'hub' for all change initiatives across the organization, which eliminates duplication and facilitates the prioritization of change activity according to business need and value for money.
- It guarantees appropriate governance and oversight, which drives consistency of standards.
- It gives the business transparency over the total cost and benefits of change.
- It helps to build and develop specialist change skills, knowledge and expertise to serve the business better.

Figure 1.3 is an example of a typical change team structure, although there are many variations.

Figure 1.3   Example of a change team structure

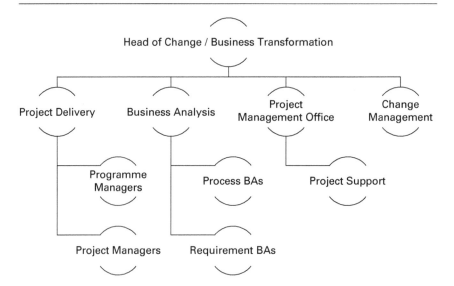

The role of the change manager

In this book we use the term 'change practitioner' to describe someone delivering organizational change. However, some change teams include dedicated change managers.

Change management is a professional discipline rooted in psychology and the science of human behaviour. It is aimed at supporting employees who are, or will be, impacted by organizational change through activities such as:

- impact analyses
- business readiness analyses
- stakeholder management
- training
- communication and engagement.

In essence, a change manager lays the foundation for the change and clears a path for organizational change to be delivered successfully. The importance of this role is frequently overlooked or conflated with that of a Project Manager. However, according to Britain's biggest job board, Indeed. co.uk, between February 2014 and August 2018, the number of change management roles being advertised more than tripled, increasing from 870 to 2,857 postings. This bodes well for the discipline.

Finally, a change team is most effective if it has a reporting line that is as function neutral as possible. It has to occupy a place in the organization and, given the nature of many change initiatives, IT or Operations are arguably logical places. Therefore, the team often falls under the responsibility of the chief operating officer (COO) or the chief information officer (CIO). However, this does not mean that the change team prioritizes the demands and needs of those functions over others.

Conclusion

By now the reader will have an appreciation of the 'macro' change trends the world is faced with, the volume of change organizations are faced with and the root causes of the change. We have also looked at some of

the reasons why organizational change can be problematic for many people. Later we will take a more in-depth look at five specific challenges
resulting from organizational change, together with some models, tools
and techniques practitioners can keep in their 'tool box' to help them
overcome these challenges.

We have reviewed the vehicles for organizational change – projects and
programmes – and how they can be structured to deliver change initiatives
effectively. Finally, the reader has been introduced to the benefits of investing in a dedicated change team, as well as a potential change team structure.

References

Ashkenas, R (2015) We still don't know the difference between change and
    transformation, *Harvard Business Review*, https://hbr.org/2015/01/we-still-
    dont-know-the-difference-between-change-and-transformation (archived at
    https://perma.cc/9HED-PDAJ)
Buchanan, D (2003) Getting the story straight: Illusions and delusions in the
    organisational change process, *Tamara: Journal of Critical Postmodern
    Organisational Science*, 58 (7), p 2
Derwan, C and Keller S (2009) The irrational side of change management,
    McKinsey Quarterly, www.mckinsey.com/business-functions/people-and-
    organizational-performance/our-insights/the-irrational-side-of-change-
    management (archived at https://perma.cc/QN6T-6MZH)
Hammer, M and Champy, J (1993) *Reengineering the Corporation: A manifesto for
    business revolution,* Nicholas Brealey Publishing, London
Hodges, J and Gill, R (2014) *Sustaining Change in Organizations*, Sage, London
Human Capital Institute (2021) Thriving through transformation: HR's roles in
    change management, www.hci.org/system/files/2021-03/2021%20Talent%20
    Pulse%208.1.pdf (archived at https://perma.cc/M7G4-XQCK)
J P Morgan (2020) Why COVID-19 could be a major turning point for ESG
    investing, www.jpmorgan.com/insights/research/covid-19-esg-investing
    (archived at https://perma.cc/C4KR-WAK3)
Kopestinsky, A (2021) Electric car statistics in the US and abroad. PolicyAdvice,
    https://policyadvice.net/insurance/insights/electric-car-statistics/ (archived at
    https://perma.cc/HM4A-TM7U)
Kotter, J (1995) *Leading Change*, Harvard Business Review Press, New York
Lewin, K (1947) *Understanding the three stages of change*, Harper & Row,
    New York

Marshak, R J and Heracleous, L (2004) Organizational development. In: Clegg, S and Bailey, J (eds) *International Encyclopaedia of Organization Studies*, Sage, Thousand Oaks, CA

Mintel (2020) Plant-based push: UK sales of meat-free foods shoot up 40% between 2014–19, www.mintel.com/press-centre/food-and-drink/plant-based-push-uk-sales-of-meat-free-foods-shoot-up-40-between-2014-19 (archived at https://perma.cc/AR8J-7243)

Mutune, G (2021) The quick and dirty history of cybersecurity, https://cyberexperts.com/history-of-cybersecurity/ (archived at https://perma.cc/U3AR-CRDN)

Oreg, S, By, R and Michel, A (2013) *The Psychology of Organisational Change,* Cambridge University Press, Cambridge

Sowden, R (2011) *Managing Successful Programmes*, Stationery Office, London

Acquisitions, digitalization and regulation

02

The change giants

Introduction

The SWOT and PESTLE analyses in Chapter 1 highlighted a range of typical change drivers and the resulting change activity. In this chapter we will explore three of those drivers in more detail:

- acquisitions
- digitalization
- regulation.

Acquisitions

What are acquisitions?

An acquisition refers to one company purchasing most or all another company's shares, thus gaining control of that company. Provided the purchasing company acquires more than 50 per cent of the target firm's stock and other assets, the acquirer can make decisions about the newly acquired assets without the approval of the acquired's shareholders. In general, acquiring companies are financially stronger (and therefore normally significantly larger) than their targets and typically, although not always, the acquired entity adopts the name and branding of its acquirer.

Often mentioned in the same breath as acquisitions, mergers refer to the fusion of two companies similar in size and scale into one new legal entity.

They are significantly rarer than acquisitions – according to the Institute of Mergers, Acquisitions and Alliances (IMAA, 2019) there were 49,849 acquisitions globally in 2019, but there were just 20 mergers globally in the same year. The primary motivator of a merger is not one of control, rather the merging companies' belief and agreement that their combined entity would be more valuable to shareholders than if they remained separate. One of the best-known examples of this is the merger of British multinational pharmaceutical companies Glaxo Wellcome and SmithKline Beecham in 2000 to become GlaxoSmithKline plc (GSK). In 2019, GSK was the world's sixth-largest pharmaceutical company according to Forbes (Industry Wired, 2020), an achievement most unlikely had they remained separate entities in competition with each other.

Why do acquisitions happen?

Why do so many organizations go through the effort and expense of acquiring another? There are various reasons including to:

- Increase market share.
- Grow turnover.
- Expand to other countries and markets.
- Reduce operating costs.
- Enhance or acquire a strategic capability.
- Obtain product or service innovation.
- Upgrade or acquire employee talent (Goedhart et al, 2017).

In practice, most transactions are motivated by more than one of the above. For example, when Vodafone acquired Mannesmann, a German conglomerate, in 2000, it became the largest acquisition in corporate history with a deal value of $180 billion. It made Vodafone the largest global mobile operator, not only increasing market share but also expanding Vodafone's geographic footprint overnight. Additionally, a significant number of talented Mannesmann engineers, developers and senior managers were acquired as a result.

AT&T was already one of the world's largest telecom giants when it acquired BellSouth for $67 billion in 2006. However, the transaction handed AT&T a ready-made domestic customer base of 70 million people, consolidating its hold over the US telecom market in a way that allowed it not only to grow but also to gain market share without the need to invest in its network.

The acquisition of a strategic capability is arguably best demonstrated by Google's 2005 purchase of the unknown wireless start-up, Android, for $50 million. By acquiring rather than developing an operating platform, Google accelerated its ability to catch and compete in a market dominated by Microsoft's Windows Mobile and Apple's iOS platform. In doing so, Google also increased its market share – Android is now the most popular mobile Operating System in the world, used in nearly 86 per cent of all smartphones manufactured in 2018. In addition, in one of the best examples of talent acquisition, Google acquired one of Android's founders, Andy Rubin, who became senior vice president of mobile and digital content (Callaham, 2021).

Product innovation was at the root of Walt Disney Co.'s 2006 acquisition of Pixar for $7.4 billion, bringing the type of animation and creative content that produced box office behemoths such as *Finding Dory* and *Monsters Inc*. In 2009 Disney spent $4 billion on Marvel Entertainment, handing it an action hero franchise that, although watched by many demographics, appealed hugely to men and young boys, an audience hitherto elusive to the Disney brand. The subsequent 11 Marvel films resulted in $3.6 billion of box office revenue for Walt Disney Co (Disney, 2009).

Finally, cost reduction is an acquisition driver most prevalent in the manufacturing and pharmaceutical sectors where overheads are high due to production space, distribution costs and the upfront cost of raw materials. One of the key drivers for the pharmaceutical industry specifically is the spiralling cost of research and development, with only the largest players able to afford multi-year drug development programmes. When Allergan sold its Actavis arm to Teva Pharmaceuticals for $40.5 billion in 2015, Teva's motivation was the ability to develop and manufacture drugs within a competitive timeframe and budget.

An upward trend

IMAA reported a record $5.8 trillion in global M&A transactions in 2021 and predicted that conditions are ripe for continued growth. This is due to several factors – corporate cashflow in 2021 was at record levels and private equity firms, responsible for 24 per cent of global transaction value in 2021, still have funds remaining for further transactions. Small and medium-sized firms, often the targets of an acquisition, are more vulnerable to the macro-economic uncertainties following the Covid-19 pandemic – likely interest rate increases, increased corporate taxation levels and the recurrence of new Covid-19 variants. At the same time, as governments dig deep to rebuild their economies after the worst of the pandemic, the state stimulus packages that would typically prop up smaller firms are disappearing as the public purse strings are tightened.

The link between acquisition activity and organizational change

Whether a firm is the acquirer or is being acquired, the transaction always brings significant change because it involves the integration of one company into another. Integration typically involves disruptive activity such as the transfer of employees and the migration of IT applications to name but a few. People on both sides of the transaction often respond with fear and resistance, creating a range of challenges, which we will examine in Chapter 6.

Digital transformation and its role in organizational change

Digital transformation is a key driver of organizational change and therefore an important one for practitioners to understand. According to research conducted by North Carolina State University (2018), the introduction of digital technology was top priority for most of the 1,063 senior executives they interviewed in 2019, demonstrating the importance of digital capabilities to the corporate change agenda.

What is digital?

The term 'digital' refers to the capture, storage or transmission of data in binary form – a number system that only uses two digits: 1 and 0. Because computers use electrical signals that are either on or off, all data processed by a computer must be converted into binary. Therefore, all information processed by a computer is a sequence of 1s and 0s. This was made possible by the invention of the transistor in the US in 1947, which enabled the control of electronic devices and paved the way for digital computers, cameras, radios and phones. Digital technology, once the exception, is now commonplace for most of us, whether we realize it or not.

The path to digital

The rise of digital technology is often referred to as the 'digital revolution', the latest milestone on a long timeline of industrial development, the first of which was the Industrial Revolution, which started in the UK in the mid-18th century. This was the era of mechanization and the shift from a largely agricultural economy to an industrial one, thanks to the invention of machinery to replace manual labour.

This new manufacturing capability helped usher in the second industrial revolution, which was characterized by mass production. This period, between 1870 and the beginning of the First World War in 1914, brought improvements to existing industries through the availability of electricity and the newly invented light bulb.

The digital revolution of the 1980s is considered the third 'industrial' revolution and was characterized by mass automation. Technology started to move away from analogue and electric with innovations such as the personal computer, the internet and mobile communications. The world wide web followed in 1989, triggering the proliferation of related technology such as web browsers, web applications and application programming interfaces (APIs), which enabled activities such as e-commerce, digital marketing and social media.

Industry insiders believe the world is now living through a fourth industrial revolution, one that will challenge humankind in a very different way from its predecessors. The type of technological breakthroughs being made are now of such magnitude that they will fundamentally alter how we live, work and socialize. This section provides an overview of the key areas of development, how digital technology is being used by different groups and how it may be applied in the future.

Artificial Intelligence

Artificial Intelligence (AI), first conceptualized in 1956 as part of a research programme at Dartmouth College in the US, is the programming of machines to think and respond like humans. It is described by its founders as the 'science of making machines clever'. AI has subsets of activity such as robotics, neuro-linguistic programming, automation and machine learning. It is already in everyday domestic use, for example the digital assistants Siri (iPhone) and Alexa (Amazon). In the business world, it is often used to reduce processing costs by undertaking low-value, repetitive tasks previously carried out by humans. According to a report by Capital Economics (Evans and Heijmann, 2022) on behalf of the Department for Digital, Culture, Media, and Sport, 1,300 UK firms invested £63 billion on AI technology in 2020. This figure is projected to reach £200 billion across 1.3 million firms by 2040 and with investment will come significant changes in ways of working for thousands of people.

Internet of Things

The term Internet of Things (IOT) was coined by Kevin Ashton of Proctor and Gamble in 1999 and refers to the inter-connectivity of smart devices. Some 8.4 billion IOT gadgets were in use in 2017 and by 2020 this number had grown to 20.4 billion. Examples are smartphones, lighting, sound systems like Sonos, central heating such as Nest, wearables like the fitness watch Fitbit and even coffee machines. The interaction between devices provides companies with rich customer data and insight, helping them to react to consumer behaviour and trends.

Cloud technology

Cloud technology refers to a network of linked remote servers, operating as a single 'ecosystem' to store and manage data, run applications and deliver content or services. It replaces files and data stored on devices and is accessible online from any internet-capable device. Businesses and consumers can choose from four different types of cloud resources – public, private, hybrid and community.

Big data

Big data are high-volume, high-velocity and high-variety data sets.

Often the data are of a personal nature, for example fitness trackers and home security. Such data can supply firms with useful insight for targeted and consumer-driven decision-making, provided they invest in the processing and analytics.

Blockchain

Blockchain was created in 2008 as a type of database storing data in 'blocks' that are 'chained' together. It is a decentralized 'peer-to-peer' network controlled by all users, providing total transparency of transactions. The most common use for blockchain so far has been as a transaction ledger for Bitcoin and in the banking sector. However, its transparency has broader appeal, such as to government bodies for audit purposes, and it has started disrupting other industries such as health, insurance, energy and travel.

3D printing

Three-dimensional (3D) printing is a manufacturing process that produces a physical object using a digital template. It works by producing several thin layers of liquid, powdered plastic, metal or cement, and then fusing them. When 3D printing scales up, it will enable consumers to print out objects at home without going out to buy them or waiting for them to be delivered. Although currently too slow for mass production, some car manufacturers use 3D printing for prototypes.

5G

5G is the new (fifth) generation of wireless technology, following previous generations of mobile technology such as 3G and 4G. 5G is faster and has greater capacity than previous generations of wireless technology, enabling thousands of devices in a small area to connect simultaneously. Consumers who use large amounts of data such as gamers will no longer experience latency. Businesses see the opportunity for new and innovative services, for example by connecting video systems that allow pharmacists to remotely check patients are taking medication.

What are the benefits of digitalization?

According to the Altimeter Group (2014), a research and strategy consulting firm specializing in disruptive technologies, digital transformation is the 'realignment of, or new investment in, technology and business models to more effectively engage digital customers at every touchpoint in the customer experience lifecycle'. Digital change can be very investment heavy and highly disruptive.

However, the application and benefits of digital technology are present in virtually every sector. Tom Goodwin pointed out in his 2018 book, *Digital Darwinism*, that digital technology has enabled start-ups such as Uber, Airbnb, Alibaba and Facebook to become tech giants in a relatively short space of time using digital development as an enabler. They have all managed this thanks to digital technology's high speed and scalability.

For organizations willing to invest in digital development, the benefits are significant. A 2011 joint study carried out by MIT School of Management's Center for Digital Business and CapGemini Consulting (Fitzgerald et al, 2013) with 157 senior leaders across 50 organizations in 15 countries identified nine key benefits of digital transformation in three main areas:

1 Enhancing the customer experience:

   a. Customer understanding – using analytics-based customer segmentation, organizations build an informed view of customer demographics so that they can develop products specifically targeted to each distinct market segment.

   b. Top-line growth – using technology to deliver digitally enhanced sales presentations and predictive marketing campaigns.

   c. Customer touchpoints – customer service can be enhanced significantly through digital initiatives, for example the use of a Twitter account to respond to client complaints.

2 Rationalizing operational processes:

   a. Process digitization – automation makes processes more efficient, cheaper and scalable.

   b. Employee enablement – technologies such as email, document and file storage services, and video conferencing enable employees to collaborate across borders and time zones.

   c. Management information – transactional systems give executives deeper insights into products, regions and customers, allowing decisions to be made on real data and not on hypotheses.

3 Transforming business models:

   a. Digitally modified business – firms can augment the physical with digital offerings, such as a supermarket launching an e-commerce service.

   b. New digital business – companies sell digital products that complement traditional products, for example a sports clothing manufacturer selling digital devices that can track and report on the customer's workout.

   c. Digital globalization – organizations can transform from multinational to fully global. Digital technology means they can benefit from global synergies such as shared services while still appealing to local clientele.

While some firms have capitalized on all the above benefits of digital transformation, others are only just beginning to see the opportunities. For many it is viewed with suspicion and seen as an expensive and unwanted distraction. Despite the benefits already noted, this view is not completely unfounded, as digital technology has the potential to be highly disruptive across all industries, sectors and activities.

Why is digital transformation so disruptive?

Companies not only need to react to technological development but also the number of competitors appearing due to the speed, agility and innovation available. As with other types of change, many digital transformation efforts end in failure or fail to meet expectations for many reasons.

First, the magnitude of change it creates. Digital transformation generally involves changing each element of the Target Operating Model (people, process and technology) because digital change is not as straightforward as decommissioning a legacy analogue system and replacing it with a digital one. It also introduces the prospect of integrating existing analogue systems with a new digital application. The impact on process and people leads to a quite different way of working and the cost is off-putting to many senior leaders. Furthermore, it means organizations need to hire employees who understand the digital technology in question while also retaining the staff with knowledge of legacy systems.

Furthermore, the velocity of digital change can be challenging. While some development is gradual, for example the evolution of autonomous vehicles, senior business leaders today are faced with so much digital innovation that many firms are simply 'running to stand still'. For example, as soon as a new customer portal is launched, further development is required to add new features and capabilities. As a result, employees experience constant change to their ways of working.

Common pitfalls

The absence of a clear objective means that many digital projects are initiated for the wrong reason, for example because an existing analogue system is coming out of warranty or support. This is used as the catalyst for change, rather than being driven by a strategic desire to innovate and become a market leader or solve a particular problem for consumers. In contrast, if organizations create and follow a digital 'roadmap' aligned to its strategic objectives then moving to digital is more likely to be successful.

A lack of vision or leadership from senior management often results in the absence of urgency to innovate and transform. The MIT research shows that 93 per cent of employees supported digital transformation after it was announced by a senior leader and discussed in an open forum. However, in practice only 36 per cent of CEOs communicated the vision sufficiently to their employees. Digital transformation represents such a big change that teams must understand why it is necessary and what the benefits are.

Innovation fatigue caused by continuous change with no discernible end date can lead to burnout within teams. Firms often seek to mitigate this by delaying or pausing digital projects to allow employees to assimilate the change. However, a more appropriate response would be to invest time before work begins to create the appropriate project and delivery structure. In the case of digital transformation, the most appropriate method is Agile – a continuous series of incremental changes delivered through 'sprint' cycles and in consultation with the impacted teams. In addition to the traditional Agile project team structure, it is also wise to engage an Agile coach who can train employees on Agile principles and help guide them through the initial stages of transformation.

A lack of preparedness means that organizations often do not carry out due diligence or feasibility studies into the impact of the digital transformation in question and as a result may implement the wrong solution or incur unnecessary additional costs. As we have already seen, launching a new digital application impacts the whole Target Operating Model and if there is no analysis of the impact on the related structure, processes and data the new solution is unlikely to be completely successful.

Finally, there is often a lack of clarity over roles and responsibilities. Many senior leaders who advocate digital transformation assume that the IT function will deliver it due to the obvious technical nature of the change. However, while digital transformation is enabled through technology, it is not the role of IT to identify and resolve the impacts throughout the value chain. Most technical teams are not close enough to the business to be able to define what problems they are trying to solve. Furthermore, not engaging with the end-user often leads to increased resistance and a lack of engagement from the business. Similarly, end-users rarely have the technical knowledge to define the optimum solution for their problem. This impasse can be overcome by involving the Change team from the start. The project manager and business analysts act as the interface between the business and technology teams, by collecting business requirements and helping to translate them into functional specifications for development.

What does the future hold?

Our world moves exceptionally fast, and businesses not only need to transform their operations to be able to keep pace with their customers, they need to anticipate change and be ready for it when it occurs.

The only certainty is that this development will continue, and at speed. Organizations will need to continue to adapt and evolve. The 2019 World Economic Forum (WEF) coined the term 'Society 5.0' as the next 'industrial' revolution. The WEF believes Society 5.0 will be an 'imagination society', where digital transformation combines with creativity to arrive at sustainable development. This will require a significant change of mindset, even for those who have already embraced the digital revolution.

It is likely that Society 5.0 will be led by the 'millennial' generation, defined by *The Economist* as the 1981 to 1996 birth cohort that reached adulthood in the early part of the 21st century. This generation is significantly more comfortable with technology and innovation than previous generations of 'digital migrants', as they grew up in a world of constant digital change.

Generation 'Z' (people born between 1995 and 2015) will have spent some of their formative years in the grip of the Covid-19 pandemic, heavily reliant on collaboration tools such as Zoom and Microsoft Teams for their home-schooling and social life. This has embedded a longer-term expectation of flexible and remote working arrangements that their predecessors would never have considered. They will likely take advantage of the existing 'gig' economy and 'portfolio career' concepts to work as independent contractors and freelancers to maximize the flexibility, variety, creativity and autonomy that they expect. In turn, this will stoke the demand for mobile digital solutions as enablers. As these demographic groups become the consumers of the future, they will expect constant innovation in both their professional and private lives. They will become challenging consumers and employees with high expectations and low loyalty. Organizations that cannot accept or embrace this relentless digital development will struggle to attract and retain them, either as employees or customers.

Regulatory compliance

As we saw throughout Chapter 1, legal and regulatory obligations feature heavily in the SWOT and PESTLE analyses of organizations in many industries. In fact, according to research carried out by Moorhouse Consulting (2012), regulatory change comprises 40 per cent of all change projects in the UK.

What is regulatory compliance?

Regulatory compliance is an organization's adherence to the rules, regulations and standards set out for its industry or sector in each country of operation.

These rules are devised and introduced through different channels, most commonly via domestic government legislation, government-appointed agencies or by supra-national bodies such as the EU.

So many industry sectors are now regulated that it would be impossible to cover them all here. Instead, this chapter will provide an overview of regulatory change through the lens of two of the most heavily regulated sectors globally – financial services and the pharmaceutical industry.

Financial services

In the UK, the financial services sector is regulated via the 'twin peaks' system of the Financial Conduct Authority (FCA) and the Prudential Regulatory Authority (PRA). Part of their remit is to define appropriate regulation for registered firms to comply with, which the FCA then monitors and oversees on an ongoing basis. Additionally, the FCA interprets, communicates and enforces legislative and regulatory requirements originating from other bodies, such as the UK government and, prior to 31 January 2021, the EU.

The sector operates under a significant volume of regulation, much of it introduced following the 2007 financial crisis. After many years of excessive risk-taking by large global banks combined with the burst of the US housing market bubble, the value of US real estate-backed securities plummeted overnight. This rocked financial institutions globally, very few of which were immune to US market forces. Many countries were affected, forcing domestic governments to bail out their financial institutions with public money, deeming them 'too big to fail'. In 2008, American Insurance Group (AIG) received a loan of $85 billion over two years to avoid the further stress its bankruptcy would place on the global economy. Similarly, the UK government injected £45.5 billion into the Royal Bank of Scotland (RBS) between October 2008 and December 2009 in a move to maintain financial stability, making the UK government RBS' majority shareholder with a 58 per cent stake in ordinary shares. Some institutions did not survive the crash, most famously the Wall Street brokerage firm Lehman Brothers, which filed for bankruptcy in September 2008.

Regulation introduced on both sides of the Atlantic has since sought to prevent a repeat of such events. In 2014 the EU introduced the Solvency II Directive to codify, standardize and strengthen the bloc's insurance sector by stipulating a minimum amount of capital that insurance companies must hold to reduce the risk of insolvency. In a similar vein, Basel III was developed by the Basel Committee on Banking Supervision to reform the regulation, supervision and risk management of banks. Factors contributing to the 2007 financial crisis such as capital adequacy and market liquidity could have been avoided if they had been more closely regulated and these changes sought to prevent history from repeating itself.

Pharmaceutical

The pharmaceutical industry is one of the world's most regulated, which is necessary to protect people from the potentially harmful effects of legal drugs and medication. Regulation ensures that medicines are developed, manufactured, stored and sold in line with a strict regulatory framework designed and monitored by health professionals such as doctors, chemists and pharmacists. To procure and retain a licence to operate, companies must comply with a complex set of laws and regulations governing activities such as clinical trials, drug development, manufacturing, packaging, distribution and quality checking. Drug companies in the UK are regulated by the Medicines and Healthcare products Regulatory Agency (MHRA), a government body established in 2003. Its oversight prevents the use of ineffective, poor-quality or harmful medicines, which could lead to illness, exacerbation of disease, mass resistance to medicines or even death. Such oversight also minimizes the undermining of confidence in health systems, health professionals and medication in general.

In the US, the Food and Drug Administration (FDA) has a wider regulatory reach because pharmaceutical companies are permitted to advertise some drugs directly to the general public. It is also commonplace to employ sales teams to distribute drugs directly to hospitals and other healthcare providers, often visiting doctors in person to encourage them to endorse and prescribe their firm's product. Large pharmaceutical companies even employ lobbyists, whose sole responsibility it is to influence politicians at local, state and federal level to enact laws which benefit the industry. In short, the scope for unethical behaviour is high and the only way to safeguard patients is through a tightly enforced regulatory framework.

Finally, in addition to the sector-specific regulation described above, there are also examples of sector-neutral rules that organizations must also comply with. Perhaps the best-known recent example of this is the EU's 2016 General Data Protection Regulations (GDPR), which govern the gathering, use and management of personal data, known as personally identifiable information (PII). The Regulations were written into UK law through the Data Protection Act 2018, sparking a flurry of activity for organizations to ensure they can access and delete personal information quickly and on request. As the legislation applies to any company that collects or stores customer data, the Act applies to virtually every organization in the country, irrespective of size or industry sector.

Why does regulation drive so much organizational change?

The above examples are only intended as a snapshot of the regulatory environment in two industries, but they are illustrative as to why regulation drives so much change. The volume of new and updated regulation creates a significant workload for compliance teams, but to become compliant with regulation such as the GDPR, Solvency II or Basel III, firms must make disruptive changes to systems, reporting, data and governance. For example, to comply with the GDPR, organizations were obliged to store personal data in a way that enabled fast identification and deletion. Depending on how the organization stored data before the GDPR was introduced, this requirement might have necessitated new processes and procedures around the collection and storage of PII, in turn requiring changes to its data storage arrangement. Additionally, many companies were obliged to invest in costly data security controls such as data-breach mechanisms and notification protocols.

In case firms are tempted to overlook new or updated regulation, there is another powerful change driver – financial penalties. In the financial services sector alone, $342 billion in banking fines have been issued between the EU and US since 2009, leading to a further collective $850 billion in erased profits. In 2019 the FCA fined Standard Chartered Bank £102.2 million for poor anti-money laundering controls and in 2012, US and UK authorities fined Barclays $450 million for attempting to manipulate the London interbank offered rate (LIBOR).

To highlight the seriousness of GDPR breaches, British Airways had the dubious distinction of being the first recipient of a large fine from the Information Commissioner's Office (ICO) in 2019. The airline faced a £183 million bill following a card-skimming data harvest attack, which accessed the payment and personal data of around 430,000 customers in June 2018. However, given the impact of Covid-19 on the travel and aviation industries, the ICO subsequently reduced the fine to £20 million.

In the US, pharmaceutical companies have paid over $25 billion in fines over the last 30 years for a range of misdemeanours such as overcharging government health programmes, unlawful promotion, concealing data, substandard manufacturing practices, financial violations, and the illegal distribution and promotion of unapproved medicines. Some of the fines are particularly punitive, for example in 2012 the FDA fined GlaxoSmithKline $3 billion to settle civil and criminal liabilities arising from its misleading promotion of drugs and its failure to report safety data. In 2013 Johnson & Johnson agreed to pay a $2.2 billion fine to resolve criminal and civil allegations relating to three prescription drugs (Buntz, 2020).

Some regulation has been introduced to ensure compliance remains a top priority for senior executives. In the UK, the senior managers and certification regime was introduced to the banking sector in 2016 and later to the insurance sector in 2018. It was designed to reduce harm to consumers by making firms and individuals more accountable and ensure organizations can demonstrate that employees clearly understand where responsibility lies.

It is unsurprising that the necessary change is given top billing in most change portfolios and investment cases, edging out strategic initiatives such as top line growth opportunities or innovation. Given the complexity of most industries' regulatory agenda and the gravity of non-compliance, the best way for a firm to ensure compliance with new or updated regulation is to ensure it is delivered via the Change portfolio. The benefits of doing this are:

- The initiative receives adequate budget.
- The project provides structure to what is usually a complex set of requirements with inflexible delivery deadlines.
- Visibility increases because a project draws in Subject Matter Experts, Change Agents and other stakeholders, as well as a dedicated internal communications work stream.
- Project governance creates engagement with senior leaders via the Steering Committee and Executive Sponsor, which generates the levels of ownership and accountability vital for a regulatory initiative.
- The documentation generated by a project provides evidence of the changes made, which can be used to demonstrate compliance to customers, regulators, shareholders and auditors.

Regtech

Companies spend a lot of time, money and effort reading and interpreting regulations to draw out the relevant and actionable sections. JWG, a London-based think tank focusing on global financial services regulations, estimated in 2016 that over 300 million pages of regulatory documents would be published by 2020, and that over 600 legislative initiatives would need to be processed and analysed by the average medium-sized firm.

Combing through such a weight of regulatory and legislative documentation manually has obvious disadvantages – not only is it time-consuming and expensive for a well-paid legal or compliance professional, but it is also highly error-prone.

To counter this, many firms are turning to the growing number of 'regtech' solutions. A portmanteau of the words 'regulatory' and 'technology', regtech has become something of a corporate buzzword in recent years. Several offerings have emerged, offering cloud-based and automated Software as a Service (SaaS) platforms which provide clients with continuous regulatory updates relevant to their industry. Using AI, they scan and analyse regulatory policies, whitepapers, news publications and other document types to extrapolate the key obligations within minutes. It is estimated to save legal and regulatory professionals hundreds of hours each year. Some software even goes on to group the requirements into tasks and allocate them to specific users in a form of project or action plan.

However, in practice, adoption of such tools is surprisingly low, and many firms still take a tactical, deadline-driven approach to regulatory compliance. If organizations begin to approach regulatory change more strategically, for example by investing in AI solutions, the adoption of regtech tools will itself become a change initiative. Furthermore, due to the nature of a modern data-driven regulatory approach, other data and technology changes would be needed at enterprise level to provide the necessary data integration, security and governance.

What does the future hold?

One thing is clear – the volume and pace of regulatory change in many industries has reached unmanageable levels and it is not uncommon for a large organization to have more than one regulatory project in flight at any one time. The increasing costs and complexity are untenable and there is no suggestion that the pace of change in this area will slow.

Since the Covid-19 pandemic struck in early 2020 there has been an increased focus on business continuity and resilience. The Business Continuity Institute (BCI) defines business continuity as 'having a plan to deal with difficult situations, so your organization can continue to function with as little disruption as possible'. Some industry sectors have introduced resilience regulation to ensure that organizations are in a position to withstand unexpected incidents such as cyberattacks, terrorist incidents or pandemics and that they are not detrimental to the consumer. As the world becomes increasingly connected and unpredictable, operational resilience regulation will likely increase and expand across multiple sectors.

There will also be new risks to contend with, such as the increasing use of robotics and AI, the impact of innovation on operational resilience, concerns around cybersecurity and questions surrounding digital ethics. The growing evidence that the ineffective implementation of non-regulatory technological change contributes to cyber and operational risk is also attracting regulatory scrutiny.

As policymakers and regulators continue to scan the landscape to ensure that their respective industry sectors are well insulated from new and existing threats, they must balance their desire to expand the regulatory agenda with macro concerns such as growth, profit and productivity.

Conclusion

In this chapter we have explored three of the most commonplace drivers of organizational change – acquisitions, digitalization and regulatory change. Not only do they trigger change, but they are also increasing in frequency and significance, which places them firmly at the top of the radar for senior leaders and change practitioners.

Like all types of organizational change, acquisitions, digitalization and regulatory projects give rise to a wide range of implementation challenges. In Chapters 6 to 11 we will examine the main challenges experienced by organizations and their employees and propose practical tips, techniques and solutions to overcoming them.

References

Altimeter Group (2014) The 2014 state of digital transformation: How companies are investing in the digital customer experience, www.prophet.com/pdf/the-2014-state-of-digital-transformation/?redirectedfrom=gatedpage (archived at https://perma.cc/GJL8-S4ZM)

Buntz, B (2020) GSK, Pfizer and J&J among the most-fined drug companies, according to study. *Pharmaceutical Processing World,* https://www. pharmaceuticalprocessingworld.com/gsk-pfizer-and-jj-among-the-most-fined-drug-companies-according-to-study/ (archived at https://perma.cc/5FS2-TC25)

Business Continuity Institute Introduction to Business Continuity, https://www.thebci. org/knowledge/introduction-to-business-continuity.html (archived at https:// perma.cc/F9T7-NF46)

Callaham, J (2021) Google made its best acquisition nearly 16 years ago: Can you guess what it was? https://www.androidauthority.com/google-android- acquisition-884194/ (archived at https://perma.cc/5Q39-MZ5F)

Cole, B (2022) Regulatory compliance, https://searchcompliance.techtarget.com/ definition/regulatory-compliance (archived at https://perma.cc/F9T7-NF46)

Disney (2009) Disney completes Marvel acquisition, https://thewaltdisneycompany. com/disney-completes-marvel-acquisition/ (archived at https://perma.cc/ GUN8-9WJM)

Evans, A and Heimann, A (2022) AI activity in UK businesses. An assessment of the scale of AI activity in UK businesses and scenarios for growth over the next twenty years, https://assets.publishing.service.gov.uk/government/uploads/ system/uploads/attachment_data/file/1045381/AI_Activity_in_UK_Businesses_ Report__Capital_Economics_and_DCMS__January_2022__Web_accessible_. pdf (archived at https://perma.cc/VD32-D58P)

Fitzgerald, M, Kruschwitz, N, Bonnet, D. and Welch, M (2013) Embracing digital technology – a new strategic imperative. *MIT Sloan Management Review*, https://sloanreview.mit.edu/projects/embracing-digital-technology/ (archived at https://perma.cc/TRK8-UT6F)

Goedhart, M, Koller, T and Wessels, D (2017) The six types of successful acquisitions, McKinsey & Company, https://www.mckinsey.com/business- functions/strategy-and-corporate-finance/our-insights/the-six-types-of- successful-acquisitions (archived at https://perma.cc/PH77-V5NG)

Goodwin, T (2018) *Digital Darwinism: Survival of the fittest in the age of business disruption*, Kogan Page, London

Groenfeldt, T (2016) Financial Regulations Will Surpass 300 Million Pages by 2020 Says JWG, https://techandfinance.com/2016/04/20/financial-regulations-will- surpass-300-million-pages-by-2020-says-jwg/ (archived at https://perma.cc/ 9MYC-FQKT)

Hughes, R (2019) Where are all the change managers delivering digitisation? www.govtechleaders.com/2019/06/25/where-are-all-the-change-managers- delivering-digitisation/ (archived at https://perma.cc/CV5B-2BTE)

Industry Wired (2020) World's Largest Pharmaceutical Companies by Revenue in 2020, https://industrywired.com/worlds-largest-pharmaceutical-companies-by- revenue-in-2020/ (archived at https://perma.cc/324C-84PL)

Information Commissioner's Office (n.d.) Enforcement Action, https://ico.org.uk/ action-weve-taken/enforcement/ (archived at https://perma.cc/R6R5-JBL2)

Institute of Mergers, Acquisitions and Alliances (2019) Join the global number one in M&A, imaa-institute.org (archived at https://perma.cc/G24S-X32T)

LaPedus, (M) AT&T buys BellSouth for $67 billion, https://www.eetimes.com/att-buys-bellsouth-for-67-billion/ (archived at https://perma.cc/4NRT-DN4Q)

Maini, F (2014) Deloitte, risk and regulation: A wave of change for pharma [Blog] Deloitte. 30 July. Available from: https://blogs.deloitte.co.uk/health/2014/07/risk-and-regulation-a-wave-of-change-for-pharma.html (archived at https://perma.cc/CY4P-YJG5) [Last accessed: 31 January 2021]

Moorhouse Consulting (2012) Asking too much of financial services? https://www.mca.org.uk/updates/asking-too-much-of-financial-services (archived at https://perma.cc/WGU7-PZR7)

National Audit Office (2017) The first sale of shares in Royal Bank of Scotland, https://www.nao.org.uk/wp-content/uploads/2017/07/The-first-sale-of-shares-in-Royal-Bank-of-Scotland-Summary.pdf (archived at https://perma.cc/L8VV-4GB8)

North Carolina State University (2018) Top Risks Report 2019: Executive perspectives on top risks for 2019, https://erm.ncsu.edu/library/article/top-risks-report-2019-executive-perspectives-on-top-risks-for-2019 (archived at https://perma.cc/UM9J-49B8)

Teva to Acquire Allergan Generics for $40.5 Billion Creating a Transformative Generics and Specialty Company Well Positioned to Win in Global Healthcare, https://www.tevapharm.com/news-and-media/latest-news/teva-to-acquire-allergan-generics-for-$40.5-billion-creating-a-transformative-generics-and-specialty-comp/ (archived at https://perma.cc/9G8H-XVKY)

The Economist (2018) *How established firms are winning over millennial consumers,* https://www.economist.com/the-economist-explains/2018/10/10/how-established-firms-are-winning-over-millennial-consumers (archived at https://perma.cc/B868-9JA6)

Vodafone Acquires Mannesmann in the Largest Acquisition in History, https://www.goldmansachs.com/our-firm/history/moments/2000-vodafone-mannesmann-merger.html (archived at https://perma.cc/MS7A-QX8N)

Coaching in a change context   03

Introduction

Coaching is about change and as we have already seen, change is one of the most complex things that some people find hard to accept. The aim of this chapter is to define, simplify and unravel exactly what coaching is, what coaches do and why these coaching techniques are so important within the context of organizational change.

Although the emphasis of this chapter and indeed the book is on how to coach people through change, mentoring has its place too. The authors have been mindful to mention and include other interventions, including mentoring where they believe the intervention will add more value than coaching. What will become evident is how coaching is more powerful in facilitating change and has sustainable and long-term impact. The ultimate aim is to build confidence, competence and credibility in how to use a variety of newly defined skills and techniques to support and develop the role of change practitioner.

The relevance of coaching for change practitioners

Change practitioners have responsibility for supporting and guiding the organization through change and will typically serve, manage and influence a diverse range of people and personalities throughout their working day. These people may include the main sponsor, a project team and of course the target audience for the change. Ultimately, successful delivery and embedding of change will involve influencing people and their behaviour, particularly when resistance is present.

During the course of their work, change practitioners will draw on a vast range of communication, influencing skills and techniques. Learning the skills and nuances of coaching will enhance and refine these. Coaching will equip change practitioners with powerful techniques to support people through change and uncertainty and to navigate conscious and unconscious patterns of behaviour. The ultimate aim is to deliver change that is understood and accepted by the majority.

Furthermore, many employees, particularly on non-managerial grades, have little or no opportunity to access coaching, even though this intervention would prove highly useful for them. Coaching is typically offered to the senior management team and is usually delivered by a qualified and experienced external coach. This may not be the most practical or cost-effective solution, especially when the organization is going through a significant change programme and there is a need to expand the coaching to more employees. The change practitioner, with their newly developed coaching skills can help support more people within the organization and so offer these techniques to the many instead of the few.

Chapter 11 explores the subject of building an internal coaching capability in more detail with appendixes offering suggestions on how to gain a qualification in coaching.

Defining coaching and mentoring

Coaching and mentoring are two different disciplines, with overlapping and complementary skills but with different processes, expectations and outcomes. At the heart of mentoring is the idea of transferring learning from a more experienced to a less experienced person. The mentor has subject matter knowledge and experience to support the learner. What sets coaching apart from mentoring is that the coach does not need subject matter knowledge because the role of the coach is not to give advice or suggestions. Indeed, the less the coach knows about the person and what they do, the better. Any in-depth knowledge can prevent the coach remaining impartial and detached from the process and the person. Too much knowledge can draw the coach into giving advice and suggestions, usually because they have 'been there', 'done it' and know best. Change practitioners using a coaching approach can sometimes be viewed as a challenge, but it is possible to overcome these challenges with the right mindset, practice and experience. Coaching is as much a mindset as it is a skill. This chapter will guide the change practitioner in adopting coaching skills, mindsets, tools and techniques.

Coaching

There are numerous definitions of coaching written by experts in their field, including Peter Hawkins, David Clutterbuck, Julie Hodges et al, as well as coaching institutions such as European Mentoring and Coaching Council (EMCC), Association for Coaching (AC), International Coaching Federation (ICF). Two definitions are offered below:

> ... *partnering with clients in a thought-provoking and creative process that inspires them to maximise their personal and professional potential.* (ICF)

> ... *is a professionally guided process that inspires clients to maximise their personal and professional potential. It is a structured, purposeful and transformational process, helping clients to see and test alternative ways for improvement and competence, decision making and enhancement of quality of life.* (EMCC)

From these definitions, we would suggest that coaching is primarily a conversation between two people (the coach and client) and a 'thinking partnership' that is:

- goal and future-focussed
- person-centred
- structured and planned
- contracted and confidential.

For coaching to be successful there needs to be a recognition that change is desirable and to do something or many things differently. For example, taking steps towards a goal or aspiration. This may include growing and developing within their role, navigating blockers and barriers, and trying new ways of thinking or communicating. The coaching can help the client to be aware of unhelpful behaviours and habits, and supporting them in learning a new set of helpful behaviours and habits.

The role of the coach

The coach will facilitate the coaching process and conversation to help the client formulate their ideas and solutions in a confidential and safe environment. The coach:

- Provides a psychologically safe environment without shame or judgement.
- Helps individuals in transition, change and transformation.

- Facilitates open and honest conversations around anxiety, uncertainty and fixed mindsets.
- Facilitates a conversation to improve performance.
- Holds the mirror up to the client and holds them accountable.
- Supports the client to bridge the gap between where they are now and where they want to be in terms of a goal or desired outcome.
- Explores what the client needs in order to gain buy-in to the change and look at how they will benefit.

Internal blocks and barriers, resistance and/or limiting beliefs can prevent goals from being reached. As previously mentioned, one of the main differences between coaching and mentoring is that the coach is not there to give advice, suggestions or to influence the client in any way. A good coach trusts that their client can work out a solution or work towards a goal, without being directed or being told what to do and how to do it. The coach asks questions from a place of curiosity, patience and considering different perspectives. This allows the client to think and reflect on their situation and any possible feelings, triggers and associated behaviours.

Mentoring

The origin of the term 'mentor' is believed to date back to Greek mythology and specifically Homer's *Odyssey*, where Odysseus left his son Telemachus in the care of his best friend Mentor while Odysseus went off to fight the Trojan War. Mentor was asked to pass on everything he knew as a wise, trusted friend and adviser and show Telemachus the ways of the world so that the young man would be prepared for life.

David Clutterbuck, an expert in this field, offers a modern-day definition:

A mentor is a more experienced individual willing to share knowledge with someone less experienced in a relationship of mutual trust. The holistic nature of the mentoring role distinguishes it from other learning or supporting roles, such as coaching. The mentor provides a very different kind of support – one based on reflective learning and something akin to pastoral. (Clutterbuck et al, 2016)

As Clutterbuck et al confirm, at the heart of mentoring (in the traditional sense) is the idea of transferring learning from a more experienced and older person to a less experienced, younger person to support their understanding, learning, professional and career development (although in contemporary workforces, the age divide may not be as relevant).

A mentor is often seen as a 'role model' with the mentee assessing what it is that makes their mentor so successful. The mentor will support the mentee with a career plan and will explore the skills and mindset the mentee needs to adopt and develop their career.

A mentor is usually more senior than the mentee and so has influence at the higher levels of the organization and/or profession. The mentor, particularly if they work within the same organization, can therefore 'open doors' and offer the mentee opportunities, such as attending meetings and meeting senior people, which would otherwise be inaccessible.

Creating an effective mentoring relationship

Although coaching and mentoring skills are of equal importance, the intent and expectation when mentoring is that the mentor will share their wisdom, indicating to the mentee what has worked for them in the past and how this might work in the mentee's situation. However, this can, and often does, get in the way of high level listening. Although mentoring has a pivotal place within organizations, what mentoring does not do quite so well is encouraging others to think for themselves. A committed and excellent mentor will regularly use a coaching approach to build rapport, show interest, ask questions and understand the mentee first before any advice is offered. Mentors might fall into the trap of making *assumptions* about what the mentee wants to know instead of *asking* what the mentee wants to know. A useful and incisive question for the mentor to ask is quite simply, 'What questions do you have for me as your mentor?' or 'What advice do you need from me?'

To clarify mentoring is a two-way process where both the mentor and the mentee learn from each other. For example, the mentee may generate an idea the mentor has not previously thought of, or the mentee may be able to help the mentor view a particular situation from another perspective. Building a rapport from the start with open and honest dialogue and two-way feedback is the key quality of an effective mentoring relationship.

Expectations of the coach and mentor

The following list summarizes the expectations and role of the coach and mentor. The term 'client' is used to describe the person being coached (coachee) or mentored (mentee).

The coach:

- Is not an expert and does not need subject knowledge to support the client.
- Is focussed on the client and their end goal and solutions.

- Is not focussed on problems or blame.
- Enters into a short-term relationship and usually lasts for six sessions over six to eight months.
- Empowers the client to take responsibility for their actions and decisions without giving advice or suggestions.
- Asks open and challenging questions to help the client to think from different perspectives.
- Facilitates questions and helps the client to make sense of what is going on and find a solution.
- Does not hold the wisdom. The wisdom comes from the client, not the coach.

The mentor:

- Is seen as an expert and has subject matter knowledge to support the mentee.
- Has a more holistic relationship with the mentee and will explore other aspects of the mentee's work and life.
- Enters into a long-term relationship and usually lasts for two plus years.
- Empowers the mentee to think of what they want from their career while offering advice, suggestions and guidance based on the mentor's own experience.
- Asks open and challenging questions as well as giving advice from their own experience.
- Holds the wisdom. Wisdom can also come from the mentee but the emphasis is on the mentor and their experience.

A useful way of knowing if you are coaching or mentoring is to ask yourself 'which way is the wisdom flowing?'

Can anyone be a coach or mentor?

In principle, anyone is capable of coaching and mentoring if they have the right skills and mindset. With mentoring, age and experience do not always matter. Peer group mentoring is a good example of where people on the same career grade can mentor each other by sharing what they do and how they do it. Reverse mentoring is thought to have originated from Jack Welch, a business executive within General Electric, and flips the traditional relationship by pairing younger workers with more experienced employees on topics they are more familiar with, such as technology, social media, gender and diversity.

The skills and mindset required to coach someone else is more complex. Coaching requires complete objectivity and the ability to 'not get in the way' of the conversation. Since the coach typically asks questions for just 10–20 per cent of the time with most of the thinking and talking coming from the client, the ability to listen carefully to what is said and not being said is an important skill and takes many hours and indeed years of practice to achieve. Suspending judgement and knowledge about the person is another challenge, possible with practice.

A word about sports coaching

Although a lot can be learnt from sports coaching – particularly around the commitment to encourage, motivate and develop skills, potential and performance – sports coaching is a different type of coaching altogether. The role of the sports coach is to assist athletes in developing their full potential and peak performance. The sports coach is responsible for training, demonstrating, encouraging, motivating and energizing the athlete or sports team by analysing their performance and instructing them in relevant skills to reach their goal. Sports coaching tends to be aligned to mentoring and training.

This style of coaching is not always beneficial in the business world as it encourages a mentality of dependency on the manager and or coach and therefore the individual is not empowered to think for themselves.

Essential skills for change practitioners

The change practitioner will already be using a refined set of skills including consulting, influencing and negotiating. They will no doubt have a high level of intuition, integrity, and the ability to listen and question. The aim of this section is to highlight additional essential skills that trained coaches will be familiar with and that will also be invaluable for change practitioners. We start with emotional intelligence as this underpins everything human beings do and has substantial relevance for the organization as a whole, not just when going through change

Emotional intelligence

As a subject, emotional intelligence has grown out of the rapid advances in scientific research over the last 25 years, into subjects such as brain functioning and neuroscience and empirical evidence on the importance of discussing feelings and emotions in a psychologically safe environment.

Emotional intelligence was developed as a concept by two psychologists, Peter Salovey and John Mayer in 1990, although it was the psychologist, Daniel Goleman who is credited with making the term more widely known in his book *Emotional Intelligence: Why it can matter more than IQ* (1995). Emotional intelligence refers to a set of skills that define our moods, feelings and emotions and how these influence people in everyday personal and professional life. Emotions can influence job satisfaction, engagement, and the development of team morale and adaptation to change.

An organization relies on emotionally intelligent leaders to be fully aware of how to manage themselves, to be aware and understand others and to build trusting relationships. This level of emotional maturity can make a significant difference to the outcome and success of the change initiative. As it is such an important skill, the authors would like to delve a little deeper into the theory and practice of emotional intelligence.

Emotional intelligence has relevance at all levels within organizations from senior leadership level through to the general workforce. Consider how emotionally intelligent or aware your organization is in:

- Managing the change process and its impact on the organization as a whole.
- Observing the impact this change is having on individuals and teams.
- Knowing how the behaviours of senior leaders are perceived by others.
- The way that change impacts on the relationships between departments and stakeholders.

It is important to make emotional intelligence integral to any change programme to fully embed these principles. This is where coaching has particular relevance. The change practitioner can help raise awareness when using coaching techniques to help stakeholders step into the shoes of others, to manage unhelpful behaviours and to help them build trusting relationships. The Emotional Intelligence model and concepts can be shared by the change practitioner during a one-to-one or team coaching session.

The four components of emotional intelligence

There are four component areas of the Emotional Intelligence model with empathy being an important factor of emotional intelligence.

These four areas as typically depicted in a four box matrix, as seen in Figure 3.1.

Self-awareness: Noticing and naming our emotions and feelings in the moment. Being aware of who we are, our reputation, our personality traits and our impact on others. Awareness of our beliefs and values which may impact our communication.

Social-awareness: Stepping into the shoes of others and empathizing with their situation. Noticing the emotions in others, both verbal and non-verbal and adapting our behaviour to enable effective rapport building and communication.

Self-management: Being aware of triggers that cause a negative reaction and possible outburst in us. Ability to regulate our moods and behaviours to enable successful communication and rapport.

Relationship management: The willingness and ability to build rapport and trusting relationships. To adapt to other's styles and the willingness to work collaboratively with individuals for successful working relationships.

Figure 3.1   Emotional Intelligence matrix

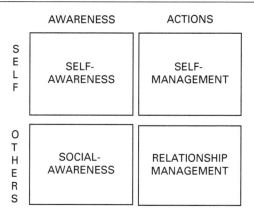

Coaching skills essential for change practitioners

The following essential skills have been guided by the core coaching competencies as set out by the three main coaching bodies (EMCC, AC and ICF), and they are by no means complete. These essential skills are required and expected for professional coaches to operate at their best and in this context are useful for change practitioners as well. They offer the opportunity for change practitioners to evaluate their level of awareness and competence in using each of these skills when using a coaching style and approach with their stakeholders. Consider also that a high level of emotional intelligence is required to be aware of and to use these skills and understand the potential barriers to using them:

- rapport
- listening
- questioning
- summarizing
- impartiality
- challenging assumptions
- open, not leading, questions
- using silence
- avoiding advice giving.

The authors would recommend as part of the change practitioner's professional development, to measure their current competence for each of the above essential skills out of 10 (10 being high). For example:

On a scale of 1 – 10, what is your skill level in building rapport? When might this level increase or decrease?

On a scale of 1 – 10, how would you rate your level of listening? What might affect your level of listening?

On a scale of 1 – 10, what is your skill level in using open questions? What needs to happen for this skill to increase?

Asking a trusted friend or colleague to evaluate the scores from their perspective will also help to raise self-awareness.

Although these skills may seem straightforward, there are potential challenges or barriers to using each of them. These challenges may be a conscious decision not to use the particular skill, a blind spot or a lack of confidence for fear of what might happen if that skill is used. An example of this is the use of silence.

Some change practitioners may not feel comfortable with silence after asking a question and when the stakeholder is thinking about how to respond.

The need to fill the void may result in the change practitioner asking another question before the stakeholder has finished thinking and reflecting on the previous question. Being comfortable with silence will allow space and time for reflection for both the stakeholder and the change practitioner.

Potential barriers and how to overcome them

Rapport building

Consider the rapport you have with the individual. Do you like this person and do you get on well with them? Lack of rapport will have a negative impact on the quality of listening and the willingness to be impartial and non-judgmental. Your body language will be a sign of how you think and feel about this person.

Change the mindset about the individual. Forget what might have happened in the past or what others say about them. Imagine that this is the first time you have seen this person and so have not made a judgement about their character.

Listen with interest and intent

Are you listening or just waiting to speak? What is the chatter going on in your head as you are listening to the individual? How many questions are you thinking of before the individual has finished speaking?

Pick up on the words spoken, the tone of voice and the emotional message behind the words. Pay attention to what is *not* being said as much as what is being said.

Summarize what you have heard

If the level of listening has been low then it will be difficult to summarize what has been heard or the summary may be wrong. Impatience to finish the meeting quickly could also prevent the change practitioner from summarizing fully.

Do not wait until the very end of the meeting. Knowing that summarizing is going to happen will encourage careful listening. Once the conversation has been summarized, an incisive question often follows.

Question incisively and curiously

Questions can sometimes feel like an interrogation when they come from a place of judgement or shame, particularly when asking 'why?'

Allow your tone of voice to ask the question in a curious way, not judgementally. Consider what response you are wanting from your question. Ask questions that move the person to a goal or ideal outcome. Don't dwell on problems or blame.

Impartial and non-judgemental

When you know too much, impartiality can be a challenge. The more information that is known about the person or their problem, the more likely it is that advice and suggestions will be offered.

Make a conscious decision to suspend all you know about the person and situation. When an opinion or piece of advice comes into your head, push it away so that you can remain impartial and objective.

Challenging assumptions

This links closely to the ability to listen to the language used and to be aware if the individual is assuming something without fact. People are very good at making up stories to justify a thought or feeling.

Check the facts. Be bold and do not shy away from asking challenging questions and to challenge any assumptions you think are being made. Check your own assumptions too. Ask the question 'is this true?' 'How do you know it to be true?'

Open not leading questions

Leading questions are a way of giving advice 'through the back door'. They are usually long, closed questions that lead the individual to a solution or idea that you would like them to have. The idea or solution is likely to be yours and not theirs. An example is 'Do you think that speaking with your manager would help?', which is another way of saying 'I think you should speak with your manager.' An open question would be 'who else could you speak to?'

Having an awareness of the style of questions being asked is the first step to changing this habit. Does the question elicit a yes or no response? In which case it is likely to be a closed and leading question. Ask questions starting with What, Where, When, How and Who?

Silence is your friend

A challenge for all those who are uncomfortable with silence. The need to fill the silence is likely to be your issue not theirs. The meeting can feel rushed and, at worst, an interrogation. Silence is used to support reflection and the thought process. If you think the individual is uncomfortable with silence then it is best to ask them.

Relax and pace your meeting. Take a deep breath and count to three before asking the next question. Give the individual a chance to think about your question before you ask another. If their eyes are looking away from you and focussed mid-distance, this shows the person is thinking about the question. Stay silent until they are ready to reply.

Suggest with caution, do not give advice

An eagerness to give advice and offer suggestions is not as helpful as may be intended. Only offer ideas and suggestions when the individual is truly stuck.

Ask questions first to gain understanding and to test their thinking. The best person to come up with ideas is the person with the problem or issue.

A useful model to help change practitioners know if they are being directive or non-directive in their approach is the Coaching Spectrum of Push and Pull

Figure 3.2   The coaching spectrum of Push and Pull questions

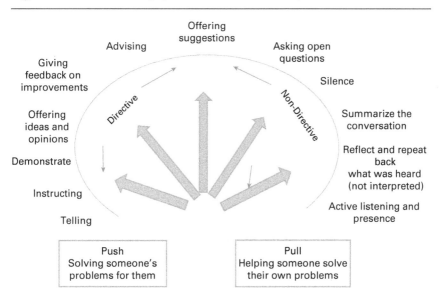

SOURCE Miles Downey, 2014

questions adapted by Miles Downey (2014). This shows the Push and Pull type questions and confirms that instructing, advising, suggesting sit on the directive or 'push' end of the spectrum. Used sparingly this might work, but if this style is used to excess it may result in the individual not being encouraged to think for themselves or may be dependent on the change practitioner to come up with the answers. The 'push' style of questioning is usually used when people are stressed, busy and just want the problem sorted quickly. The consequence of this is that the individual returns multiple times asking the same or more questions.

In contrast, a coaching style focuses on the 'pull' side of the model, which helps the individual to think of what they can and are willing to do to solve their own problem, issue or concern. This is a non-directive style using incisive questions, summarizing and active listening to encourage the individual to work through the issue. This requires a far more developed set of skills and a particular mindset.

The potential pitfalls of giving advice

Alison Hardingham et al's book *The Coach's Coach* (2004) suggests that 'advice is not coaching'. Hardingham sees advice as being disrespectful to the client.

To explore this subject further, it is useful to know the reason why advice is usually given in the first place.

Justifications are:

- If I'm asked for advice then the person must surely need or want it.
- It's my job to give advice – I'm the expert after all.
- If I know the answer to the problem then it makes sense for me to advise others.
- I don't have time to ask lots of questions – it's quicker to just tell others what to do.
- It makes me feel good when I am asked for my advice and I know the answer.
- I know better than the person asking.
- I want to help and guide the person.
- The advice I give would work for me so it's likely to be right for someone else.
- If I am asked by a senior person for advice then I don't want to patronize them by 'coaching' them.

The list could go on. For most people, there is good intent behind giving advice. For some people, however, the need to be right and to prove how much they know is the real reason. This can be problematic; it can be viewed as egotistical and arrogant. Any subconscious need to be right is likely to be revealed in the tone of voice used and the way the advice is delivered.

When we give advice, we are saying to others 'I know better than you. If you do it my way, then you can't go wrong.' This approach is based on judgements and opinion and things can, and do, often go wrong. Such as:

- If someone has taken your advice and it goes wrong, you are to blame. It wasn't their idea, it was yours.

- Your advice was ignored, and someone else's advice was used instead. How does this leave you feeling and thinking? Why were you asked for your advice if it's not going to be used?

- Were you asked for the advice or did you just feel the need to express your opinion? How might the other person feel about this unsolicited information?

- The advice is accepted because the other person wants to please you, but they are not committed to the ideas you have given.

- The advice often comes from what *you* think is best and what *you* would do in a similar situation rather than what is best for the other person and what is right for them.

Advice versus suggestions

An alternative to offering advice is to give suggestions: whereas advice is a judgement, a suggestion is offered for consideration.

When a suggestion is offered it is often worded and delivered in a different way and has a different intent. It is a recommendation based on a concern about the other person's ideas or decisions, and sounds like it is coming from a place of wanting to help:

Might I make a suggestion?

or

My suggestion would be.

Advice can often sound like a judgement and opinion:

What you should do is X.

or

I think you should do X.

The importance of using the right language, tone of voice, energy and pace when delivering the words makes a big difference to how others perceive and hear what is being said and this can have a dramatic effect on the outcome of the meeting.

Conclusion

In this chapter we have evaluated:

- The relevance of coaching for the change practitioner.
- Defining what coaching and mentoring is.
- Who can coach and mentor.
- Essential coaching skills for the change practitioner.
- The importance of emotional intelligence.
- The pitfalls of giving advice.

What is evident from the wider research is that coaching requires a different level of skill to that of mentoring, influencing or negotiating, not necessarily more superior. The ability to coach requires the need to remain completely objective in a conversation and to trust that the stakeholder, for example, is the best person to find the answers without the need to be told. By developing these high level skills, the change practitioner will enrich their communication skills and have far more influence with those they work with.

References

Clutterbuck, D, Megginson, D and Bajer, A (2016) *Building and Sustaining a Coaching Culture*, CIPD, London

Coachingfederation.org. 2022. [Online] https://coachingfederation.org/ (archived at https://perma.cc/Z84W-94FS)

Effective Modern Coaching, Downey, M (2014) LID Publishing, London

Goleman, D (2020) *Emotional Intelligence: Why it can matter more than IQ*, Bloomsbury Publishing, London

Hardingham, A, Brearley, M, Moorhouse, A and Venter, B (2004) *The Coach's Coach – Personal development for personal developers*, CIPD, London

Best practice coaching methods for change practitioners

04

Introduction

Experienced coaches will naturally follow a set of guiding principles, models, theories and frameworks to help support them in their profession. A guiding principle will also help change practitioners to decide what to do in different situations and ensures clear values and best practices are maintained. In this instance having a set of clear models and frameworks will ensure that any potentially difficult conversation has been thought through and planned.

Included within this chapter are themes covering:

- contracting and agreements
- structure and frameworks
- preparing for the session
- avoiding ethical dilemmas.

Contracting, agreements and setting the scene

Contracting is arguably one of the most important aspects of coaching and is defined as one of the first guiding principles that, when done well, will avoid any potential problems later on in the coaching relationship. Contracting 'sets the scene' for successful meetings.

The word 'contract' has many definitions and in the coaching context refers to the agreement between attendee(s) of a meeting to confirm:

- The purpose of the session.

- What is expected between the coach and the client.

- What the confidentiality clauses are and what happens if confidentiality is broken.

Contracting during a coaching session is a widely used practice. However, in terms of corporate meetings (including meetings between the change practitioner and stakeholder), contracting is often overlooked or seen as unnecessary and taking up valuable time. Because of this, meetings often don't start well and problems occur later. These problems are difficult to unpick because a clear agreement was not put in place as guidance at the time and there is nothing to refer back to when things go wrong. If the term 'contract' seems a bit formal then using a less formal name will achieve the same outcome. Explaining to an individual that you will be 'setting the scene' before you start the conversation is likely to receive a better response than saying, for example, 'I am going to contract the session first.'

You are a change practitioner and have set up a meeting with a team member who has some concerns about a restructure that you are managing. As part of this meeting, you agree:

- What can and can't be said outside of the meeting.

- What to do if a senior manager asks you for pertinent information about the individual attending the meeting.

- What to do if the team member is asked to talk about the meeting with their manager.

It is important to discuss these issues as part of the contracting agreement to ensure an open and transparent conversation takes place from the start and so each party knows what is expected going forward.

Confidentiality and breaking the confidentiality clause

Confidentiality is an essential part of this process. Agreeing what can and can't be said and repeated outside of the room is essential to gain trust as well as working within ethical guidelines.

There are times when it is advisable to break confidentiality agreements, particularly if the individual discloses something to the change practitioner that is of harm to themselves, to others or is a criminal act. The individual attending the meeting needs to know about this clause at the start of the session because it is impossible to know what they may want to off-load to the change practitioner, as a way of unburdening guilt, fear, concerns and even gossip. The individual may consider the change practitioner to be un-biased and someone they can trust with their information. This may be the case, but only if the information is legal. It is important to add here that instances like this are very rare. Anything left undisclosed and that needs to be discussed is known as a *psychological* contract.

Psychological contract

A psychological contract is not useful in a coaching conversation and should be avoided. A psychological contract happens when things which need to be said and explicitly defined or expressed are ignored or assumed that it is not important. Both parties *think* that they know what the other is thinking, feeling and expecting from the meeting. It is impossible to know what some-one else is thinking if they have not verbally said what is on their mind. Having a clear verbal contract and agreement at the start of the meeting is essential to avoid problems later. There is a saying in the coaching community that when things go wrong in coaching it's because the contract has not been fully established, or has not been understood or agreed.

The contract or agreement can change over time. This is often referred to as 're-contracting' or 'spot contracting' where the relationship or the goals and expectations shift over time and will need to be re-established.

Three-way contract

Three-way contracting is widely used when an individual is recommended for coaching as part of an organizational change by their manager. Unless the individual is fully committed to the coaching then there is often a resistance to being coached and the outcomes of the sessions are rarely successful. The three-way contract at the start of the process with the coach, coachee and manager will help ensure that everyone involved is clear as to why the coaching has been recommended and what the expected outcomes are. The coachee will have the opportunity to express concerns in the contracting meeting which gives the coach the chance to agree an open confidentiality agreement with the individual's manager.

Resistance to coaching and how this can be overcome will be discussed later in this book. The following two scenarios using the same problem demonstrate what can happen when three-way contracting is not followed through.

Scenario 1: example of coaching using three-way contracting

The situation

Mel manages a small team and has a team member called Sam. Sam has been working in the team for a few years and Mel has started to notice some negative language being used by Sam during a recent restructure of the team. Mel has also noticed that Sam's time management has started to suffer. Mel thinks that an external coach will help Sam with time management and to develop some emotional intelligence. However, Sam has never had coaching and does not understand what it is. When Mel mentions the coaching idea to Sam the first reaction is 'Is there something wrong with me? I thought I was doing OK at work. Am I the only person being coached?' This is a typical reaction from those who do not understand coaching or its benefits.

The approach

Mel set up the coaching with a trusted external coach who recommended a three-way discussion for the first 15 minutes of the first coaching session, where Mel was invited into the room with Sam and the coach. The coach facilitated a discussion with Mel and Sam where they agreed expectations and what a good outcome would be for both of them. During the session, the coach encouraged both Mel and Sam to be honest about what was on their minds and what some of the past issues had been, to encourage Sam's buy-in to the coaching and to commit to the change in behaviour which Mel was asking of Sam. This three-way discussion also enabled the coach to explain confidentiality and contracting.

The outcome

The coaching went well as soon as Sam realized that the sessions were not a way to 'fix a problem' but to encourage an open dialogue about Sam's underlying concerns relating to the recent restructure. The opportunity to speak in confidence and with honesty to someone outside of the organization was a key benefit. Sam returned to work with a more positive mindset and with more motivation to accept the changes. Future one-to-one conversations were also improved as trust had increased between Mel and Sam.

Scenario 2: example of a meeting without the three-way contracting

Mel suggests to Sam that coaching would be useful. Mel has a conversation with the external coach to express concerns about Sam but is too busy to attend the first session. Mel does not see the relevance of contracting because the session is for Sam and it has been agreed the meeting is confidential.

The approach

When the coach meets with Sam the conversation at first is quite strained. Sam is unsure of what coaching is and why the coaching has been agreed. It would seem that Mel has not spoken to Sam about her concerns and is hoping that the coach will do this instead. Time is spent in the session exploring what Sam thinks Mel is concerned about but, overall, there is some resistance to the questions being asked as trust has not yet been established. A few weeks later Mel asks the coach how the sessions are going and expresses disappointment that Sam's behaviour has not improved.

The coach feels under pressure to justify why this might be and agrees that it is difficult to know what can be explored with Sam as a clear contract has not been established. Furthermore, Mel and Sam have not had any conversations outside of the coaching to discuss feedback. Reflecting on the coaching session, the coach realizes that insisting on a three-way contract would have avoided these problems.

Top tip

Clear contracting is essential in a coaching conversation to establish and agree everyone's role and responsibility in the meetings.

The use of frameworks and coaching models

Although there is no defined structure when having a coaching conversation, the use of a coaching model or framework can help to improve the flow and structure of the conversation.

Frameworks and models are often used interchangeably but they mean different things.

- A framework is a set of guiding and core principles to use when preparing for a coaching conversation.
- The coaching model is a structured method to use during a coaching conversation to guide the process.

This section explores how and when to use these.

When managing difficult situations and conversations, the challenge isn't so much what to do, but how to do it. It is equally important for the change practitioner to check they are ready for whatever challenges may emerge during the meeting as it is for planning for the meeting itself.

Chapter 3 explored and guided the user in the concept of using a set of essential skills that form the core principles and mindsets required by the change practitioner. These core principles enable an adult-to-adult conversation and reduce the chance of the stakeholder being resistant or defensive. The responsibility lies with the change practitioner to ensure that these core principles are used as part of their own values and beliefs.

Preparing for a coaching conversation

What is often overlooked by change practitioners, managers and other change professionals is how to prepare themselves, as much as the documentation, to ensure a meaningful conversation.

REST (Noble, 2021) is a framework that offers guidance to ensure a successful, considered and structured conversation. It stands for:

- Rapport and being present
- Empathy
- Setting the scene
- Target (stay on track).

REST

This framework may take a while to remember and to feel comfortable with, but when used alongside a coaching model or technique it will guide the change practitioner on how to ensure a successful conversation. What follows are useful ideas to make each of the REST stages effective:

Rapport and being present

- Relationship engagement. Being truly in the space with positive regard for the person you are with.
- Awareness of self and your thoughts, feelings and actions. Being fully in the room with no other distractions.
- Sitting in a way that demonstrates rapport and an interest in the other person.
- Openness and willingness to find interest and be curious. Getting to know the person better.

Empathy

- Stepping into their world. Seeing things from their perspective.
- Understanding as far as you can how things must be for them.
- Avoid sympathizing. Taking on the emotions of the other person is rarely helpful.

- Acknowledging what is going on for them.
- Not rescuing or trying to make things better.

Setting the scene

- A two-way agreement as to the purpose of the meeting, what you both want to get from the meeting and what you are both responsible for.
- Essential if you have someone resistant to having the meeting and who may not engage in the conversation.
- The meeting can only go ahead if there is a dialogue between both of you and an acceptance of the meeting.

Target (stay on track)

- Not getting 'hooked' into a conversation you didn't intend to have.
- Suspending your judgements and opinions will help you to stay on track and focussed.

What are ethical dilemmas?

As a set of guiding principles for all professionals, this chapter would not be complete without the mention of ethics and behaviours at work.

Ethics can also be described as a set of principles and conduct linked to the moral values and moral choices people make. Ethical practice, also referred to as ethical maturity, relates to the standards of professional conduct that anyone within a position of responsibility is expected to uphold (Iordanou et al, 2017).

It is likely that anyone in a senior leadership role with regular contact with anyone inside and outside of the organization, will come across an ethical dilemma at some point in their profession, possibly even daily.

Unethical behaviours at work

Much has been written around unethical workplace behaviour including the CIPD's review of unethical workplace behaviour (2019). Unethical workplace behaviour manifests itself in many ways and can vary in severity from minor transgressions to large-scale illegal activity. These behaviours are often referred to as counterproductive work behaviour (CWB) and are actions that go against the legitimate interests of the organization and its employees. CWB is often driven by self-interest and includes acts of sabotage, theft, fraud, deception, bullying and harassment. CWB can also be more passive unethical conduct such as withdrawing behaviours, lateness, absenteeism, non-compliance with rules and deliberately and knowingly reducing personal work standards. All these behaviours happen for a reason and often as a result of organizational change, especially when the change is not seen as acceptable or fair by some individuals and when it elicits fear.

Potential ethical dilemmas

There are many possible examples of change practitioners unwittingly finding themselves in an ethical dilemma and not knowing what to do next. Here are some examples of where professional ethics and boundaries may clash.

The change practitioner:

1 Is aware that a team is being removed and therefore there will be job losses for the whole team. The Head of Service is aware of this. When meeting with one of the team they mention that their Head of Service has told them that there is nothing to worry about and that no one in the team is losing their job.

2 Is in a longstanding relationship with someone in another team and has just heard that a restructure of their partner's team is going to mean job losses. This may impact the change practitioner's partner but the change practitioner has confirmed confidentiality until more is known about the changes.

3 Is having a conversation about a new system implementation. The individual suddenly, and without warning, tells the change practitioner that they are being sexually harassed in the office but is too scared to tell anyone.

4 Has been made aware of an acquisition that will take place over the next few months but is sworn to secrecy. The culture of the company acquiring the business goes completely against all of the change practitioner's

beliefs and values leading to concerns about the impact this will have on the people and how the work will change. The change practitioner can't afford to leave the company but is expected to sell the benefits to the rest of the organization.

5 Is pursuing an organizational change or transformation for their self-interest; acting outside the law or their delegated authority in planning or implementing change.

6 Coerces employees into a certain behaviour or uses manipulative tactics that involve deceit, threat, fear, secrecy or dishonesty to gain commitment to change.

7 Has agreed to speak with an employee about a change implementation. The employee is angry with the organization and is taking out their anger on the change practitioner. The behaviour is unacceptable, the change practitioner feels quite scared by the reaction of the individual but at the same time has a sense of empathy with them and does not want to abandon the meeting.

How to avoid ethical dilemmas

The nature of ethical dilemmas is that they often occur when you are least expecting them. As soon as an ethical dilemma has happened it will be in the conscious awareness of the change practitioner to make sure it does not happen again. Reading through the 'potential for ethical dilemmas' will alert the change practitioner to the potential pitfalls and how to avoid these, but there could be many more situations that are relevant within the organization and that are not on the list. Pre-planning is essential. Before any meeting think through what the potential pitfalls are and ask the questions 'Is there anything potential for an ethical dilemma to occur here? What can I do to avoid this?'

In Chapter 11 of this book the subject of coaching supervision is discussed as an important aspect of continuous professional development (CPD) for internal coaches. Discussions with a coach supervisor will helped the coach to avoid ethical dilemmas and will provide an opinion from an unbiased perspective.

Trained coaches will know the importance of being aware of their 'internal supervisor'. This is the ability to know instinctively when something is not quite right and not ignoring their feelings. With practice, the change practitioner can learn to concentrate on their own 'internal supervisor' when something does not feel right. This could simply be because of their own moral values and judgements. Some people are more intuitive than others and this ability to understand something instinctively, without the need for conscious reasoning helps them to make important decisions in the moment.

To avoid ethical dilemmas when there is no access to a coach supervisor, the change practitioner may know someone else within the organization they can speak with, in confidence, to sense-check what is happening for them or to pre-empt the situation happening in the first place. This could be a senior manager in HR or another trusted colleague.

Earlier in this chapter the subject of confidentiality was discussed and consideration should be made to who the change practitioner chooses to speak with and making sure that confidentiality is respected on either side.

To summarize, here are some practical tips the change practitioner can adopt to avoid ethical dilemmas happening or to mitigate any future situations:

- Think in advance about the appropriateness of the meeting, who you are meeting with and if there is any potential for a dilemma occurring.

- What is your 'internal supervisor' or intuition telling you either before or during the meeting?

- If you are mid-way through a meeting and you are feeling uncomfortable, let the stakeholder know and suggest that the meeting is ended.

- Seek out a coach-supervisor or trusted friend who can talk through situations either before or after the meeting to sense-check and gain perspective from a different viewpoint.

- Learn from any previous ethical dilemmas to mitigate future similar situations.

The relevance of ethics for change practitioners

The role of a change practitioner is underpinned by a set of ethical values that influences their actions and the outcomes and consequences of a change initiative. These may be personal values, a Code of Conduct set by the organization, the accreditation they have undertaken or those of a professional body.

Ethical maturity at an organizational level is essential and is defined as 'the increasing capacity to embrace ethical complexity and deal with appropriate respect and fairness to all parties involved in a situation' (Carroll and Shaw, 2013). At an organizational level, issues around ethics and boundaries can often be blurred when operating as an internal change practitioner. As an example, issues around confidentiality may arise during a conversation. The change practitioner will likely be privy to sensitive information that is relevant to their job role. When the time comes to meet with the stakeholders they may volunteer information that conflicts with the change practitioner's role. The stakeholder may also display counter-productive behaviours as they think it is safer to do so in the presence of the change practitioner as opposed to their manager. These behaviours are not necessarily the responsibility of the change practitioner to remedy but could lead to a useful conversation with the stakeholder to help them to understand what is upsetting them. If this conversation happens it is wise to take in these considerations:

● How ethical is this conversation?

● What is the intent of the change practitioner?

● Is it the change practitioner's responsibility to have this conversation?

● Who does this conversation serve, the change practitioner or the stakeholder?

● What if the conversation turned into a counselling session?

These important questions around the intent of the conversation will help avoid ethical dilemmas occurring.

Top tip

Pay attention to your 'internal supervisor' and take action. If you do not feel comfortable about what is being said to you then be honest and admit to the individual how the information is making you feel. The best question to ask in the moment is: **'What would you like me to do with that information?'** This puts the responsibility back on the individual to expressly say what they want to have happen and what their expectations are. They may ask you, as change practitioner, to fix the problem for them and it will be your responsibility to decide what to do next. Remembering that when you fix the problem for someone else, you now own the problem and they don't.

Using coaching models

A coaching model provides a structure for a coaching conversation or meeting, to guide the process and focus on the end goal. Even experienced coaches will use a coaching model to help navigate and guide the conversation through a logical sequence. Without the structure of a coaching model, the coaching can easily end up as a 'cosy chat' with no real sense of where the coaching session is going or where the client wants to get to.

Three useful questions to use at the start of a coaching conversation are:

- What is your goal?
- What do you want to achieve?
- What would be a good outcome for you?

Once the goal has been defined further questions are asked to clarify how to make these goals specific and measurable.

This section will explore three coaching models that can be used as part of a formal coaching session or an informal meeting using a coaching style and approach.

1 GROW made famous by Sir John Whitmore.

2 CLEAR developed by Peter Hawkins.

3 EMERGE developed by the co-author Sue Noble.

GROW

GROW is an acronym for:

- GOAL setting for the session as well as short- and long-term goals.
- REALITY checking to explore the current situation, blocks and barriers to success.
- OPTIONS and alternative strategies or choices.
- WRAP UP what is to be done, when and by whom and the will or motivation to do it.

The principle behind GROW is that the coach helps the client to develop and define their goal early in the coaching process. Once the goal has been established the coach can move around the GROW model to establish the reality of the situation and options to consider before ending up at 'Wrap Up' (*what, when, who, will*). Typically, experienced coaches use GROW in a more systemic way simply because the goal may take time to develop. Very few people turn up for coaching with a defined goal and forcing someone to come up with a goal can be stressful and impractical. The goal is often established through the coach's skilful questioning and can evolve over the course of the coaching sessions.

CLEAR

Clear is an acronym for:

- CONTRACT the session, how the process will work, establishing the client's desired outcomes.
- LISTEN using active and empathic listening. Establish the reality and reframing.
- EXPLORE the current situation, generate new insights and create different options.
- ACTION plan once the best option has been agreed. What are the first steps, then how to proceed?
- REVIEW the actions during the session and at the next session to check for commitment.

The focus on CLEAR is the emphasis on the contracting at the start of the session and the importance of empathic listening to enable the change practitioner to explore the current situation. This helps to guide the client to a clear plan of action and to finish the session with a review of the coaching and the importance for checking the client's commitment to coaching.

EMERGE

EMERGE is an acronym for:

- EXPECTATION. Contracting and agreeing the session, goals and ideal outcomes.
- MOTIVATION AND ENERGY to reach the goal and to change the current situation.
- EXPLORE what has been done already, what has worked, blocks and barriers.
- REVIEW AND REFLECT on the conversation. What else could be done. New insights and learning.

- GENERATE IDEAS for options and choices. Check the goal is still the same.

- EVALUATE actions and way forward. Summarize the session and check new insights and learning.

Figure 4.1 shows how the EMERGE coaching model incorporates essential elements that ensure a successful coaching outcome. Coaching is about change and for coaching to be successful the client must realize and have the motivation for change. Without the intrinsic motivation *(what compels the person to do what they want to do)* the momentum for change may diminish over time. Any process that involves change requires internal energy to get there. This is where the EMERGE coaching model which explicitly defines the *motivation and energy* to reach the goal or desired outcome can be useful.

Figure 4.1   EMERGE coaching model and framework

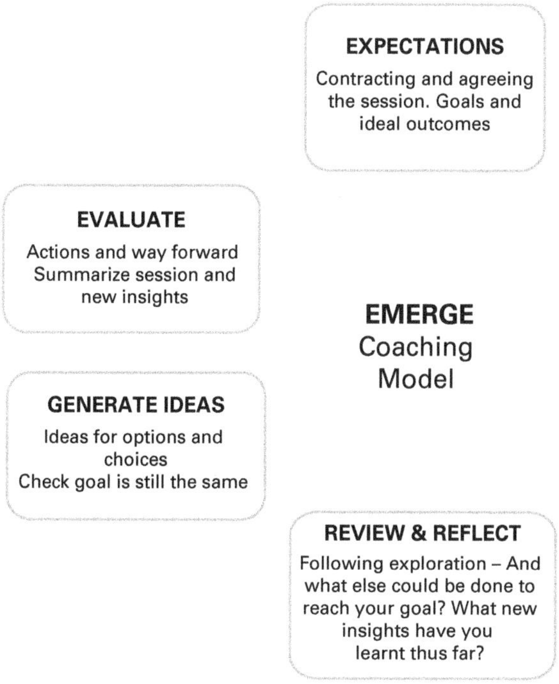

EXPECTATIONS
Contracting and agreeing the session. Goals and ideal outcomes

EVALUATE
Actions and way forward
Summarize session and new insights

MOTIVATION & ENERGY
To reach the goal and to change the current situation – intrinsic and extrinsic

EMERGE
Coaching
Model

GENERATE IDEAS
Ideas for options and choices
Check goal is still the same

EXPLORE
What have you done?, already? What has worked well, not so well? What are the blocks and barriers?

REVIEW & REFLECT
Following exploration – And what else could be done to reach your goal? What new insights have you learnt thus far?

SOURCE (Noble, 2020)

To fully embrace EMERGE as a coaching model it's important to understand not only what each stage aims to do but also why it is important to address each of the stages. EMERGE is not intended to be used in a strict, regimented way. Users can go to the stage that is most appropriate once the conversation gets underway.

However, experience shows that to optimize a coaching conversation it is best to start with *Expectations* and to end with *Evaluate*.

Appendix A offers a comprehensive understanding of why each stage is important when using the EMERGE model and how to incorporate EMERGE into a coaching conversation.

Conclusion

This chapter has explored a number of important issues of how to have successful coaching conversations either formally or informally by using structured frameworks and models to guide the process. The important but thorny issue of ethical dilemmas has also been given a spotlight because it happens, often without noticing and usually when it is too late. This chapter has offered some guidance on how to manage these situations with contracting and agreeing the session being an essential part of any conversation to ensure that psychological safety is maintained and transparent.

References

Carroll, M and Shaw, E (2013) *Ethical Maturity in the Helping Professions*, Jessica Kingsley, London

CIPD (2019) Rotten apples, bad barrels and sticky situations, www.cipd.co.uk/knowledge/culture/ethics/ethical-behaviour#gref (archived at https://perma.cc/54CT-9449)

Iordanou, I, Iordanou, C, Hawley, R (2017) *Values and Ethics in Coaching*, Sage, London

Introduction to Emergenetics® and its relevance to change and coaching 05

Introduction

In the world of change delivery, it is useful to understand the nuances of personality types, strengths and behaviours. If we have no sense of awareness of who we are and the impact change has on ourselves, how can we know how change is impacting others around us?

In each of the chapters we have highlighted the importance of offering support to those we work with, and ourselves, when experiencing organizational change. This chapter explores what is known as the 'third generation' of psychometric tools, which includes an accurate and easy to use profiling tool called Emergenetics®. The aim is to offer further support by understanding the way people think and behave when experiencing organizational change and how to support people through uncertainty and ambiguity.

This chapter does not delve into the history of personality types and psychometric testing but does help readers to understand that Emergenetics is a scientifically reliable psychometric tool that measures the way people *think* and *behave* separately. It provides clarity of how thinking attributes can impact on how information and change is processed and how behaviours become evident when change happens.

Emergenetics explained

Emergenetics tests patterns of thinking and behaving that emerge from the combination of an individual's genetic blueprint and environmental influences. The term was coined by putting two words together, 'emerge' and 'genetics'

The research behind Emergenetics began in the late 1980s by co-developers Dr Geil Browning (an educator) and Dr Wendell Williams (an organizational psychologist) and lasted for approximately 10 years. Both were interested in psychometrics and how people behaved at work. They based their research on strict database management (which preserves the validity and reliability of the tool) and also on a commitment to keep their metaphorical model of the brain current with research into neuroscience. This offers practical strategies using the theory of Emergenetics (Browning, 2006 and 2018).

How can change practitioners use Emergenetics?

Understanding someone's thinking and behavioural preferences is an incredibly powerful tool for change practitioners because it reveals how people make decisions, manage challenging situations and communicate their thoughts and feelings.

There have been many studies over the years that aim to understand what personality is and the personality traits that can help and hinder communication and decision-making. By communicating with people how *they* want to be communicated with and not how we *assume* they want to be communicated with is all part of influencing and building rapport.

How does Emergenetics work?

Emergenetics is based on seven attributes that can be separately identified and scientifically quantified for each individual. Figure 5.1 shows the four thinking and three behavioural attributes and although not represented in colour on this example, each of the thinking preferences are colour coded.

The four thinking attributes are:

- analytical (blue)
- structural (green)

Figure 5.1   Emergenetics, four thinking and three behavioural attributes

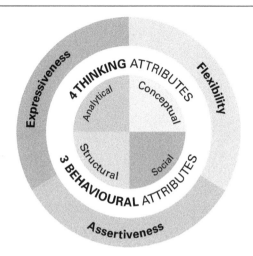

SOURCE Emergenetics International

- social (red)
- conceptual (yellow).

The three behavioural attributes are:

- expressiveness
- assertiveness
- flexibility.

The results are evaluated from the responses to an online questionnaire. As previously mentioned, each thinking attribute is represented by a colour displayed as a pie chart and a percentage for each of the attributes. An individual's profile can be made up of any combination of thinking and behavioural preferences, expressing our uniqueness and individual strengths. The behavioural attributes are represented by a percentile spectrum. This is represented on a coloured version of the model by a purple circle around the thinking attributes pie chart. This is because behaviours are often the first thing noticed in others. Understanding individual's thinking preference comes later.

Behavioural attributes and how people show up

The behavioural attributes are scored and range from 0 to 100 percentiles on three spectrums and the results are expressed by the third they fall in – first-third, second-third or third-third. The results are not measured in terms of high or low but by the degree of energy expended in each behaviour. Emergenetics is careful not to describe people as 'not assertive' or 'inflexible'. Judgemental language such as 'very' or 'not good at' is also avoided because Emergenetics measures preference, not competency or aptitude.

The spectrum is calculated as follows based on continuous validation and research:

- 33 per cent of the population will fall in the first-third (their scores are within 0–33 percentile).

- 33 per cent will fall in the second-third (their scores are within the 34–66 percentile). This is the 'It depends' group and they can flex their attribute either way depending on the circumstances.

- 33 per cent will fall in the third-third (their scores are within the 67–100 percentile).

The next section focuses in more detail at the three attributes and their significance.

Expressiveness

The degree of expressiveness indicates the outward display of emotions toward others and the world at large. Expressiveness is not what is experienced inside but what is shared with the outside. As shown in Figure 5.2, people who are on the first-third of the expressiveness spectrum may appear reserved or quiet. In a meeting with others they may be more likely to listen

Figure 5.2   Expressiveness spectrum

My thoughts are my business		I can't wait to tell everyone
Quiet, reserved, pensive		Gregarious, spontaneous
Energized by solitude		Energized by people
Facial expressions are passive		Facial expressions are animated
First-third	Second-third	Third-third

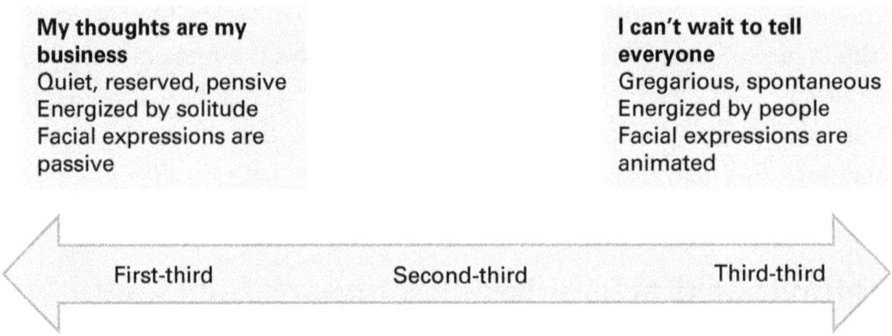

rather than talk. People who are on the third-third of the expressiveness spectrum may be more outgoing and talkative. They will happily share information about themselves.

People who are in the second-third of the expressiveness spectrum will move easily to first-third or third-third behaviour, depending upon the situation.

Assertiveness

The degree of assertiveness reflects the style and pace with which you advance your thoughts, feelings and beliefs. As shown in Figure 5.3, people who are on the first-third of the assertiveness spectrum are often easy going, amiable and calming. In a meeting with others they are likely to ask questions to bring people round to their way of thinking. People who are on the third-third of the assertiveness spectrum are more likely to be driving, competitive and do not mind confrontation. They are likely to tell others what they think should be done.

People who are in the second-third of the assertiveness spectrum will move easily to first-third or third-third behaviour, depending upon the situation.

Figure 5.3   Assertiveness spectrum

No need to get excited
Keep the status quo
Amiable, peacekeepers
Complete tasks at own pace
Even toned voice

Let's get this done now!
Set a goal, competitive
Challenging
Complete tasks at all costs
Voice becomes louder

First-third   Second-third   Third-third

Flexibility

The degree of flexibility measures the willingness to accommodate the thoughts and actions of others and to meet their needs. Flexibility can also relate to accepting and accommodating change, particularly when it has been imposed by someone else. As shown in Figure 5.4, people who are on the first-third of the flexibility spectrum tend to prefer defined situations and need a reason to change their mind, which can sometimes be misunderstood as resisting change. In a meeting with others they may question new ideas unless they are provided with a convincing rationale for the change. People on the third-third of the flexibility spectrum are likely to be accommodating and open to new suggestions. They are more likely to go with the flow and agree with the ideas put forward.

People who are in the second-third of the flexibility spectrum will move easily to first-third or third-third behaviour, depending upon the situation.

Figure 5.4   Flexibility spectrum

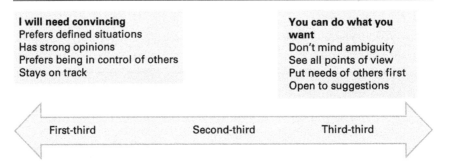

Thinking attributes and how people think

Analytical thinking (represented by the colour blue) is logical, rational, objective, factual and sceptical. This thinking attribute is not about the detail but is about the data. People with this preference can generally understand the data within a spreadsheet and be able to make sense of it. Analytical thinkers:

- Are unlikely to be comfortable moving forward without knowing the objectives of the goal and the data supporting it.

- May have a logical reason for being sceptical and may appear unemotional.

- Need to have a sound reason for change, for example the data to justify it.

The analytical part of the brain immediately looks for verification and asks 'Where's the data and research?'

Structural thinking (represented by the colour green) is practical, cautious, predictable and methodical. Structural thinkers:

- Are likely to need set plans and guidelines.
- May not be comfortable without set processes to achieve the goal.
- May be cautious about change and feel stressed unless they are convinced the change is an improvement and know how the change will affect the future.
- May need background information and a plan with clear steps.

The structural part of the brain looks for a workable solution and asks, 'How can I apply this practically?'

Social thinking (represented by the colour red) is sympathetic, connected, socially aware and intuitive about other people. Social thinkers:

- May have an emotional reaction to change and may take the change personally.
- Are likely to be concerned about how it will affect others.
- May need to use stories and have conversations with others to process the information.

The social part of the brain has a concern for others and asks, 'Who else needs to be involved in this?'

Conceptual thinking (represented by the colour yellow) is imaginative, creative, innovative, visionary and intuitive about ideas. Conceptual thinkers:

- May be early adapters and energized by change in the beginning.
- Are likely to connect with the ideology or big picture.
- May summarize the change with a picture, word or motto.

The conceptual part of the brain may immediately grasp essential ideas, likes to see where things lead and asks: 'What's the concept here and where can I go with it?'

What is each thinking attribute motivated by?

Motivation has been an important theme throughout this book as just one of the drivers for change. Understanding how each attribute is motivated will help change practitioners when working with stakeholders. This is particularly useful if the thinking and behavioural preferences are known in advance. However, it is possible to pick up on clues when speaking with individuals, listening to the language they use and watching out for their gestures and expressions.

Analytical thinkers are best motivated by a leader they believe has credibility or a track-record of being right – someone who excels in a particular area and whose expertise they believe will benefit the group. If they do well, they prefer to be rewarded in a way that is commensurate with their contribution.

Structural thinkers like to implement projects and want to know that time spent will add to the organization's progress. They are best motivated by a leader who is organized, thoughtful, competent and meticulous. They might prefer to be rewarded in writing, in a timely manner, in a precise way that is specific to the task.

Social thinkers want to feel valued and need to know that what they do has an impact. They are best motivated by someone they respect, and they will always go the extra mile for people who express trust, faith and belief in their abilities. They prefer to be rewarded in person with a gesture that is from the heart.

Conceptual thinkers must be invested in the cause or they will not feel motivated. The big picture matters more than who is leading the change. They also prefer unconventional and imaginative rewards.

Expressiveness. Third-third preference employees are more motivated when things are openly discussed and an open door environment. They may prefer public recognition. The first-third preference employees may not like a lot of fanfare, but they appreciate one-on-one and private encouragement.

Assertiveness. Third-third assertiveness preference employees are likely to let you know what they want as a reward. First-third assertiveness preference employees may hope that everyone will move in the same direction and may find recognition by being thanked for gaining consensus.

Flexibility. Those with a third-third preference in flexibility will likely go along with the team as long as a project does not contradict their morals or beliefs. They may be happy with many kinds of recognition. First-third flexibility preference employees will be pleased with recognition and seeing something through. They may also want to know in advance what kind of reward they can expect.

No excuses

With Emergenetics there is a saying: 'no whining or no excuses'. Because the focus is on preference rather than personality, if an individual does not have a preference for an attribute, this is not an excuse to disengage with a particular task or an excuse for non-performance.

It is possible to accomplish a task that is not appealing to a particular strength or preference, but it may take more concentration. There is no ideal Emergenetics profile for a role. Someone on the third-third of the assertiveness spectrum does not necessarily make a good leader, despite some common stereotypes. Likewise, someone on the first-third of the flexibility spectrum is not necessarily resistant to change. It is important to remember that with Emergenetics everyone can move up and down the behavioural spectrum depending on the situation and everyone has the ability to think in different ways. This is evident when individuals have more than one Thinking preference which then leads them to make decisions based on their two or more preferences.

The following case studies offer two different examples of how the Emergenetics thinking preferences and behavioural spectrum may work in practice.

CASE STUDY

Jaylin:

- Manages a small team of four people in the marketing department of a shipping company.
- Has a preference for conceptual and social thinking.
- Leadership style is strategic, visionary, inclusive and people focussed.
- Can allow emotions to get in the way of making the right decision.
- Does not have a preference for analytical or structural thinking.

Behaviour attributes:

- second-third expressiveness
- second-third assertiveness
- second-third flexibility.

When Jaylin was told by his manager of a possible restructuring of the team, his first thoughts led him to think about the future, the vision of the new team. His thoughts then turned to his team and how they may be impacted by this news.

Jaylin is keen to meet up with his team to explain the news he has been given and is aware that not everyone has a preference for conceptual and social thinking.

Jaylin:

- Will use his knowledge of the team's profile to make sure that his communication meets as many of his teams' preferences as possible.
- Is aware that his behavioural preferences will help him to 'walk the spectrum' and to manage the meeting using a range of behavioural attributes which enable a successful outcome.
- Is aware of the importance of using his least preferred attributes (analytical and structural) to help him to structure the next steps in the process.
- Is aware that he should study and communicate the data logically and rationally, which is not his natural preference.
- Knows that this may take more concentration and will take him out of his comfort zone.
- Considered ways of managing his energy levels appropriately.

CASE STUDY

Amba:

- Is Head of Service for Highways and Transport within a local authority and she directly manages four team leaders.
- Has a preference for structural and analytical thinking and in terms of leadership style is focussed on facts, is pragmatic and action-oriented.
- Can allow her logical thinking to dismiss the emotions of her team.
- Does not have a preference for social or conceptual thinking.

Behavioural attributes:

- first-third expressiveness
- third-third assertiveness
- second-third flexibility.

When Amba was told by her director about a new IT system and the changes in procedures for the team as a result, her first thoughts were to gather the facts and data to enable her to make an informed decision as to whether these new procedures were right for the team. Amba then made a list of all the things that she and her team needed to do before the implementation started. Although communicating with the team was not her natural style, Amba realized that her team was made up of people with a preference for social thinking.

Amba:

- Made a list of when and how she would meet with her team.
- Is aware to put more thought into the future of the implementation and how it might look once the changes had all been completed.
- Is aware of the need to 'dial-up' her conceptual thinking.

During Amba's first meeting with her team, she demonstrated her first-third expressiveness by being calm, poised and quiet. She thought carefully about the pros and cons of the change and was willing to listen to her team's concerns.

Amba:

- Allowed her team to speak and she did not interrupt.
- Increased the momentum and energy by sharing her concerns about the new system and by stating very clearly and directly that she would speak with the director about her concerns.

How to recognize thinking and behavioural attributes

An ideal situation would be for everyone within the organization to undertake the online Emergenetics questionnaire and for the results to be shared and evaluated as part of a team 'Meeting of the Minds' event. The purpose and advantage of this would be that the organization is consistent in its approach to understanding how to use the Emergenetics psychometric tool and that everyone in the team is talking the same language. It is far easier to work out the behavioural preferences of someone else because of what we can see, hear and observe about them and their behaviours. It is less easy to decipher someone else's thinking preference but this can be achieved by observing and listening to the words used and the way they are expressed. A good way to start this process is to evaluate yourself first, before evaluating the thinking of someone else.

Using the following list:

- Select the words in Table 5.1 that best describe you. You may select a few or many.

- The more words you circle in a certain attribute the more likely you will have it as a preference.

- Remember to be honest with your evaluation. This is not about what you would like your thinking preference to be but an honest reflection of your thinking preference based on what you know about yourself.

Top tip

When evaluating someone else, remember that this is from your perspective and a more accurate way is to ask the individual to complete the list evaluation for themselves.

Table 5.1   Evaluating the thinking and behavioural attributes of Self and others

Analytical	Conceptual
Reasoned	Inventive
Rational	Original
Intellectual	Innovative
Objective	Imaginative
Follows logical thinking	Intuitive about ideas
Questioning	Unconventional
Critical thinker	Global
Investigative	Seeks change
Inquiring	Bored easily

(*continued*)

Table 5.1   (Continued)

Structural		Social
Detailed		Sensitive
Disciplined		Giving
Methodical		Friendly
Rule follower		Supportive
Follows process		Intuitive about people
Organized		Compassionate
Traditional		Caring
Predictable		Empathic
Practical		Feeling

Expressiveness

First-third	Second-third	Third-third
Avoids spotlight		Talkative
One to one		Performer
Keeps feelings private	It depends	Talks to strangers
Calm		Chatty
Reserved		Outgoing
Quiet		Gregarious

Assertiveness

First-third	Second-third	Third-third
Compliant		Tough
Peacekeeper		Telling
Avoids confrontation	It depends	Forceful
Accepting		Determined
Deliberate		Competitive
Amiable		Driving

Flexibility

First-third	Second-third	Third-third
Focussed		Easy going
Narrows options		Adaptable
Prefers defined situations	It depends	Accommodating
Dislikes change		Handles ambiguity
Decides easily		Sees many options

Table 5.2 Phrases to use for each thinking preference

Analytical	Conceptual
I'll get to the point	I have this wild idea
What is the cost/benefit ratio?	Let's brainstorm new ways to solve this
I have been analysing the situation	What is the bigger picture here?
What is the bottom line?	How does this connect to the vision?
I'll skip the details and just give you an executive summary	This has the right flow
What does the research say?	I value your ingenious ideas
I value your investigation of the facts	Let's be creative here

Structural	Social
Here are more details	How are you feeling about this?
Organization and order are the keys to the solution	I'm concerned about how others will react
Let's take this one step at a time	I'm sure you want to be involved in the discussion
What does the policy say?	Have all the right people been included?
Are we on schedule?	Let's work through this together
Let's take an inventory	How does that grab you?
I appreciate your efficiency	I love your contribution to this team

Communicating with Emergenetics

This chapter has explored the importance of being more aware of the way our thinking and behavioural preferences have an impact on our communication and decision-making motivation. Table 5.2 aims to help change practitioners consider the language to use to maximize communication impact and to more successfully influence and motivate individuals in each of the thinking attributes.

Understanding the language patterns people use and how this might relate to their thinking preferences can help build a better understanding of others as well as ourselves.

Conclusion

This chapter has highlighted the importance of understanding what makes us, as individuals, unique and that what is important for ourselves is not necessarily the same for others. Treating people how they want to be treated is essential for building rapport, trust, understanding and tolerance. Understanding that different people think and behave differently, make decisions and generally are motivated depending on the uniqueness and combination of the way our brains process thought and display behaviours will support the change practitioner in understanding themselves as well their stakeholders. The use of Emergenetics offers an additional tool to support organizational change. Used alongside previously mentioned tools within this book will provide a rich toolbox of skills to draw upon in different situations.

Emergenetics is explored again in terms of resistance to change in Chapter 7 and business transformation and ambiguity in Chapter 8.

References

Browning, G (2006) *Emergenetics®: Tap into the New Science of Success*, Harper Collins, New York

Browning, G (2018) *Work That Works: Emergeneering a positive organizational culture, an Emergenetics guide*, John Wiley & Sons, Hoboken

Change challenges and coaching solutions

This section explores practical coaching techniques to manage five key change challenges faced by organizations. These are challenges that arise as a result of change, as opposed to being the root causes of change. They are:

- post-acquisition integration
- resistance
- ambiguity
- stakeholder engagement
- making change stick.

Each challenge is described in a stand-alone chapter and is followed first by some traditional change interventions and second by practical coaching tools and techniques.

Not all problems are suited to a coaching intervention. The authors have highlighted where an external coach will add value and situations which can equally be managed internally by employees with the requisite skills and knowledge.

Post-acquisition 06
challenges

Introduction

The eye-watering transaction figures and acquisition success stories described in Chapter 2 may make for compelling reading, but, in reality, such headlines are only the tip of the iceberg. Every transaction is predicated on a business case that promises to deliver financial and non-financial benefits far greater than the purchase price. The key to these benefits being realized, and to what extent, lies in the smooth integration of the acquired firm into the acquiring entity.

Much is written about identifying acquisition targets, carrying out due diligence and negotiating the deal, but there is considerably less focus on what takes place post-completion. Many organizations are so focussed on activities such as due diligence and financing, they under-estimate, or do not recognize at all, the challenges of planning and carrying out the integration. Compare it to a house move – we search for a house we like, research the area for schools and other amenities and then secure a competitive mortgage. When completion and moving day arrive, we leave some of our belongings behind in the old house and then fail to unpack our possessions in the new house.

It sounds ridiculous and yet that is what many organizations do. The act of moving one company into another is far more complex than moving house. From a purely practical point of view, transferring staff members, IT applications and services from one entity to another, terminating office leases and harmonising employment contracts are all time-consuming and costly activities.

The other and arguably more challenging aspects of integration relate to people and their reaction to the transaction. Employees from both sides of the transaction often respond with fear and resistance. If we layer external stakeholders such as clients and shareholders, the result is a complex and nuanced change challenge. The fact that the two firms have sufficient shared synergies to enable the transaction does not necessarily make for a wrinkle-free integration.

The complexity of this organizational change coupled with the high financial stakes means that there is a significant role to be played by change practitioners. According to Ken Smith and Alexandra Reed Lajoux in *The Art of M&A Strategy* (2012), nearly $1 trillion in shareholder value has been lost through deals with poor integration results in the last 10 years alone.

However, it is surprising how many acquiring firms underestimate the size of the task and the need for a dedicated project led by a strong change practitioner. In their book *The Complete Guide to Mergers and Acquisitions* (2018), Timothy Galpin and Mark Herndon reference a CEO who declared his company was 'now in the big leagues of change management'. Sadly, this level of enlightenment is something of an anomaly and he understood what many still do not – insufficient attention to and poor handling of the organizational change is one of the main reasons integration efforts flounder and sometimes fail. How do acquiring firms bring employees on the journey? How do they minimize disruption for their clients? How do they achieve a smooth integration in the shortest possible timeframe? Using a blend of personal experience and research, this chapter will explore the various ways in which change practitioners can help organizations to overcome these challenges, mitigating and often eliminating the barriers to success.

Acquisition stages

There are several stages in an acquisition which can be broadly split into pre and post-deal.

Prior to the transaction completing, there is normally a long process of due diligence, followed by structuring, financing and closing the deal. After the transaction completes, attention naturally turns to the integration of the acquired entity and realizing the business case benefits. If an integration plan has already been developed, it can be deployed on day one. Furthermore, as we will see later, there are key activities such as communications that should be initiated before completion, which further strengthens the case for planning in the pre completion phases. An example flow model is shown in Figure 6.1.

Figure 6.1 Acquisition deal flow model

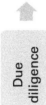

Strategic need	Identify	Due diligence	Make deal	Integration	Realize benefits
• Strategy discussions highlight a need/ opportunity to acquire. • Involve key pre-deal teams such as Legal & Corporate Finance.	• Locate & evaluate long list of potential targets. • Research the targets (early due diligence). • Engage external professional services.	• Short list targets. • Deep-dive valuation of possible targets.	• Negotiate. • Draw up legal documents. • Plan the integration.	• Integrate the acquisition in the relevant part of the business.	• Track, report and capitalize on benefits. • Lessons learned.

Transaction

SOURCE Inspired by Timothy Galpin and Mark Herndon, 2018

> ## A word about culture
>
> It is not the intention of this chapter to bypass the obvious cultural challenges posed by an acquisition. As culture comprises many aspects such as strategy, vision and mission, core values, systems and procedures, it seems more logical to address cultural aspects throughout the chapter, rather than as a stand-alone section. This reflects the nature of organizational culture – it is woven throughout every aspect of an organization and therefore to treat it as a stand-alone section would be misleading.

Integration speed and timing

One of the simplest and most advantageous things a firm can do to reduce integration headaches is to begin planning the integration project activity before the deal completes. This enables the change practitioner to work with stakeholders on both sides of the transaction to identify all the relevant deliverables and carry out an impact analysis.

> ## Top change tip
>
> Prior to discussing integration-related topics with the selling party pre completion, seek advice from legal counsel to ensure no sensitive information is inadvertently shared.

However, the concept of planning integration tasks prior to the transaction completing is not as common as it should be. According to research by Galpin and Herndon, 24.6 per cent of 153 companies canvassed reported that they wait until completion to begin even planning the integration.

This statistic is surprising given the time-sensitivity of integrations due to the pressure from the Board and shareholders to realize the business case benefits. Additionally, Transitional Service Agreements (TSAs) bring another time-related pressure. TSAs are a feature of many acquisition agreements and are designed to ensure a level of service continuity from a divesting parent company during the integration period. They usually apply to group or shared services which, if switched off by the divesting company on completion day, could not be replicated by the acquiring entity on day one. For example, a large IT estate could take 6 to 12 months to move from a divesting party and therefore it makes sense to pay a service fee to 'keep the lights on'. Crucially, TSAs represent a significant cost to the acquiring company, and it is in their interest to progress integration activity as quickly as possible to eliminate this reliance and therefore reduce the cost.

Bearing in mind these pressures, the integration planning should include an in-depth prioritization exercise. For example, if the transaction is driven by the desire to access a desirable client base, the most urgent focus should be client retention. If the priority is talent acquisition, an employee retention plan can be put in place to safeguard against key talent leaving the business.

Summary

Integration planning can and should begin before the deal closes and activities should be prioritized according to the benefits stated in the business case.

Integration resourcing and plan

Resources

When questioning senior executives about the greatest obstacles or challenges to integration, the most common gripe in Galpin and Herndon's research was the lack of dedicated project resources made available for such a big task – only 32.5 per cent reported always establishing a traditional project structure. Unsurprisingly, the companies that reported increased success at integrations cited availability of project resources as the top reason for this.

This raises a further question – what constitutes appropriate resources for an integration? This depends on the size and complexity of the transaction. For a large acquisition impacting most or all business functions, the ideal model is a Project Manager to represent each of the functions (see Figure 6.2) Additionally, each Project Manager requires access to

Figure 6.2 Integration project structure

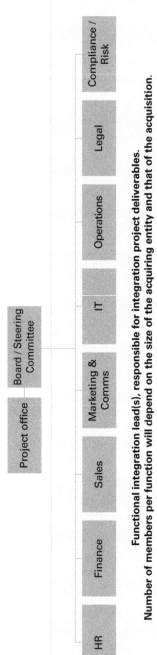

Functional integration lead(s), responsible for integration project deliverables.
Number of members per function will depend on the size of the acquiring entity and that of the acquisition.

appropriate Subject Matter Experts (SMEs) whose time has been freed up to work on the project. Unfortunately, Galpin and Herndon's research shows what many project managers already know – that 60 per cent of companies expect their SMEs to input knowledge and expertise to integration projects on top of their day job with no allowance made for the additional call on their time.

For a large integration, a Programme Manager, also sitting in the Project Office, may be required. While this may not be a full-time post, the presence of a central figure avoids duplication between business areas or, worse, important activity slipping between the cracks completely.

Finally, there is a very strong business case to be made for a Change Manager to be allocated to activity as disruptive as an acquisition. The specific activities a Change Manager should contribute to (and often lead) will become clear throughout the remaining sections in this chapter.

Top change tip

Be realistic about the size of the integration activity – it is a project and project and business resources should be assigned accordingly.

Planning

It is not sufficient merely to bring together appropriate resources in a structure chart. All project tasks must be tracked, monitored and reported with a detailed project plan. In Hodges' (2016) research of 270 M&A transactions, he found that companies with a structured plan to manage integrations generated shareholder returns above the pre-deal industry expectations.

Summary

Sufficient and appropriate project resources are key, backed by a robust and well-managed project plan.

The role of leadership

A transaction as important as an acquisition is generally a highly political time for senior leaders in both the acquired and acquiring organization. Concerns about retaining their senior position are a significant distraction for leaders at this time. Unfortunately, when many senior managers are jockeying for position in the new world this is the very time when organizations need senior leaders to step up. To be clear – this is in addition to and not instead of a Programme or Project Manager. They become the integration Project Sponsor, taking accountability for the delivery of the integration project.

Typically, the most appropriate candidate for this sponsorship role is the person who leads the function most impacted by the acquisition. For example, if a financial services organization purchases a technology start-up, the Chief Information Officer or Chief Technology Officer is the logical leader. Crucially, though, the key requirement is for a charismatic individual who embodies the qualities of a genuine leader – a consensus builder who can communicate and influence at all levels of the organization and who has a decision-making mandate.

Often overlooked, the Chief Financial Officer (CFO) can be the ideal choice. In McKinsey's 2020 survey of integrations (Agrawal et al, 2020), 49 per cent of 200 respondents reported their CFO having designed the company's post-acquisition road map and 47 per cent said the finance chief took the lead in developing the capabilities required to support integration. The same body of research suggested that when the CFO was 'very involved' in integrations, companies were much more likely to realize the expected benefits of the transaction. This is somewhat unsurprising, given that this role is responsible for establishing an end-to-end process for capturing the most value from a deal, for example by assessing the full range of potential synergies, building realistic forecasts and ensuring the financial and strategic objectives can be met and reported once the deal is completed.

Top change tip

Select the most appropriate senior leader to take the lead on the integration – this person is responsible for taking people on a change journey like no other.

Decision-making

In addition to the senior leader or Sponsor, a 'Steering Committee' should be established for the duration of the integration project. The existence of this group ensures a cross-section of the organization's leaders are not only consulted on key decisions but more importantly it is accountable for project oversight and acts as an escalation point for risks, issues and decisions.

Finally, the Steering Committee can and should include senior leaders from the acquired entity. They will have in-depth knowledge in some areas that the acquiring leadership team does not have.

Summary

The most successful integrations have strong senior leadership, project management and executive sponsorship.

Retaining key talent

From an organizational change perspective, one of the most challenging areas of an acquisition is the retention of high-performing employees. Inevitably, an acquisition brings new employees, some of whom will not accept that they will be employed by a different company to the one that interviewed them, offered them a job and trained them. The existing (legacy) employees often feel threatened by new staff coming into their organization, particularly if talent acquisition was a factor in the purchase. At the same time, both sets of employees are likely to be approached by competitors taking advantage of any job security fears they may have.

Both sets of employees will have concerns about job retention, reporting lines, salary, bonus, pay rises, benefits, holiday allowance, parental leave, hybrid working and all manner of other questions. This applies to both sets of employees but in reality will trouble the acquired employees more and they will keep asking these questions until they have an answer. Companies lose thousands of hours to these informal conversations that, in the absence of hard facts, tend to involve a lot of rumour and conjecture. This is a huge distraction for senior leaders but, because they usually have their own concerns in this arena addressed very early in the integration process (and often before the deal completes), they may overlook the need to cascade information down to middle managers and employees. This is exacerbated by the fundamental disconnect in priorities between the organization and the employees. Most of senior management's time and energy in the pre-deal phases falls on legal, regulatory, technical and financial concerns, whereas post-completion, attention turns to the urgent need to realize the financial and non-financial benefits of the transaction in the shortest possible timeframe. Throughout this period, very little time and energy is spent on peoples' likely reaction to the change.

Top change tip

Develop an employee retention plan in the period leading up to completion and be clear about the top talent you wish to retain from both entities.

Since people at all levels of their organization prioritize their personal uncertainty, it is best to address these concerns pro-actively. A plan can be developed to outline a timeframe for dealing with practicalities such as the alignment of employment contracts, pay and benefits, which will set many peoples' minds at rest.

Summary

Do not underestimate the size of the organizational change and plan ahead to reduce employee fears.

Communication

Internal communications

There are so many communication hurdles before, during and after an acquisition – misinformation, rumour, conjecture. Most can be overcome through a strong internal communications strategy incorporating regular and appropriate communication. This begs the question as to why 60 per cent of Galpin and Herndon's respondents reported a 'poor' or 'very poor' communication strategy.

A structured and multi-channel internal communications strategy is not a difficult task and can make or break an integration. It serves two key purposes:

- On a practical level, internal communications engage the entire organization in the integration – they inform and update employees on key elements of the acquisition, such as the rationale for the transaction, the timeframe, who is leading it and how the integration will unfold.

- On an emotional level, they help to reinforce new branding, changed strategy, corporate values, new ways of working and what it means for them.

An additional error often made at such times is to gloss over or somehow sugar-coat important messages for fear of upsetting people. Jack Welch oversaw some 600 acquisitions during his time as CEO of General Electric and, in a 1993 interview on the subject, he made the case for transparency and clarity: *'how do you bring people into the change process? Start with reality, get all the facts out. Give people the rationale for change… when everybody gets the same facts, they'll generally come to the same conclusion.'* (Markovits, 2020).

The timing and frequency of internal communications are as important as the content and format. Communication must begin before the transaction completes and must continue throughout the integration, not just when the deal closes or when there is something important to say. In addition to traditional communication vehicles like email and intranet, there are some very effective and inclusive ways of communicating with employees, depending on how closely impacted they are likely to be by the transaction. In a sales-led organization, the full list of communications should be directed at sales staff – email, team meetings, desk drops, Q&A sessions, meet and greet events. Other parts of the organization can probably suffice with the minimum emails outlining timeframe and rationale for the transaction.

Top change tip

Set up a central email mailbox and use it for all outbound communications relating to the integration project.

Finally, internal communications apply to both parties in the transaction. It is unacceptable to communicate well with the employees of the acquiring entity while keeping those of the entity being acquired in the dark. Wherever possible, in the lead-up to the transaction when the two sets of employees are still separate, electronic message distribution and face-to-face meetings should take place simultaneously. Post completion, the acquired entity's employees are legally part of the acquiring entity, although in practice they will probably still need to use their legacy email addresses for several weeks. A common pitfall during this period is sending an email with a team distribution list that the new teams do not receive. It is important to avoid one set of employees receiving key messages but not others.

External communication

While external stakeholders are not experiencing change and upheaval to the same extent as their internal counterparts, there are many groups of external stakeholders who need information about an acquisition, for example:

- customers
- shareholders, where relevant
- investors
- market analysts
- the press.

The subject of customer or client retention is so intrinsic to the success of an integration that it warrants a section of its own later in this chapter. With regards to the other external stakeholder groups, only senior leaders should handle interaction with external parties such as the press or market analysts. They are arguably closest to the original deal objectives and therefore best placed to craft and deliver compelling communications throughout the timeline in a way that is tailored to different stakeholders. These leaders are also more likely to have received media training and they must be armed with professionally written statements and heavily rehearsed presentations.

It is not necessarily the CEO who performs this task. Often, CFOs come into their own in front of shareholders, investors and market analysts. If in doubt, a senior leader with a charismatic style will win the day as these interactions rely on persuasive delivery.

Summary

A clear internal and external communication strategy is the key to the success of an integration and should be initiated prior to deal completion.

Training

Top tip

Combine the training plan with the internal communications strategy – they can complement each other.

Alongside the internal communications plan, training is a key integration activity. Organizational change is about asking people to work differently, and training is the enabler that eliminates the legacy policies and practices that do not support the new ways of working.

There is usually a disproportionately heavy focus on the training needs of the new employees from the acquired company and their urgent need to learn to use new systems. Most organizations use email, an HR portal and a client or sales database such as a Client Relationship Management (CRM) tool. On top of that will be telephony and collaboration tools such as Zoom, WebEx or Teams. They cannot integrate into the team, work effectively and feel part of the new organization if they are unable to carry out simple tasks.

In addition to systems and applications, new employees are also met with a whole raft of new policies and procedures, which can be trained in a way that supports the communication of core values and helps to eliminate behaviours from their 'old world', for example:

- agile working
- desk booking and clear desk policies
- dress code
- remote working arrangements.

Often, the needs of the acquiring entity's employees are overlooked here, although they are sometimes required to unlearn old habits and learn new ones. For example, the acquired entity may have a state-of-the-art sales tool that was a key reason the organization was such an attractive acquisition target in the first instance. This opens up a training requirement for the legacy employees, many of whom will react with scepticism to being asked to use a system from the acquired, probably smaller, entity.

How this training is developed and delivered has a significant impact on how these practical and cultural change elements are adopted and embedded, so it is vital to be prepared. An impact analysis and training needs assessment can be conducted before the integration phase, ready to roll out on day one. For optimum success, the appropriate people must deliver the training. For example, while many employees could provide a demonstration of the HR portal, it is obvious that questions will arise during the session which HR would be best placed to answer.

Summary

Training is a core change activity for both sets of employees, especially those coming in. It is also an ideal area for advance planning.

Client retention

The major risk for the acquiring organization is that, in many cases, the business case for the acquisition rests partly or wholly on the target's client base. A study by consulting firm Bain & Company (Miles and Rouse, 2011) shows that customer defections are a major contributor to some acquisitions failing to realize the expected benefits. The same study found that 25 per cent of all retail banking customers have experienced M&A in the last three years and, of these, 15 per cent moved to a competitor as a result.

If customers get cold feet they may go to a competitor, cancel or fail to renew, making it impossible for the acquiring entity to realize the expected benefits of the transaction. This would be a disaster for the Board and shareholders.

However, irrespective of the original rationale for the acquisition, many organizations overlook the fact that customers are also being taken on a change journey, one that they did not sign up to. If a small bespoke firm is acquired by a large organization, its customers may assume they will lose the 'personal touch' and the dedicated account management they have previously bought in to. On the acquiring side, there is a risk that the distraction of the acquisition process inadvertently leads to a reduction in client visits and rushed or late proposals, triggering falling sales or increased complaints.

Top change tip

Recognize that customers on both sides of the transaction are also on a change journey. Focus on standards of sales and service.

In the lead-up to the transaction, the relevant senior managers on both sides should define and agree a client strategy to minimize this risk. This includes:

- Early communication to both sets of clients before and immediately after the transaction has completed, articulating the benefits and expected timeline.
- Providing scripted statements to sales staff to ensure a consistent message to customers.
- Identifying potential customer 'flight risks' and designing mitigation activity such as joint sales visits and renewal incentives.
- Prioritizing large accounts or those with growth potential and match them with the top salespeople.
- Running a report of contract expiration or renewal dates (or any relevant milestone when a customer could start shopping around) and prioritize according to this chronology.
- Understanding the optimum team structure – the strongest salespeople may be from the acquired entity.
- Working with the Marketing and Brand team to update sales materials and organize client events.

Summary

The client portfolio may be one of the key drivers for the acquisition. It is therefore critical to have a retention plan.

Coaching solutions for post-acquisition challenges

In Bruce Peltier's *The Psychology of Executive Coaching* (2010), he discusses four stages where coaching is useful. He specifically refers to coaching being 'of special importance during mergers and acquisitions' and an 'organizational sea change [which] can become a disaster without outside help'.

Outside help in the form of a qualified executive coach is highly beneficial. However, it is also possible for those involved in change and who are non-qualified coaches to play a supportive coaching style role in these situations.

It is easy to feel overwhelmed by the complexity and number of challenges experienced by the organization and individuals following an acquisition. There are many internal and external factors that at times may feel impossible to solve, outside of the change practitioners' control and finding a specific coaching solution by way of a tool or technique is a challenge.

Some of these challenges can either be managed by bringing together teams or by supporting the individuals responsible for delivering the post-integration project. To get to grips with these challenges, the next part of this chapter will explore:

- supporting senior leaders
- team coaching and team facilitation – the how and the why.

Supporting senior leaders

With a focus on the role of leadership in an integration, this is a perfect example of where the expertise of an external coach is invaluable. As mentioned previously in this chapter, a senior leader will need to step into their authority (not autocracy) as the integration project sponsor and take accountability for the delivery of the integration project whilst other senior executives will form the Steering Committee.

It can be a tough and lonely world at the top and with the lack of peer group support the senior leader may feel isolated and vulnerable. An executive coach plays a pivotal role in working with the Project Sponsor and/or senior leader to help them navigate this challenging role. The executive coach will:

- Hold the leader to account by challenging thoughts, ideas and assumptions in a supportive and useful way for the leader.

- Hold a mirror up to highlight blind spots and skills and behaviours known to the leader, which have been hidden and possibly ignored for fear of shame or embarrassment.

- Provide useful tools and techniques to bring insight and understanding to particular challenges to help move ideas and projects forward.

- Use provocative questions to gently move the client out of their comfort zone to develop new skills and confidence.

- Encourage the leader to take responsibility for their thinking and actions and hold the client accountable for any actions not met – this may be a sign of disengagement with the coaching process and is important to discuss with the coach.

- Be a sounding board, a listening ear and the person who can be trusted with personal information which the client may not be comfortable sharing with anyone else. For example, an admission of imposter syndrome and possibly admission of a skills gap.

Knowing when to use an external coach

The intensity and value of a coaching session with a qualified, experienced and confident coach can only be achieved by someone who has had many years of coaching experience, has the confidence to challenge senior leaders and who receives continual personal and professional development in the form of coaching supervision. The coach will have worked with a selection of complex characters at different levels of seniority and with varying personality types. However, if the organization has a team of highly trained, qualified and experienced internal coaches, this resource can be utilized to good effect.

> **Top tip**
>
> Choose your executive coach carefully. Expensive does not always mean good quality. Check for qualifications, accreditations, experience and, importantly, whether the executive coach is receiving coaching supervision and how often. Check also if their coach supervisor is qualified and experienced. If possible, find out the coach's view on coaching supervision (for example, are they only having this intervention to get through a tendering process or accreditation?). This CPD ensures their skills are fresh, relevant and ethically sound.

Supporting larger groups

There are times when communication can only realistically be effective in group or team gatherings to ensure the whole message reaches as many people as possible. However, imagine a room full of 50 people, hearing exactly the same message at the same time from the same person. Groups of this size can be problematic. Information can be open to interpretation particularly when the brain is so adept at filtering information to ensure it hears only what it wants to hear. Deletion, generalization and distortion of information is highly likely. This is an obvious challenge if the aim for those attending the meeting is to listen and understand the message intended.

Working with smaller groups will result in a more satisfactory outcome because the facilitator will have the time and space to manage questions from the whole team and will be able to manage the process more efficiently. Dealing with resistance in a smaller group is more manageable. If those attending the meeting feel that their concerns can be voiced and understood, this will help the process to move forward instead of going over old ground and old stories.

When working with groups of more than 20 it is advisable to employ more facilitators to manage the process and to observe the behaviours in the room when one speaker is talking. The rule of thumb is generally one facilitator for each cohort of 12 to 15 people but that largely depends on the subject, the mindset of those attending and the level of resistance likely to be demonstrated.

Team coaching versus team facilitation

There is much confusion between team coaching and team facilitation. David Clutterbuck confirms that team coaching 'is a relatively new concept that lacks a consistency of definition, practice and empirical evidence' (Clutterbuck, 2020). In contrast, team facilitation is a well-known intervention and has been used for many years by trainers and coaches alike.

This section aims to demystify these two very important interventions and to help the change practitioner to understand how and when to use these skills and at what point external intervention is recommended. The two interventions are explained separately in the next section to help clarify the differences, although it is difficult to write about one intervention without mentioning the other and the authors have made reference to the two interventions in both sections.

Team coaching

Even some of the leading experts in the coaching world, (Clutterbuck et al) found it challenging to define team coaching and realized that although some coaches advertised team coaching, they found a combined approach of coaching and non-coaching with some not even coaching the whole team. As a consequence, they captured the essence of team coaching, defining it as:

partnering with an entire team in an on-going relationship, for the purpose of collectively raising awareness and building better connections in the team's internal and external systems and enhancing the team's capability to cope with current and future challenges.

David Clutterbuck continues to say that team coaching focuses on growing long-term team capacity and helping the team co-create value with and for all their stakeholders.

In contrast, in their recently published book, *Building Top-Performing Teams* (2021), Lucy Widdowson and Paul Barbour define team coaching as:

helping teams work together, with others and within their wider environment to create lasting change by developing safe and trusting relationships, better ways of working and new thinking, so that they maximize their collective potential, purpose and performance goals.

This definition is echoed by Georgina Woudstra, Director of Team Coaching Studio (2021):

Team coaching should not be confused with training, mentoring or consultation. Effective team coaching cannot fit into an away day and those who try (from either side of the divide) are disappointed.

To add further clarity, team coaching can be described as when the coach works with the whole team instead of a coach working with one person. The quality of the team coaching is defined by the quality of the team coach. There is a different set of skills required to be a team coach rather than team facilitator. As we will see in the next section, the team facilitator does not necessarily need to be a trained coach, although these skills would certainly enhance their practice. In contrast, the team coach will be an experienced coach and use a similar set of skills to those adopted when working with one client. They may possibly be an experienced trainer with the various skills and experience of managing larger teams and team dynamics, while still using their coaching skills.

Team coach research

Widdowson and Barbour (2021) interviewed 36 team coaches to explore what they did as team coach practitioners. They concluded that most team coaches focus on:

- process
- interpersonal relationships
- relational dynamics
- systemic context.

These all relate to the team as a whole and not task-based performance. What defines team coaching is that the team will be made up of either:

- An existing team working together in the same department and made up of a team leader and a team of direct reports.
- A team of managers/leaders who are a peer group and have the same or similar responsibilities.

In the coaching session, the team agree to:

- Take full responsibility for the agreed goals, outcomes and discussion.

- Take full and joint responsibility for how they would like the session(s) to develop.

- Take full responsibility for any actions defined and who is assigned to those actions.

- Engage with a trained and experienced team coach over a number of weeks or months.

Returning to the challenge presented by acquisitions, team coaching lends itself perfectly to this scenario and has particular relevance when the team has a situation that is preventing them from working at their best or where the team want to move forward with a team goal, project or action.

The intended outcome of these sessions is to re-align the team to build psychological safety, trust and an open channel of communication. The coach works with the team as a whole, not individuals within the team, to define the underlying issues that prevent the team from succeeding. The team coach will skilfully work with a helicopter vision of the situation, for example where team members are in conflict with each other. The coach will look closely at team dynamics and give feedback on what is observed. The detail of who said what and why, is of little interest to the coach who will take a more holistic approach and aim to talk more about the symptomatic issues and how to regain trust, rapport and an open communication with each other.

Typically, a team coach will work with a team over longer periods of time, maybe weeks or sometimes months. This is unlikely to be a one-off session, unlike team facilitation that is often commissioned as a one or half-day session. The shorter session is more cost effective but does not foster sustainable change.

As with team facilitation, the success of team coaching relies on a strong partnership between the team coach, the sponsor, the team leader / manager and the team members. This partnership is most effective when ground rules, clear expectations, timeframes and goals are established at the start of the process. Trust, rapport and open, honest communication is an essential part of this process.

Team facilitation

David Clutterbuck in his book, *Coaching the Team at Work* (2020), agrees with the Association of Facilitators that the description of team facilitation has many overlaps with team coaching and many experienced team coaches he has interviewed use facilitation skills within their portfolio of approaches.

One key difference is that the facilitator steers and manages the conversation whereby the team coach assists the team to manage their own conversation.

Clutterbuck goes on to say that there are significant differences between team coaching and facilitation, although these are not universally agreed. These differences are that facilitation:

- Has a focus to solve a specific, current or near future problem (team coaching aims to build the team's capability to solve its own problem).
- Places greater emphasis on process (team coaching on generating questions that stimulate insight).
- Typically aims to achieve a solution within the session (team coaching, when done well, lays down the foundations from which the team can find its own solutions in its own time).

Team facilitation is the process of moving a team from where they are now to where they need to be through a structured, meaningful discussion where the team interacts and takes responsibility for actions and outcomes. The facilitator will be highly skilled in:

- Managing the process, time, pace, techniques.
- Managing team dynamics.
- Managing and organizing larger groups who demonstrate a range of resistance and engagement.
- Challenging mindsets and assumptions through incisive, judgement-free questions.
- Having the confidence to move in and out of the structure at the right time.
- Listening to what is being said and not being said.
- Noticing behaviours: active, inactive, engaged, disengaged.
- Regularly checking in with the team to hear what is on their minds (particularly when there is silence or low energy in the room).

An external and neutral facilitator could help the team decide on their employee and client retention strategy. The facilitator will have a mental and physical 'toolkit' of tried and tested tools and techniques to work with the team in this goal-focussed discussion. As the team asks questions and identifies potential problems, the facilitator draws upon their many years of experience and knowledge of various communication, leadership and psychological models and techniques. This is shared with the team which may be useful for understanding why things are as they are. The facilitator will know the importance of not dwelling on the past and will encourage the team to move toward a solution or a set of agreed actions to work on outside of the session.

The success of a facilitated team session relies on a strong partnership between the facilitator, the sponsor, the team leader and the team members. In the same way that one-to-one coaching relies on effective contracting, team coaching and facilitation is no different. Trust, rapport and open, honest communication are an essential part of this process. The facilitator takes responsibility for the process and for the techniques used. The team are passive in this respect but are active when it comes to discussions, agreed outcomes and goals.

Team facilitation and acquisitions

Team facilitation can be made up of one team or a number of smaller teams who work within the same organization and who are experiencing the same challenge with the same or similar overall outcome, for example following an acquisition. In this situation the multiple teams may be made up of both organizations. The aim is for the team facilitator to work with these two merging teams who may see themselves as a 'group' and work towards them becoming a strong and collaborative team.

The team facilitator will usually be an experienced trainer, used to working with challenging groups. They will have highly developed skills in listening and questioning.

Top tip

Decide first what the outcomes and desired goals of the team are before deciding if a team facilitator or a team coach is required. How likely is it that the team will want to work together in a collaborative and mature way? Be clear who you are employing to carry out these sessions. If you are looking specifically for a team coach to work with a team over time then a qualified coach who is experienced in working with teams and ideally qualified as a team coach, is likely to be the right choice. If you are looking for a quick one-day session bringing either one or more teams together then it would be wise to employ an experienced facilitator who will adopt a range of facilitation and team techniques, unless there was internal capacity for someone within the organization to fulfil this facilitator role.

The pros and cons of using internal and external coach and facilitators to support the integration process

One of the key benefits of employing an external consultant, coach or facilitator is that they are unlikely to get swept into the politics of the organization. Some independent external facilitators have earned their stripes as an internal facilitator before becoming freelance and will know how difficult it is to remain impartial and to avoid being the 'scapegoat' for anything that goes wrong, either on the day or afterwards. The group can often see the internal facilitator as 'part of management' and therefore do not engage with them as easily as they might do with an external facilitator. Even so, an external facilitator can sometimes feel as if they are there to fix a problem that, in one day, is impossible. They are often treading a fine line between meeting the needs of the group or team and meeting the needs of the client (the organization).

It is possible to use an internally trained and experienced team facilitator if they have the confidence and assertiveness to deal with the challenges of managing large group gatherings. Having more than one facilitator to manage questions and opposition is a wise move in these circumstances. When it comes to team coaching, it is possible to use an internal resource – ideally someone who is a trained coach and has experience of previously facilitating team sessions. However, consider how well this person knows the team and if there is potential for a conflict of interest as a result. One of the benefits of using an internal coach, apart from cost, is that any immediate team needs can be met far quicker than having to find and contract with an external team coach.

Conclusion

The act of acquiring another company is the catalyst for arguably the most disruptive change an organization can undertake. This change impacts employees on both sides of the transaction in a range of ways and there are many change and coaching techniques a change practitioner can deploy to reduce, eliminate or avoid the biggest pitfalls.

In terms of coaching, with the wide-ranging challenges acquisitions inevitably experience, it is clear to see that one size does not fit all. The change practitioner will need to consider the best intervention required to meet the needs of teams and individuals. A flexible approach with consideration given to the emotional as well as logical outcomes is essential for success. What we have seen in this chapter is that supporting the team through the integration process requires time, effort and the right intervention. Providing a variety of individual coaching and team/group support will ensure success but may not necessarily lead to everyone being content with the integration process.

The next change challenge looks at the reasons why some people resist organizational change and proposes techniques to reduce resistance.

References

Agrawal, A, Dinneen, B, Kim E and Uhlaner, R (2020) The one task the CFO should not delegate: Integrations, McKinsey & Company, https://www.mckinsey.com/business-functions/m-and-a/our-insights/the-one-task-the-cfo-should-not-delegate-integrations (archived at https://perma.cc/B92T-MSZA)

Clutterbuck, D (2020) *Coaching the Team at Work: The definitive guide to team coaching*, Nicholas Brealey, London

Galpin, T and Herndon, M (2018) *The Complete Guide to Mergers & Acquisitions: Process tools to support M&A integration at every level*, Jossey-Bass Professional Management, San Francisco

Hawkins, P (2012) *Creating a Coaching Culture*, McGraw-Hill, Berkshire

Hills, J You can do anything if you can change behaviour Part 1, https://headheartbrain.com/brain-savvy-business/you-can-do-anything-if-you-can-change-behaviour-part-1/ (archived at https://perma.cc/4VGK-F5YT)

International Association of Facilitators IAF World, https://www.iaf-world.org/site/ (archived at https://perma.cc/F3XV-A3GG)

Markovits, M (2020) Reflections on Jack Welch, Achieve Mission, https://www. achievemission.org/blog/reflections-on-jack-welch/#:~:text=One%20 quote%20from%20Jack%20that,the%20clearest%2C%20most%20 dramatic%20terms (archived at https://perma.cc/KV5G-N33W)

Miles, L and Rouse, T (2011) Keeping customers first in merger integration, Bain & Company, https://www.bain.com/contentassets/7964ed171ae74917a5cd5ec 4d0638315/bain_brief_keeping_customers_first_in_merger_integration.pdf (archived at https://perma.cc/AH9T-V5MR)

Peltier, B (2010) *The Psychology of Executive Coaching: Theory & Application*, Routledge, London

Smith, K and Reed Lajoux, A (2012) *The Art of M&A Strategy: A guide to building your company's future through mergers, acquisitions and divestitures*, McGraw-Hill, San Francisco

Widdowson, L and Barbour, P (2021) *Building Top Performing Teams: A practical guide to team coaching to improve collaboration and drive organizational success*, Kogan Page, London

Woudstra, G (2021) *Mastering the Art of Team Coaching: A comprehensive guide to unleashing the power, purpose and potential in any team*, Team Coaching Studio Press, Winchester

Resistance to organizational change   07

Introduction

This chapter considers what is arguably the largest challenge facing any organizational change practitioner – resistance. In his 1969 *Harvard Business Review* paper, Paul Lawrence dubbed it 'one of the most baffling and recalcitrant of problems which businesses face' and any seasoned change professional knows how true this is.

Many of us will have encountered resistance in our personal lives and instinctively know what it means.

In an organizational change context, there are several definitions from different academics, theorists and practitioners but in his 2003 research at Cornell University, Shaul Oreg provides perhaps the most comprehensive:

> [an] *individual's tendency to resist and avoid making changes, to devalue change generally, and to find change aversive across diverse context and types of change.*

This resonates because it not only correctly identifies the individual's negative reaction to all types of change but also highlights the tendency to devalue change as a concept. The latter is crucial because it increases the likelihood of detractors sharing this sentiment with others and spreading resistance.

The aim of this chapter is to:

- Describe the scenarios that resistance causes in the delivery of change.
- Highlight some of the key root causes to the resistance, using a variety of models and frameworks to understand why people react the way they do.

- Share practical change management tools to mitigate and sometimes remove resistance.

- Propose coaching and mentoring frameworks and techniques that can be applied in conjunction with the traditional change approach.

Over the years, countless resistance models and frameworks have been put forward by academics and practitioners alike and it is not the authors' intention to include them all. On the contrary, this is a hand-picked set of change and coaching techniques which have proved invaluable to the authors and which work well together.

Why people resist change

There is a significant body of research relating to the psychological and sociological reasons people resist change and it is insightful to step back temporarily from organizational change and consider peoples' responses to change in general.

In his 1995 book *Leading Change: Overcoming the ideology of comfort and the tyranny of custom*, James O'Toole acknowledges that to resist change is a normal human reaction. He lists 33 hypotheses as to the reasons for this, such as fear of the unknown and contentment with the *status quo*. Ultimately, he argues, the deep-rooted human desire to protect established social relations is at the root of resistance behaviours. Research carried out by neuroscientist Jan Hills at the consultancy Head Heart + Brain sets out the theory that humans resist change because they are social, not economic, beings and survive best in social groups. Social recognition within these groups creates a reward response in the brain. As the human brain scans for threat and reward, it notices threat five times more than reward, therefore humans are more likely to notice threats. As the logical and rational part of the brain does not work well with threats, it processes them as the equivalent to stress.

In a corporate setting there may be several factors contributing to the 'threat' while at the same time the factors that create the reward response in the brain are being removed. The SCARF model developed by David Rock in 2008 illustrates perfectly how organizational change inadvertently damages or removes the factors that create the reward response and provides an overview of the five stimuli that drive our response to minimize threats and maximize rewards.

1 Status

Description: our sense of importance to our self and others.

Creates reward response by: promotion, change in job title.

Creates threat response by: demotion, devaluing the job title.

2 Certainty

Description: being able to predict the future.

Creates reward response by: job security and clear communication about the future.

Creates threat response by: not sharing what people need to know about the change and its consequences.

3 Autonomy

Description: a sense of control over events.

Creates reward response by: empowering people to make decisions and be in control of their work and lives.

Creates threat response by: telling people what they should do and how to do it and removing their sense of control.

4 Relatedness

Description: a sense of safety and connection with others.

Creates reward response by: respecting working relationships and social interaction.

Creates threat response by: breaking teams up, making people redundant.

5 Fairness

Description: a perception of fair exchanges between people.

Creates reward response by: demonstrating authenticity, empathy and logic.

Creates threat response by: communicating a view of the change which is neither logical or fair.

The SCARF model demonstrates that any positive emotion or reward generally creates a reward stimulus that leads to action. When we perceive a personal reward then serotonin is released. This well-known 'feel-good' chemical creates a sense of hope and optimism. However, a negative emotion or punishment causes a threat stimulus that leads to avoidance. This is because when a threat is perceived, cortisol is released in the brain that acts as a blocker leading people to resist. People do not necessarily react badly to change *per se* but they do react negatively to having change *done* to them. The SCARF model is a game-changer in articulating why resistance to organizational change happens and we will re-visit it later in this chapter.

The Change Iceberg

One of the most useful ways of understanding why change professionals so frequently encounter resistance to organizational change is through the Change Iceberg. It was developed in 1996 by Wilfred Krüger who argues that change practitioners often only consider the tip of the change iceberg – project cost, quality and time (Value Based Management). However, this delivery-focussed view does not consider what resides 'below the surface', namely:

- management of perceptions and belief
- power and politics management.

Also lurking 'below the surface' are four different types of stakeholders with the ability to support or frustrate the change.

- *Opponents* have a negative attitude towards change generally and are also negative about this specific change. Change practitioners can work to influence their perceptions and beliefs to help provoke a change of mind.

- *Hidden opponents*, otherwise known as opportunists, have a negative attitude towards change generally but are supportive of this particular change. Management of their perceptions and beliefs is not enough here and must be coupled with data and information to change their viewpoint.

- *Promoters* have a positive attitude towards change generally and are positive about the change in question. These individuals are the ideal change agent, a concept we will explore later in this chapter.

- *Potential promoters* have a generally positive attitude towards change but for certain reasons they are not convinced about this particular change. The appropriate tools to bring to bear are power and politics management.

Krüger's Change Iceberg is a useful illustration of resistance to organizational change – managing 'above the surface' only delivers basic acceptance. The nuances that reside beneath the surface – attitudes, behaviours and personality types – are far more complex and it is these which coalesce to create resistance.

Figure 7.1   Resistance Pyramid (reproduced with kind permission of Timothy Galpin)

Resistance Pyramid

The authors' favourite resistance model is Timothy Galpin's Resistance Pyramid (see Figure 7.1). This simple model helps the user to home in on the reason people are being resistant. Galpin believes that the reasons can be distilled in to three broad groups.

- Not knowing – they do not understand the proposed changes or the rationale behind them. This may manifest as a team member who is quieter than usual or is showing a lack of commitment.

- Not able – they do not have the skills or capabilities required to make the change or there may be too many new things happening simultaneously. This comes through in behaviours such as reduced motivation, working more slowly or increased absenteeism.

- Not willing – the most powerful of the three reasons and often a response to having change 'done' to them. This can lead to behaviours from simple 'water cooler' chatter, withdrawing support, missing meetings and negative verbal and body language, to more drastic action such as direct sabotage, direct defiance and refusal to work.

The key benefit of using the resistance pyramid is that its three categories allow change practitioners to simplify a situation that often feels ambiguous and overwhelming. By understanding the level of the Resistance Pyramid the employees are in, we are one step closer to it. It is also quick to use, to the extent that the user can even mentally match someone to one of the reasons for resistance while they are interacting with them and potentially take immediate action. Additionally, there may be several stakeholders reacting in different ways and the model reduces the temptation to treat everyone in the same way.

Some people believe it is too simplistic as it forces the user to place people in one of three categories. It is worth pointing out, however, that there is nothing to prevent the user from allocating someone to more than one layer of the pyramid. For example, if someone is not willing to do something, it is often because they are not able.

Types of resistance

It is a generalization to suggest that everyone fears change but we do know that people tend to be resistant when the change is not in their best interest or doesn't align with their beliefs or values. Change does not necessarily provoke a binary response of embrace or resist. It elicits a spectrum of responses from apathy to outright aggression, depending on the characteristics of the proposed change rather than the individuals involved. There are four main drivers to peoples' reactions:

1 Size – people are more likely to resist a significant disruption, for example an office move that adds more time to their daily commute than, say, the introduction of an office desk booking system.

2 Timing – most change practitioners are familiar with the term 'change fatigue', which relates to implementing multiple changes with the same stakeholder group in quick succession. If change is planned when an organization or team is still digesting the after-effects of the last project they are more likely to resist than if an appropriate gap were planned.

3 Downstream impact – this is linked to the size of the change. Taking the example of a new accounting system, it is easy to imagine that resistance will be greater if the new system automates a lot of processes (thereby eliminating some jobs), necessitates the complete reengineering of all remaining processes and requires significant training, rather than if the system was simply introduced and other factors remain unchanged.

4 Organizational context – this relates to characteristics such as the age of the organization, the industry sector or the culture. For example, an agile digital start-up founded a matter of months ago will naturally be more receptive to change than a more established organization. Some sectors are naturally geared for change, such as fintechs or online retailers.

In summary, it is completely normal for people to resist change of all kinds and there are a whole host of reasons for doing so. How does a change professional recently arrived in a new organization cut through the theory, pinpoint the source of resistance and formulate a plan to overcome it?

Overcoming resistance

The good news is that it is possible to overcome resistance, or at least mitigate it. However, there is no simple solution and instead the authors favour a blended approach. This section aims to distil the numerous models, frameworks, tools and techniques to illustrate how a 'portfolio approach' of traditional change tools can be paired with coaching tools for the most effective outcome.

Returning to Galpin

Galpin used the same Change Pyramid to propose ways in which we can help overcome resistance, depending on which of the three layers the person fits in (see Figure 7.2).

If an individual or team is showing signs of resistance due to a lack of knowledge, the most logical solution is the development of a communication and engagement plan.

If the issue is one of ability, the likely mitigation is a training plan to address the gaps in knowledge and build end-user confidence.

If the individual or team is simply not willing to be part of the change, the challenge is to change their mind. There are many ways to approach this, which we will explore throughout this chapter.

Figure 7.2   Resistance Pyramid with solutions (reproduced with the kind permission of Timothy Galpin)

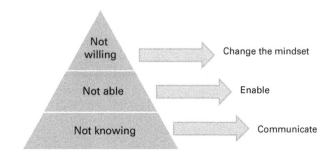

Trust as a change enabler

Trust is a vital ingredient in overcoming resistance and delivering change successfully. Professor Frances Frei at Harvard Business School has developed a useful model for a change practitioner (and indeed anyone) to have at their fingertips (Frei and Morriss, 2020). The Trust Triangle illustrates the three key components required to build (and even re-build) trust over a period (see Figure 7.3).

Authenticity – if people feel you are consistently authentic, they are more likely to trust you. What this means in practice is two-fold:

1 Behaviour – by being ourselves and not engaging in disingenuous or duplicitous behaviour, we show people who we really are.

2 Spoken word – by consistently speaking the truth and dealing only in facts, people feel confident in the message. In short – they believe us and we gain credibility in their eyes.

Empathy – the ability to understand and acknowledge another person's situation and 'walk a mile in their shoes'. Some people are naturally more empathetic than others, but empathy is a key personality trait for a change practitioner. It can be developed by spending time with others and understanding their lived experiences.

Rigour and logic – having a structured and data-led rationale for a decision or action is more likely to make it land successfully. However, it is equally important to be able to communicate the rationale. Professor Frei proposes two different approaches, depending on the speaker's natural communication preference:

Figure 7.3 Trust Triangle

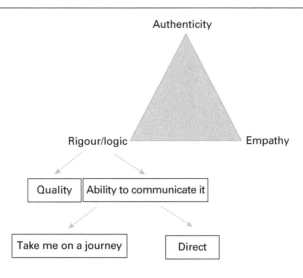

1 Direct – start with the decision or conclusion and follow with the supporting rationale, data and evidence. This approach works well for people who are worried they will lose their train of thought or in small group discussions where interruptions are more likely.

2 Take me on a journey – start by building a platform of rationale, data and evidence and work up to the decision, recommendation or conclusion. This works well with large captive audiences where interruptions are less likely or when painting a picture for people is an important part of bringing them on a 'journey' through the logic.

Resistance as an opportunity

People who are resistant to change are often viewed negatively and as the blockers to any form of vision or organizational improvement. However, according to Paul Gibbons in *The Science of Successful Organizational Change* (2019), people who resist may simply be the victim of bad habits: 'habits are like gravity, it never takes a day off'.

There is a body of neuroscience which has discovered that the brain consumes more than 20 per cent of our energy. To conserve energy, the brain has become adept at identifying patterns and creating habits. Resistance is no different – it has simply become a habit for some people.

This is not necessarily a bad thing. In their 2009 *Harvard Business Review* paper, 'Decoding Resistance to Change', Ford and Ford point out that resistance can be an important form of feedback and should not be dismissed. They framed it as a valuable 'resource' that can be used to the practitioner's advantage when treated as feedback, even from the most difficult stakeholders.

From their research of large and medium-sized firms they defined six ways that resistance can be harnessed to facilitate change.

1 Work on increasing awareness

Scenario

- Change practitioners are so deeply embedded in the change they are delivering that they often overlook the fact that others have not had the same amount of time to process the consequences.

- Organizational change is about asking people to change their ways of working and yet few change practitioners understand end-users' current tasks and therefore how they will change.

- As a result, valuable opportunities to gain employee buy-in are missed.

Solution

Listen and respond to feedback, often articulated in the form of complaints, as an opportunity to start and maintain a change dialogue.

2 The power of why

Scenario

- Many change communications focus on the 'what' – the change that is coming, timeframe and practical information about procedures and training.
- Often the purpose is overlooked – why is this change happening? Most employees are not involved in the analysis and planning work leading to a change being initiated and have no reason to understand why their ways of working are being disrupted.

Solution

- Ensure that the project vision communicated to the organization includes an articulation of the reason for the change.

3 Change the change

Scenario

- As counter-intuitive as it may seem, resistance to change genuinely can lead to better results – better adoption, more sustained adoption and therefore a better return on the business case benefits.
- Very often the employees who are most vocal in their objections are those who care the most.
- Additionally, they are often also the same employees who understand the day-to-day operation in-depth and can highlight potential pitfalls.

Solution

- Consult with this group often and be open to alternative paths forward, provided they still meet the project deliverables.

4 Build engagement

Scenario

- People feel their views are not important and are disengaged from the change.

Solution

- Provide a forum for people to share their concerns and document them.
- This is a useful way of identifying common concerns between different teams, which makes reaching an acceptable resolution much more likely.

5 Complete the past

Scenario

- Employees always remember previous change and 70 per cent of change initiatives fail.
- Therefore, people are sceptical and have low expectations when new initiatives are announced.

Solution

- Consult with team members about the history and context of prior change.

6 Reinterpret the resistance

Scenario

- People who resist change often do so because they care about the outcome.
- They may have the energy and courage to say what others are not sufficiently engaged or assertive to say.

Solution

- Involve them directly in the project, either as a subject matter expert if appropriate or in another advisory capacity.

This section has focussed on some of the traditional change tools and techniques that can be used individually or combined to reduce resistance to change. The next section illustrates the power of coaching by not only illustrating how coaching can be used to apply these tools but also how coaching can be used in isolation to reduce resistance.

Coaching solutions for resistance to change

Introduction

Traditional change techniques and tools have been used successfully by change practitioners over the years to manage resistance to organizational change but they only go part way to addressing the psychological aspects of the transition people experience when change is imposed on them.

The following coaching tools and techniques provide the ideal complement for change practitioners when supporting stakeholders to overcome their resistance to change and what help they need to move forward with their internal psychological process.

Each technique is described in more detail in Chapter 14 of this book and although each is deployed differently, what they have in common is that a strong rapport between the change practitioner and the stakeholder is essential. Typically, these techniques are most effective when used in one-to-one conversations. However, if a team has a strong dynamic and the change practitioner is a strong facilitator, these techniques can also work well with small peer groups, as each team member can share their concerns and frustrations freely.

Change and transition models: techniques to coach people resistant to change

One of the most famous and widely used change and transition models is *the change curve*, attributed to Elisabeth Kubler-Ross originally as a therapeutic tool to help people through the grieving process. The change curve was quickly picked up by businesses and change practitioners as the stages of grief laid out in the model are similar to the stages some people experience as a result of organizational change. This is why this particular model is still used and is popular today.

This section will be reviewing other change and transition models including:

- the change cycle
- Bridges' transition model
- neurological levels.

Kubler-Ross change curve

This well-known model describes the four stages most people go through as they adjust to change. People often display behaviours that are triggered by an emotional state at each of the four stages. Some people become stuck at stage 2, commonly known as the 'valley of despair'. Depending on the individual this could mean not wanting to, or not feeling able to move forward. Change is unlikely to be successful if people are not willing to at least move towards stage 3 and ideally on to stage 4. Here is an outline of the four stages and behaviours:

- Stage 1: Shock, denial, business as usual, it is not happening or going to happen.
- Stage 2: Resistance, anger, blame, anxiety, depression, apathy.
- Stage 3: Exploration, acceptance, confusion, uncertainty, energy, ideas with no structure.
- Stage 4: Commitment, cooperation, goal clarity, action planning, future focus.

The authors would like to share some more current and what they believe are more useful change and transition models, which can be used to support stakeholders who are particularly resistant to change.

The change cycle

This modern-day transition model is an adaptation of the Kubler-Ross change curve and originates from Graham Lee (2007). Lee explains that people go through both conscious and unconscious patterns of feelings, behaviours and emotions when any type of change happens. Conscious awareness ultimately leads to choice and depends on if the individual wants to accept the change or not.

There are five stages to this model (see Figure 7.4):

- uninformed optimism
- unconscious resistance
- conscious realism
- conscious optimism
- conscious integration of changes.

Figure 7.4 The change cycle

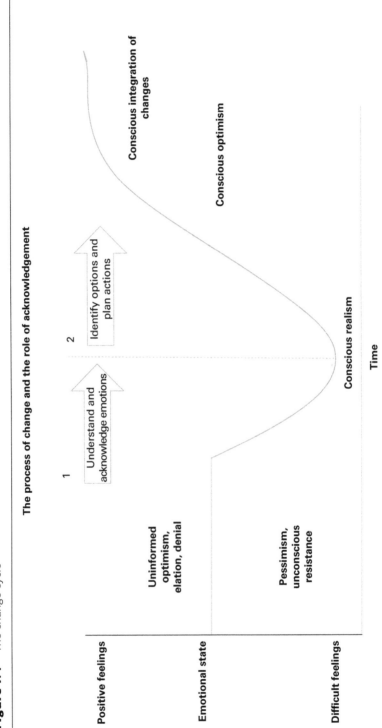

The process of change and the role of acknowledgement

Positive feelings

Uninformed optimism, elation, denial

Emotional state

Pessimism, unconscious resistance

Difficult feelings

1

Understand and acknowledge emotions

2

Identify options and plan actions

Conscious integration of changes

Conscious optimism

Conscious realism

Time

SOURCE Lee, 2007

This model is explained in more detail in Chapter 14, technique 7 of this book describing each of the five stages and possible questions to ask at each stage with additional interventions to support the change process. A summary is given below as context to how this model can be used to manage resistance to change in the following example between Alison and Josh.

The vertical axis represents a person's emotional state, ranging from positive feelings to difficult feelings. The horizontal axis represents time. Peoples' experience of change varies; therefore this cycle is dependent on the individual and the impact the change has on them. To explain the model it is useful to consider a typical situation where someone is likely to experience resistance to change, for example being asked to do a different job following a restructure.

The change cycle in practice

Alison noticed that one of her team, Josh, was acting out of character following a post-acquisition team restructure. Usually outgoing and cheerful, Josh was showing signs of moodiness and generally being quite negative about the change. Alison set up a meeting with Josh and offered him the chance to talk through what was on his mind.

Alison: Josh, I am rather concerned about you lately. You don't seem your usual cheerful self and I wondered if you would like to talk through what is on your mind at the moment? There is no rush with time.

Josh: You are right, I haven't been feeling great about the recent acquisition. There are so many changes and I am feeling uncertain about the whole thing.

Alison: Would you mind if I shared with you this useful transition model? It may help both of us to understand what is happening and how I might support you as your manager. (Alison shares the change cycle model and talks through each of the stages.)

Josh: Well yes, I am usually on the right of this model, committed, enthusiastic and always looking for the next project to work on. Before all of these changes and much to the annoyance of my peers, I was often really positive and enjoying the challenge of the job.

Alison: I agree this is where I have always seen you. Where do you feel you are now?

Josh: I do feel that I have dipped and have some difficult feelings to manage. I feel pessimistic about the changes and I admit to being resistant which is not really where I want to be. Things were going well and so why does the restructure need to happen? I am just trying to make sense of it all now. I think I just need some more clarity about what my job will involve and if I should be looking for a new job.

Alison: What support do you need from me to help you with this transition and for you to return to conscious optimism?

Josh: Regular talks with you would be great to revisit the change cycle and to see if I have slipped back at all. I like the fact that you have given me the time and space to talk this through. When we next meet can we talk about what options I have and where the acquisition leaves me, work wise?

Alison: Yes, of course, lets book another meeting in two weeks.

Summary of using the change cycle with Alison and Josh

Before the acquisition and subsequent restructure, Josh's emotional state was one of elation, optimism and positivity. He had heard a few weeks before about the changes but it didn't affect him at that moment and so it could be said that he was in denial.

The restructure was announced, which led Josh to move quickly to pessimism and concern for himself and his team. He was not fully aware of his resistance until his coaching conversation with Alison, which brought him into conscious awareness of how the change was affecting his emotions and behaviours. Alison's coaching conversation was important in helping Josh to understand and acknowledge what the impact his mindset was having on himself and others and how he could take responsibility for moving forward when he was ready.

The dip in emotions (conscious realism), came for Josh at the point when he understood the potential challenges and situation ahead of him. The realization was that he might lose status, his friends, his motivation. For some people this is where the resistance is at its most noticeable. That sense of loss and having to change habits and identity is too much and so the heels are firmly dug in to the ground. Moving into conscious optimism feels too much, too soon for some.

For Josh, the coaching session with Alison helped him to understand and acknowledge the need to start identifying options and plan actions. He also had his team to think about. This change was not just about him. With further coaching, this would eventually lead to Josh being in the final two stages of the cycle, conscious optimism and conscious integration of changes.

Bridges' transition model

An alternative transition model that is worth considering is Bridges' transition model (2017), which helps organizations and individuals understand and more effectively manage and work through the personal and human side of change. This model is described in more detail in Chapter 14, technique 8 exploring the three stages an individual experiences during change with suggested questions to ask during each stage. A summary of each stage is given below to give context and meaning to the discussion between Alison and Megan below.

Taking a closer look at figure 7.5, the Bridges' transition model might at first appear to be linear and transactional in its approach, it does in fact take in to account that people go through a roller coaster of emotions and behaviours during each of these three phases of change and transition.

The three stages are:

- **Endings:** What people are losing and letting go of and managing these losses.
- **Neutral Zone:** What happens after Endings and letting go? The Neutral Zone is the transition between Endings and New Beginnings.
- **New Beginnings:** New understandings, values and attitudes resulting in a release of energy in a new direction.

Figure 7.5 Bridges' transition model (2017)

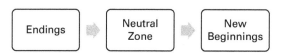

Bridges' transition model in practice

Returning to Alison and the coaching conversations that she is having with her team, she turned her attention to Megan who is also demonstrating negative behaviour. Alison is curious to know how the restructure is affecting her. However, Megan is generally not as positive as some team members and can bring the mood of the team down when she expresses her negative views. This behaviour has been dealt with in the past, but it has returned again since the acquisition. Alison invites Megan for a one-hour meeting, which Megan agrees to reluctantly. Alison is keen to see how Bridges' transition model will resonate with Megan.

Alison: Megan, I have set aside enough time for us to talk. I know that some of the team are not happy with the acquisition and I wondered how this is impacting on you?

Megan: Oh here we go, my negative attitude, yes, I know but it's not surprising I've been negative given all the changes recently and I don't think the acquisition was the right thing for the company. Of course I am going to be angry and upset.

Alison: It sounds like you are struggling with these changes. What else is on your mind?

Megan: Nothing that I want to talk about here. I'm OK.

Alison: Would you mind if I shared something which you may find useful to make sense of what is going on?

Megan: Have you been on one of those leadership programmes again? Another technique to try out on your team no doubt.

Alison ignores these remarks and focuses on introducing Bridges' transition model. She talks through the three phases of the model while Megan reluctantly listens.

Alison: If we start with endings, what are you potentially losing by this change and how do you feel about this?

Megan: This is ridiculous. It's only a model, it's not real and it does not describe what is happening to me with these changes.

Alison: I hear what you are saying but it can sometimes be helpful to use a visual model to make sense of what is going on at a personal level. What thoughts come to mind with regards this question?

Megan: If you insist I answer then what I think I am losing is certainty of what my job will be like and what I am expected to do after the restructure. I am going to potentially lose my work colleagues and possibly interest in my job.

Alison: That sounds quite stressful. Can you think of anything you might gain from the change?

Megan: Well, most of what I am thinking is supposition as I don't really know what is going to happen. If I was forced to be positive then I could say that what I am gaining is a new and fresh opportunity and maybe career progression.

Alison: Once you have got through the worst and are in the Neutral Zone, how do you want to be feeling and what might stop you from exploring new opportunities at the time?

Megan: I would like to be feeling less anxious about the changes and this will come with time but again, there is uncertainty about that. Maybe if I can let you know when I am ready for another chat like this?

Alison: Yes, of course. I will check in with you from time to time. If I could ask you to be aware of your mindset and how this is impacting on you. Maybe refer to this model from time to time and work out what your triggers are?

Summary of using Bridges' transition model with Alison and Megan

When the restructure was announced Megan felt a sense of loss but was not able to express it in that way. She may well have been going through denial to avoid thinking about the uncertainty of the future. Her emotional state impacted on her negative language and behaviour. Having a coaching conversation with Alison, although initially resistant to the meeting, enabled Megan to express how she was really feeling about the changes and restructure. At this point Megan was going through the Endings stage of the Bridges' transition model. There was no way of knowing how long this process would take. Over time and with further coaching Megan may eventually move into the Neutral Zone – feeling a sense of numbness and acceptance without agreeing to the changes; however, there is likely to be a lack of motivation. The New Beginnings will only happen once there is an acknowledgement of emotions and a willingness to identify options and actions. If there is a sense of reward or something in it for Megan then this process and moving to New Beginnings may not take that long. Not forgetting that moving into New Beginnings does not necessarily mean Megan will stay with the organization.

Overlaying these two transition models

Figure 7.6 shows how the Bridges' transition model could be used in combination with Lee's change cycle to identify the conscious and unconscious processes people are going through. This is an example of how possible it is to integrate the two models and to merge the language and understanding of each during a coaching conversation.

Top tip

Always finish the session with a few questions to help the stakeholder reflect on their experience and to check for new insights. For example, 'What new insights do you have now?' and 'What are your thoughts and feeling right now?'

Figure 7.6 Change cycle overlaid with Bridges' transition model

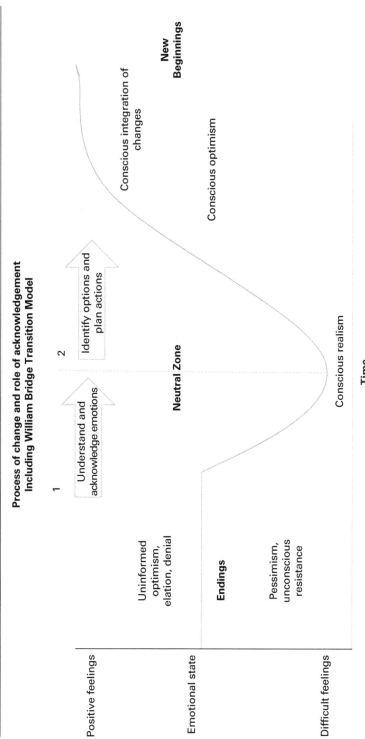

Conclusion

This chapter has identified three change and transition models for overcoming resistance and has demonstrated practical ways in which to use these models. It is worth remembering that people can easily move backward and forward with their emotions and behaviours. The importance of having coaching conversations and making use of transition tools to support and coach others through change is essential. Organizations that fail to provide this type of support may find that their employees take longer to accept change and this is one of many reasons why change fails.

For optimum results, a blend of traditional change tools and coaching techniques support the change practitioner in understanding the underlying causes of resistance with strategies to work towards acceptance and commitment.

References

Bridges, W (2017) *Managing Transitions: Making the most of change*. Nicholas Brealey, London, Boston

Ford, J and Ford, L (2009) Decoding resistance to change, *Harvard Business Review*, https://hbr.org/2009/04/decoding-resistance-to-change (archived at https://perma.cc/D2TW-Q2J7)

Franklin, M (2014) *Agile Change Management*, Kogan Page, London

Frei, F and Morriss, A (2020) Begin with trust, *Harvard Business Review*, https://hbr.org/2020/05/begin-with-trust (archived at https://perma.cc/EFS6-H3JG)

Galpin, T (1996) *The Human Side of Change: A practical guide to organization redesign*, John Wiley & Sons, San Francisco

Gibbons, P (2019) *The Science of Successful Organizational Change: How Leaders Set Strategy, Change Behavior, and Create an Agile Culture*, Phronesis Media, London

Goleman, D (1995) *Emotional Intelligence*, Bantam, New York

Hills, J (no date) You can do anything if you can change behaviour Part 1, https://headheartbrain.com/brain-savvy-business/you-can-do-anything-if-you-can-change-behaviour-part-1/ (archived at https://perma.cc/4VGK-F5YT)

Hodges, J (2016) *Managing and Leading People through Organizational Change: The theory and practice of sustaining change through people*, Kogan Page, London

Johansen, S and Selart, M (2014) *Expanding the Role of Trust in the Management of Organisational Change: New perspectives on organisational change and learning*, Fagbokforlaget, Bergen

Kahneman, D (2011) *Thinking Fast and Slow*, Penguin, London

Kotter, J and Schlesinger, L (1979) Choosing strategies for change, *Harvard Business Review*, https://hbr.org/2008/07/choosing-strategies-for-change (archived at https://perma.cc/8GGG-ELYZ)

Kubler-Ross, E and Kessler, D (2014) *On Grief and Grieving*, Simon & Schuster, New York

Lawrence, P (1969) How to deal with resistance to change, *Harvard Business Review*, https://hbr.org/1969/01/how-to-deal-with-resistance-to-change (archived at https://perma.cc/Y4VY-AH6Z)

Lee, G (2007) *Leadership Coaching: From personal insight to organisational performance*, CIPD, London

Morris, K and Raben, D (1995) *Discontinuous Change: Leading organizational transformation*, Jossey-Bass Inc, San Francisco

Oreg, S (2003) Resistance to change: Developing an individual differences measure, *Journal of Applied Psychology*, https://doi.org/10.1037/0021-9010.88.4.680 (archived at https://perma.cc/6Y4V-775L)

O'Toole, J (1995) *Leading Change: Overcoming the ideology of comfort and the tyranny of custom*, Jossey-Bass Inc, San Francisco

Rock, D., SCARF: A Brain-Based Model for Collaborating with and Influencing Others. David Rock Journal Papers, 1

Value Based Management (n.d) cited in Value Based Management Summary of the Change Iceberg by Krüger, https://www.valuebasedmanagement.net/methods_change_management_iceberg.html (archived at https://perma.cc/QMH3-42YK)

Business transformation and ambiguity

Introduction

We inhabit a world of constant flux and ambiguity. In Chapter 1 we examined the myriad ways in which global trends are driving more change than ever before, for example climate change, social justice movements, financial uncertainty and innovation. The devastating arrival of the Covid-19 pandemic has further reinforced how unpredictable the future is.

In this chapter, we will delve more deeply into:

- The ways in which external forces out of the organizations' control lead to ambiguity and uncertainty.
- How firms can mitigate this uncertainty.

Meet VUCA, the new normal

VUCA is an acronym for Volatility, Uncertainty, Complexity and Ambiguity. Its original use can be traced back to the US Army War College in the 1980s but the term was plucked from the archives by Judith Hicks Stiehm and Nicholas Townsend in 2002 to describe the complex and uncertain post 9/11 environment. The term promptly made its way into the corporate vernacular as a catch-all for the ever-changing world around us and can be defined as follows:

Volatility

- Turbulence – things are changing quickly and in an unpredictable way.

Uncertainty

- Unpredictability – experience is no longer an indication of likely future events, therefore planning and decision-making is very difficult for leaders.

Complexity

- Difficult – a problem has many internal and external causes, all of which are difficult to understand.
- Taken in combination with the unpredictability of the future, the waters are muddied further.

Ambiguity

- Lack of clarity – the various causes of events are unclear and hard to establish. Dr John Sullivan (2012) described this as the 'inability to accurately conceptualize threats and opportunities before they become lethal'.

Tales of the unexpected

Why is VUCA a problem? Companies used to be able to initiate change on their own terms, introducing new software or developing new products along a self-imposed timeline. However, the speed with which the world is changing means this is no longer the case. The reality is an almost continuous cycle of change driven by factors largely outside an organization's control. It makes the discipline of managing change extremely difficult for many reasons:

- Planning – a portfolio of projects cannot be reliably planned as it is virtually guaranteed that an unforeseen requirement will emerge leading to the whole portfolio being re-prioritized.
- Resourcing – change teams are notoriously hard to resource given the speed at which the portfolio can change. Running a Change team over-capacity by keeping resources 'on the bench' is not a viable option for any but the largest firms and therefore capacity often needs to be re-shuffled or bolstered with a short-term or interim resource at short notice.

- Talent – if a requirement emerges that has a specialist skillset, a Change team is unlikely to be able to accommodate it with existing resources. This is especially true of regulatory projects or nascent sectors such as Artificial Intelligence or specialist coding languages.

- Budget – the above points mean that confirming and sticking to an annual change budget is challenging.

- Business as usual – it becomes harder to manage the expectations of stakeholders who have day jobs but are still expected to lend subject matter expertise to projects.

- Change fatigue – VUCA creates such a never-ending cycle of change that change is never 'done'. Stakeholders waiting to reach the end of a project so they can be left in peace are disappointed when the next project begins almost straight away.

The feeling of being in a perpetual change vortex where things are never allowed to settle is very challenging for many people. However, the world is not likely to return to certainty and predictability. Most experts agree that VUCA is the status quo.

Learning to live with VUCA

If we can accept that VUCA is here to stay, the only viable path forward is acceptance, mitigation and risk management. In his 2021 book, *Leaders Make the Future: Ten new leadership skills for an uncertain world* (2012), Dr Bob Johansen introduced the concept of VUCA Prime – a way for an organizations' leaders to 'flip' the original VUCA model to the more positive notions of Vision, Understanding, Clarity and Agility.

Vision:

- Leaders with a clear strategic vision are better equipped against volatility.

Understanding:

- Leaders must look beyond their immediate business area to rationalize the volatility and to lead with vision.

Clarity:

- Leaders need to be able to receive and synthesize information quickly so that they can make data-led decisions quickly.

Agility:

- Leaders require the ability to mobilize their decisions quickly, typically by communicating and influencing at the right level.

Let us consider a few of the different ways a change practitioner can help mitigate the challenges of VUCA, using Johansen's positive model.

Vision

According to Johansen, leaders are more likely to weather economic downturns or new competition if they make business decisions in the context of the organization's strategic vision. It stands to reason that if decisions are anchored to the core strategy, even if made in response to unforeseen circumstances, the resulting action will not steer firms off course.

We have already seen that a project or programme requires a strong central vision for the business to coalesce around. This vision should always be linked to the overarching strategic direction of the business and therefore can pivot in tandem with any decisions taken in response to the unexpected. If this is not the case, an initiative is vulnerable to being paused or stopped completely as soon as an unplanned event occurs.

Understanding

Surviving uncertainty is only possible in the long term if business leaders can see beyond their immediate functional area and think in a broader organizational context. This requires collaboration and an absence of the type of 'silo' thinking common in many firms. By extension, this requires leaders to communicate with all levels of employees in their organization.

Clarity

Leaders need to be able to cut through confusion quickly and make informed business decisions, even under pressure. Using reliable data sources to make decisions which are tied to the strategic vision leads to good outcomes. When those decisions are made, they must be cascaded throughout the organization quickly and clearly.

Agility

The ability to make decisions quickly, based on data is critical but on its own is not enough. An organization also needs to 'make continuous shifts in people, process, technology, and structure' (Horney et al, 2010). This relies on flexibility and speed, which is a particular challenge for large firms. It is no coincidence that start-ups are well equipped in this regard.

Although VUCA Prime was designed with senior leaders in mind, the model can be adopted and applied by change practitioners.

Vision

The change practitioner can ensure that senior leadership commits to a strong central vision for the project or programme. They can guide the sponsor in developing the vision and linking it to the strategy, explaining the importance of the central vision as a way of making the activity less vulnerable to closure.

Understanding

Change teams are uniquely placed in a firm – they tend to be function agnostic and often have a broader organizational vista than other teams. Part of the change practitioner's remit is also to communicate upwards and downwards, thereby shaping the messaging and, with it, people's understanding.

Clarity

When leaders need to make a decision impacting a change initiative, a strong change practitioner can enable this by defining the possible scenarios and direction of travel based on different data sources. When decisions have been taken, change practitioners can be instrumental in shaping the communication to the business.

Agility

The flexibility and speed required to 'make continuous shifts' can be greatly facilitated by a strong change team. Even large firms can become nimble across people, process, technology and structure with the appropriate change procedures in place. For example, successful change teams generally have a vehicle for delivering small change (either below a certain monetary threshold or number of days effort), to prevent quick wins from being hobbled by unnecessary project governance. Similarly, if a project in flight needs to pivot quickly, Change team governance can provide the appropriate level of oversight without compromising on speed of delivery.

Leading the way

Dr Johansen's VUCA Prime model focuses heavily on leaders and leadership. In *The World Is Flat* (2011), Thomas Friedman stated that companies that 'lack the leadership, flexibility and imagination to adapt' will be overwhelmed by the speed of change. It is encouraging to note some multinationals recognizing and embracing this. In 2010, Procter & Gamble announced it was revising its supply chain strategy to facilitate its response to VUCA events and the following year it rolled the approach out company wide. In 2012, Unilever's CEO, Keith Weed, went a step further and changed the firm's leadership development model in direct response to the VUCA challenge. Weed said the firm looks 'at the world through a lens, which we call VUCA... the digital revolution, the shift in consumer spending, all this suggests that companies have to reinvent the way they do business'. It is no coincidence that both these organizations are fast-moving consumer goods (FMCG) firms reliant on slick supply chain management. Less traditionally dynamic industry sectors would do well to adopt similar strategies in the face of an increasingly unpredictable world.

A seasoned change practitioner can help here by working with senior leaders across the organization on an activity known as *horizon scanning*. It starts with a simple 'roadmap' stretching out across two to three years. The present day is a well-developed picture of the status quo, including the company's business as usual (BAU) activity and projects in flight. Year one will consist of projects in the pipeline and at various stages of approval. As the roadmap stretches out to years two and three, activity can be planned in but it becomes less certain and more subject to change. A good change practitioner can work with leaders to use strategic tools such as SWOT, PESTEL and Michael Porter's Five Forces model on a regular basis as a way of defining and tracking potential change drivers. This exercise mitigates uncertainty by anticipating it and enables appropriate responses to be developed and communicated. The other benefit of frequently scanning the horizon is that it decreases sensitivity to the unknown and, done well, horizon scanning can actively build the organization-wide embracing of VUCA.

Coaching solutions for business transformation and ambiguity

Introduction

The original VUCA definitions go hand in hand with a lack of control, anxiety and even fear. Although some people regard ambiguity, change and uncertainty as an opportunity, many struggle to function at all. We can harness this intelligence to develop strategies that enhance communication and boost performance and resilience.

Who needs support and why?

The change practitioner: Managing ambiguity is complex. There are many factors to consider. The easiest and most effective form of support is from an external coach or even a mentor. If the organization has qualified and trained internal coaches, this could work well too. The coach or mentor will work with the individual to identify personal and professional challenges and to help the change practitioner to work through the complexities of change towards a workable solution. The coach will untap blocks and barriers to success and any limiting belief that may be a blind spot or hidden (possibly, in denial). The mentor will add support in the way of advice and guidance from their own experience of dealing with a similar situation.

Stakeholders: This is even more complex. As we have seen, not everyone reacts to change and uncertainty in the same way. However, we can learn a lot from understanding personality types, thinking styles and the way people behave at work which may or may not be out of character.

Chapter 14 of this book offers a selection of additional change and transition tools and techniques to support those who are experiencing ambiguity due to business transformation. Neurological Levels is one useful technique to support people who are resistant to change or have a sense of being stuck.

To offer a fresh perspective to managing ambiguity, the following section demonstrates the importance of Emergenetics to mitigate ambiguity.

Using Emergenetics to mitigate ambiguity

In Chapter 5 the subject of Emergenetics is explored and distinguishes between the way we think and the way we behave. The four Emergenetics thinking attributes are Analytical, Structural, Social and Conceptual. Understanding these four thinking attributes can help the change practitioner to work with individuals and teams and to consider different ways of communicating and coaching to meet their needs. Considering how someone with an analytical preference compared to someone with a social preference copes with ambiguity will help change practitioners' work with individuals by tapping into their language patterns and how they process information. The following examples show how this can work.

Analytical thinking preference

Jeff is a clear thinker, interested in data and prefers objective analysis of a situation. He can come across as sceptical and he might try to find one right answer to a situation. He struggles with change if not presented with clear evidence, facts or figures to justify it. In short, VUCA is the stuff of nightmares for those with an analytical preference, like Jeff.

Because Jeff does not like being rushed, patience and an understanding of how his thinking preference is informing his experience is essential. He may also resist some questions that he sees as fanciful or lacking in logic, becoming quite defensive. So avoid questions such as 'Imagine if you were CEO in three years' time. What would you do differently?' You may experience Jeff over-analysing your questions by trying to make logical sense of what you mean. The response to your questions may be met with a hasty 'I don't know.' Although the temptation here is to offer a suggestion or advice, do avoid this – commitment and buy-in is more powerful when coming directly from the stakeholder, not the change practitioner.

Four incisive questions for those with an analytical thinking preference

1 Thinking rationally, what sense are you making of this situation right now?

2 What evidence do you need to support you through this situation?

3 What three options do you have? Which one is most relevant to you?

4 What are the pros and cons of what is happening for you?

> **Top tip**
>
> Analytical thinkers prefer time to think carefully about questions before responding. Re-grouping a couple of days later will allow them to formulate their own ideas instead of feeling pressurized to respond immediately.

Structural thinking preference

Sonal is practical, cautious and methodical. She likes set plans and guidelines, goals to work towards and background information with clear steps. Sonal will happily make lists of the tasks she needs to complete and even those she has already completed, crossing them off as she goes through each one.

Four incisive questions for those with a structural thinking preference

1 What checklist and timeline do you need from me to help support you with this?

2 What more, in terms of detail, do you need from me at this stage?

3 What is your overall goal and what do you want to achieve from this?

4 What is the first step to achieving your outcome?... and what is the next?

> **Top tip**
>
> Structural thinkers like working with people who are professional, organized, precise and on time. Be direct and demonstrate a clear list of priorities and actions.

Social thinking preference

Mosi has a social preference. He is sympathetic, connected, socially aware and intuitive about other people. Mosi is likely to have an emotional reaction to change and could take the result of the change personally. He is likely to be concerned for others and wonder how their feelings are affected by this change, as well as his own.

Mosi would value time to talk through his concerns with someone who is a good listener and is empathetic to his needs. Mosi is likely to be open to questions particularly if they are related to a concern for others, not necessarily the logical facts of the situation. Questions to avoid are 'What are the pros and cons of this situation for you?' You may experience Mosi being emotional in your conversations. Do not shy away at this stage but show empathy and work through this emotion. The temptation here is to sympathize, but instead work with Mosi to be more empathetic and find a workable solution and the support he needs.

Four incisive questions for those with a social thinking preference

1 How is this change impacting on you?

2 What support do you need from me or others?

3 What would be a good outcome that is within your control?

4 Who else could you connect with to share your experience?

Top tip

Social thinkers need more connection with others. They like to work through people, with people. Relationships are important, as is the need to be heard and understood. This same technique can be applied to the other two thinking preferences: conceptual and structural.

Conceptual thinking preference

Jia is inventive, future focussed, unconventional and prefers formulating ideas using mindmaps. In addition with coming up with her own ideas, Jia will often take ideas from others with the aim to improving on them. Jia does not have a preference for detail and would rather spend time in thinking of how things could work given the time and opportunity.

Four incisive questions for those with a conceptual thinking preference

1 Imagine this situation in six months' time, what do you see, hear and feel?

2 What ideas do you have which you'd like to share?

3 How does this connect with the vision of the organization?

4 If you could change one thing for the better, what would it be?

Top tip

Conceptual thinkers like to invest in the cause to feel motivated in the change. Big picture thinking matters more than who is leading the project. Allow them to come up with their own ideas that are met with interest, not dismissed.

Conclusion

If we accept that VUCA is the status quo, the need to continually support and lead individuals will grow. This is a tall order, but coaching can and should play a significant role. Change practitioners can build the trust, rapport and resilience that are crucial to overcoming a fear of VUCA by adopting skills in:

- Being present and engaged in conversation with the stakeholder.
- Listening with good intent.
- Being curious and interested.
- Asking questions that focus on the future not on the problem.
- Showing empathy and understanding.

References

Friedman, T (2005) *The World Is Flat: The globalized world in the 21st century*, Ernst Klett Sprachen GmbH, Munich

Hicks Stiehm, J and Townsend, N (2002) *The US Army War College: Military education in a democracy*, Temple University Press, Philadelphia

Horney, N, Pasmore, B and O'Shea, T (2010) Leadership agility: A business imperative for a VUCA world, https://luxorgroup.fr/coaching/wp-content/uploads/Leadership-agility-model.pdf (archived at https://perma.cc/M7WT-V5ED)

Johansen, R (2012) *Leaders Make the Future: Ten new leadership skills for an uncertain world*, Berrett-Koehler, Oakland

Lawrence, K (2013) Developing leaders in a VUCA environment, https://www.emergingrnleader.com/wp-content/uploads/2013/02/developing-leaders-in-a-vuca-environment.pdf (archived at https://perma.cc/99NW-QDFA)

OECD (2020) Global economy faces gravest threat since the crisis as coronavirus spreads, https://www.oecd.org/economy/global-economy-faces-gravest-threat-since-the-crisis-as-coronavirus-spreads.htm (archived at https://perma.cc/VP4B-SDN9)

Sullivan, J (2012) Talent strategies for a turbulent VUCA world – shifting to an adaptive approach, https://www.ere.net/talent-strategies-for-a-turbulent-vuca-world-shifting-to-an-adaptive-approach/ (archived at https://perma.cc/839U-WG9C)

Whiting, K (2020) Coronavirus isn't an outlier, it's part of our interconnected viral age, https://www.weforum.org/agenda/2020/03/coronavirus-global-epidemics-health-pandemic-covid-19/ (archived at https://perma.cc/CS47-9LFQ)

Stakeholder engagement 09

Introduction

As we have seen throughout this book, stakeholders of all levels often prefer to ignore change initiatives for numerous reasons. However, it is extremely challenging to deliver change if the individuals and teams impacted are not engaged. In this chapter we will:

- Understand what stakeholder engagement is and why it is important in the delivery of change.
- Learn how to identify stakeholders and define the optimum tools and techniques to engage them.
- Learn how to overcome the challenges associated with engaging different groups.
- Understand how senior leaders can help.

What is a stakeholder?

In a change environment, it is common to use the word 'stakeholder' as a catch-all for anyone with a 'stake' in the change, typically because their department or team is impacted in some way. There are different ways to organize or categorize stakeholders including:

- Internal stakeholders are inside the organization, for example managers, senior managers, executives, heads of departments, team members and end-users.
- External stakeholders are outside the organization, for example customers, suppliers, strategic partners and shareholders.

- Primary or 'key' stakeholders refers to any individual or group who can influence the change because of their ability to enable or hinder it, irrespective of whether they are internal or external.

- Secondary stakeholders are usually external, do not have a direct interest in the organizational change but can often have some influence over a business's dealings, for example software suppliers, regulators or the media.

What is stakeholder engagement and why is it important?

The Association of Project Management (APM) defines stakeholder engagement as the 'systematic identification, analysis, planning and implementation of actions designed to influence stakeholders'. In other words, it is the activity of:

- Identifying anyone with a stake in the change.
- Determining the size and type of the 'stake'.
- Defining how best to influence them throughout the project.

It is a 'hearts and minds' relationship-based activity of influencing outcomes via consultation, communication and relationship building. Failure to engage with stakeholders throughout a project means we are delivering change in a vacuum. Since delivering change is about asking people to alter their ways of working, it is impossible for any successful project to thrive in such a vacuum.

Taking a pro-active approach to stakeholder engagement has practical and emotional benefits which we will outline here.

Practical benefits:

- Reduces wasted time and effort, as people impacted by the change are involved in and contributing to the end state, for example workshopping requirements or providing subject matter expertise.

- Provides the opportunity for early and continuous validation of the approach and end goal by using a 'test and learn' approach of pilots and proof of concept with the end-user.

- Facilitates training and final roll-out by producing a set of 'super users' who have been involved in the development of the solution from the start.

- Creates a ready-made internal communications channel, as every interaction passes on information relating to the project.

Emotional benefits:

- Increases transparency of the end-product or solution, which reduces uncertainty, ambiguity, stress and fear.
- Builds trust and credibility in the solution being delivered.
- Speeds up the tipping point to adoption of the new normal.
- Provides those involved with an opportunity for personal development.

Identifying who our stakeholders are

Stakeholder analysis is a structured and popular way for change practitioners to identify stakeholders, segment their different needs and determine how best to engage with them from the start of a change initiative to achieve the desired objectives. This activity is sometimes carried out by a Change Manager but also often by the Project Manager and sometimes by both.

The most effective way to carry out this exercise is to think of it as a framework of the following questions:

- Who?
- What?
- How?
- When?

Who: stakeholder identification

Start by making a list of all potential internal and external stakeholders across the project or programme, including their function and job title. If the Change Manager has already carried out an impact analysis, this is a useful artefact too as it already captures many relevant stakeholders.

What: stakeholder assessment

Mendelow's stakeholder matrix is a useful tool for this exercise. Created in 1991 by Aubrey Mendelow, it helps to evaluate and plot stakeholders according to:

- their level of power and influence in the project

- their level of interest in getting the project off the ground and maintaining it throughout the project lifecycle.

Here is a useful guide (see Figure 9.1):

Figure 9.1   Mendelow's stakeholder matrix

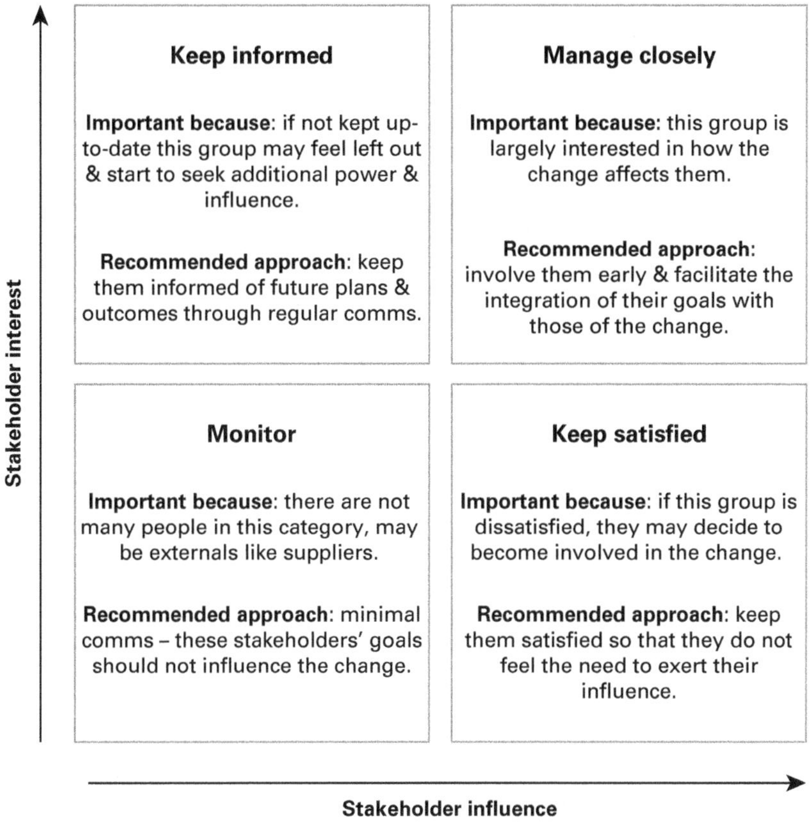

Keep informed	**Manage closely**
Important because: if not kept up-to-date this group may feel left out & start to seek additional power & influence. **Recommended approach**: keep them informed of future plans & outcomes through regular comms.	**Important because**: this group is largely interested in how the change affects them. **Recommended approach**: involve them early & facilitate the integration of their goals with those of the change.
Monitor	**Keep satisfied**
Important because: there are not many people in this category, may be externals like suppliers. **Recommended approach**: minimal comms – these stakeholders' goals should not influence the change.	**Important because**: if this group is dissatisfied, they may decide to become involved in the change. **Recommended approach**: keep them satisfied so that they do not feel the need to exert their influence.

Stakeholder interest (vertical axis)

Stakeholder influence (horizontal axis)

SOURCE Aubrey Mendelow (1991)

Group A – monitor

- Low power, low interest: a junior or middle manager in another part of the organization.

Group B – keep informed

- Low power, high interest: for example an end-user.

Group C – keep satisfied

- High power, low interest: a senior leader from a different part of the organization.

Group D – manage closely

- High power, high interest: senior leaders such as the Project Sponsor, other Steering Committee members, other senior leaders in the same part of the organization.

How and when: stakeholder engagement

Once the stakeholders have been identified and plotted in the matrix, it is time to develop the optimum engagement method for each stakeholder group. Table 9.1 offers a suggested overview of how to manage each group. In the section entitled, 'Coaching solutions for stakeholder engagement', we offer a checklist of the level of effort and the type of intervention change practitioners may use with each group.

Table 9.1   Suggestions for managing stakeholder groups

Group	Suggestions
A – Monitor	Update via internal communications vehicles such as company-wide e-Newsletters or town halls.
	Monitor to check if their levels of interest or power change as the project progresses.
B – Keep informed	These stakeholders can offer insight into areas that may need improving and may be overlooked.
	Facilitate two-way communication little and often using various methods, such as email, verbal updates at team meetings and via Change Agents.
C – Keep satisfied	Communicate in an unintrusive way that is short and to the point.
D – Manage closely	Spend most time communicating here.
	Tailor engagement to each individual in this group.
	Blend face-to-face interaction with written updates.

CASE STUDY

The Project Manager at EazyGlaze has been tasked with implementing a Customer Relationship Management (CRM) tool that has been designed specifically for the Sales Team, headed up by Jeremy who sits on the project Steering Committee and is, therefore, an important stakeholder. Jeremy recognizes his position of power and influence and has made no secret of the fact that he and his team do not see the value of the new CRM tool, he has not agreed to its introduction and does not wish to use the tool when it goes live. Jeremy reports directly to the Managing Director, Saskia, who wants to keep Jeremy on her side and not rock the boat. Saskia, originally agreed the CRM tool's introduction at a time when Jeremy was on sabbatical and now regrets not getting him involved sooner.

Although Jeremy is an important figure on the project Steering Committee, he rarely attends the meetings and never cascades important messages about the project's progress to his team. He has previously mentioned to Saskia he does not attend the meetings because he does not have a good working relationship with the other senior members of the group. In particular, it is well known in the organization that there is long-running friction between Jeremy and the Finance Director, Alan, as a result of a series of disagreements about commission payments. Jeremy thinks Alan is a 'control freak' who is too obsessed with doing things by the book. Alan believes Jeremy has been over-promoted to a role too senior for his experience and skillset and that he needs to be reined in by Saskia.

Saskia is finding the tension within her leadership team frustrating and although she knows her role is to try to manage the situation, she decides to ignore it instead. She can do without the internal fighting but is not sure what to do next.

We will return to this case study later in the chapter, but, for now, here are some things to consider. Who are the key stakeholders here and where do they belong in the stakeholder matrix? How can the Project Manager help Saskia to resolve some of the tension and conflict? Does the project have the right Sponsor?

Evolving the stakeholder management approach

The ADKAR model, developed by the Prosci® founder Jeff Hiatt in 2003, is a useful tool to monitor stakeholder engagement. The model's core principle is that organizational change can only happen when individuals change. Prosci states that 'by outlining the goals and outcomes of successful change, the ADKAR model enables leaders and change practitioners to focus their activities on what will drive individual change and therefore achieve organisational results'. ADKAR is an acronym of the five tangible and concrete outcomes:

- **Awareness** of the need to change.
- **Desire** to participate and support the change.
- **Knowledge** on how to change.
- **Ability** to implement desired skills and behaviours.
- **Reinforcement** to sustain the change.

Many change practitioners use the ADKAR model to guide their stakeholder management approach for two reasons:

1 The linear five-step model creates a set of unofficial 'stage gates' at which stakeholder engagement levels can be evaluated and the approach can be amended if necessary.

2 The best practice activities recommended at each stage can inform the engagement approach as many of them involve communication, training or other stakeholder touchpoints.

Stakeholder engagement at different levels of the organization

In addition to the distinctions created by internal and external stakeholders and their position within Mendelow's matrix, there are further considerations. By taking into account the stakeholder's position within the organizational structure, change practitioners can develop a more tailored engagement approach.

Junior management

Employees who occupy the lower rungs of the corporate ladder can be an interesting group of stakeholders. They do not generally wield a lot of power in the corporate structure, can often be young and inexperienced, and generally do not have teams of their own to lead, which can further limit their influence. However, wherever people sit within the organization, they can influence change and should never be dismissed.

The fact that they are more junior can make stakeholder engagement easier as it opens up a range of informal touchpoints such as desk-side discussions, coffee chats or even a drink after work. In a more formal setting, junior team members are generally the 'doers' – the people at the coal face using the system or following the process at the heart of the change. For this reason, they are often asked to act as project Subject Matter Experts and Change Agents (see separate sections).

The frozen middle

Many change initiatives have 'crashed upon the rocks of middle management', according to Paul Lawrence in his 2014 book *Leading Change: How successful leaders approach change management*. It stands to reason that middle managers can make or break change – they can cooperate, and their teams go with them. Alternatively, they can resist and protect their patch if they feel the change does not benefit them or their immediate team.

The interventions for this group are more complex than for junior management. Their time is more precious as they usually have teams to manage and a desk-side visit may not be welcomed. Nevertheless, opportunities exist to create engagement touchpoints through decision-making bodies like Design Boards or targeted management updates. Additionally, this group often also acts as project Subject Matter Experts (SMEs) and Change Agents.

Subject Matter Experts

As we have already seen, junior and middle management have something in common – both groups are often nominated as SMEs on projects. Outside of the immediate project team and Steering Committee, these are the people who are closest to the detail of a project. SMEs are generally a cross-functional group of people who represent the functions and departments impacted by the change. They need to be close to the day-to-day workings of the business to help the project team understand the status quo and then to feed in the future requirements effectively.

The authors' research with change practitioners based in the UK generated some common challenges on the subject of SMEs:

- There are none available to help define or advise on the change.

- They are available but have insufficient time to perform the task well.

This suggests the role of the SME has yet to be fully embraced or understood by firms, which is a significant missed opportunity for a change initiative of any size. Not only does it rob the project of the business knowledge this group possesses but it also strips out a whole stakeholder group who could help spread the vision, either informally or more formally as Change Agents.

A successful SME needs:

- The specialist knowledge for the workstream they are involved in. For example, a large data migration project would need, among others, an end-user of the system or systems in question with in-depth knowledge at a field level, as well as a data expert who understands the underlying data.

- Sufficient time to devote to the project. The Project or Programme Manager must be clear at the start of the nomination process what the likely time commitment will be, including any peaks when the SME's time will be particularly in demand. For example, in a traditional waterfall project, which has defined initiation, design, implementation and closure stages, they need to contribute to the gathering of requirements in an early stageand testing of the solution in a later phase. However, an SME may not be required as much in the middle phases when the solution is being developed. In contrast, a project following an agile delivery methodology develops and delivers over successive cycles (sprints), which requires resources to be available more often.

- Commitment to the project's success. They need to believe in the project's vision and goals. If SMEs do not believe it, not only will their commitment be half-hearted, they may become vocal and influential detractors.

- Influence over the employees impacted by the change so that they can act as a change agent wherever possible (see next section).

Change agents

This group of employees is often key to a project's success. Throughout the project lifecycle (and post project closure) they communicate and reinforce the vision, articulate the more granular project objectives and help to garner support from others who may be disengaged or resistant. Post-implementation, change agents embody the new ways of working which helps to bring others on the change journey.

Change agents can be drawn from different functions and departments across the wider organization and in common with the SMEs, the project team should select the group of people most appropriate to the change that is being delivered. There may be overlap between the two groups, though it is important to consider the individual's capacity to act as both a change agent and SME.

The role of senior leadership

It is surprising how people underestimate the role senior leaders can play in supporting and facilitating stakeholder management and engagement. In addition to the governance and decision-making role the executive sponsor and Steering Committee members take on, senior leaders can support the project manager in a variety of ways.

The vision

Arguably the most important contribution is via the creation and dissemination of the project or programme vision. The existence of a clear and strong vision enables the project team to harness it for all engagement and communication. This not only provides consistency of message but also provides a security blanket for the project team, knowing that the vision has come directly from the senior leadership. As Jack Welch said, 'Good business leaders create a vision, articulate that vision, passionately own the vision and relentlessly drive it to completion' (cited in Thangarathinam, 2020). However, many senior leaders fail to recognize how important the vision is and confuse it with a simple goal or objective, for example:

- Grow turnover by 10 per cent in three years.
- Increase profitability by 5 per cent in five years.
- Grow customer base by 20 per cent.

These are sound project outcomes but they lack the 'big picture' strategic view that engages people. MSP® defines the vision as a 'postcard from the future' with the following characteristics:

- Written as a desirable future state, not as objectives. It describes the state as if the firm is already there, in the present tense.

- Articulates in a short and memorable statement why the current state is not feasible – this acts as the rationale for the change.

- Specifically omits quantifiable metrics and targets as they can be off-putting to some stakeholders (but come later in the business case and project charter).

- Is easy to understand by all stakeholder groups and can act as the central message for all programme communications.

In the 1980s, Bill Gates' vision was for Microsoft to put a 'computer on every desktop and in every home'. There is no mention of sales targets, turnover or profit margins and is broad enough that every project, programme or initiative in Microsoft could be tied back to that vision. When that vision became outdated, in 2013 the new CEO Steve Ballmer rallied employees and shareholders around a new, 'One Microsoft' strategy, which focussed on creating 'a family of devices and services for individuals and businesses that empower people around the globe at home, at work and on the go, for the activities they value the most'. Again, there is no mention of tangible targets, but there is a strong vision that all projects and programmes can deliver towards – business and individuals, hardware and software, desktop and mobile, work and leisure.

Actions speak louder than words

Another key role senior leaders can play is to embody the change with their actions by role modelling the new behaviour. This sounds obvious but, in practice, senior executives often support a change on a superficial level but do not match their actions to their words. For example, many firms initiate projects to move to an agile office set-up where employees do not have their own desk and must book one as part of a 'hot desking' arrangement. This is an attractive project for firms as it generates cost savings due to the reduction in floor space. However, when senior managers realize this means losing a private office, they withdraw their support or start creating exceptions which undermine the central principle. When employees observe this behaviour, it sends a message that non-compliance to the new ways of working will be acceptable. Hence, trust in leadership is eroded and employees withdraw their support for the change.

Coaching solutions for stakeholder engagement

We have seen how important stakeholder engagement is in the delivery of sustained change. Therefore it is essential that the change practitioner quickly identifies barriers to engagement in the change initiative. Coaching is one way to support barriers to change, although it is not the case of 'one size fits all', as there are many ways to engage stakeholders.

Using coaching with the Mendelow matrix

Earlier in this chapter, Mendelow's matrix was introduced as a useful tool for change practitioners to assess and evaluate each stakeholder's power and influence, compared with their level of interest in the change.

Each of the four groups can be managed differently, and it is important not to disregard or ignore people who are perceived as having low influence and low interest (Group A). This group of stakeholders may increase their level of power and influence throughout the life of the project and connecting with this group early on is recommended. Remember that groups of employees, for example on the first line of hierarchy, can yield some element of power due to their numbers and solidarity, by working to rule, withdrawing labour and generally damaging customer relations. It could be argued that these groups have the most influence purely by the damage they can generate where it matters most.

The following checklist offers suggestions on the level of effort and the type of intervention change practitioners may use with each group in the Mendelow matrix. Building rapport and connecting with as many different people early in the project will help the change practitioner with future conversations, accepting that these conversations may become more challenging as the project evolves.

Group A – low power and low interest

- The level of power and interest with this group can change over time so it is best to maintain rapport from the start and check in from time to time to see how things are.

- A coaching conversation with some of these stakeholders may help to reveal underlying tensions within the workforce or to help mitigate any issues which may unfold later in the project. Overall, not much effort should be expended on this group.

Group B – low power and high interest

- Keep stakeholders in this group on your side and keep communication flowing.

- Set up regular meetings with those who are keen to work on the project. Although not wielding much power, these stakeholders are generally closer to what is happening.

- Stakeholders in this group may be able to offer insight into areas that need improving further down the organization, which will influence the change project and which may be overlooked by those higher up. The change practitioner's networking influence here can be crucial. Overall, keep this group informed.

Group C – high power and low interest

- Keep this group satisfied. Knowing how to keep this group satisfied, and what that means for each stakeholder is part of the challenge.

- Stakeholders in this group are senior leaders with power and influence but are not so interested in the change initiative or have not had it sold to them yet. They may simply not be directly impacted.

- These stakeholders could be the most challenging to manage as they may not be open to attending meetings or want to hear what needs to be heard.

- Meeting with stakeholders within this group will allow the change practitioner to ask questions and discover the level of input needed. Ensure the stakeholder doesn't get bored or frustrated with the message by keeping them engaged and interested. Asking questions will avoid assumptions being made by the change practitioner and will check the assumptions made by the stakeholder.

Group D – high power and high interest

- Manage this group closely. These are the 'key players' and the most important stakeholders.

- Make the most of their level of engagement and level of influence. This requires more time and effort to be spent on these stakeholders than any other group.

- Set up regular meetings and use both an influencing and coaching style and approach by asking relevant questions about their level of interest.

- Show interest in the stakeholder's position and what they can do to help. Also remember to ask the stakeholder what they need from you as change practitioner, how much time these stakeholders are willing to give to the change project and how you can both work collaboratively.

> Meeting in private, either in person or virtually, with the stakeholder will have the most success. Team gatherings in the early stages are unlikely to be successful in gaining commitment and engagement but can be introduced once all relevant stakeholders have been met individually. It is also worth considering using a coaching technique at the meeting when the conversation would benefit from another intervention or focus.

Coaching versus influencing

Coaching and influencing has been mentioned throughout this chapter but what is the difference between these two interventions? Although the focus of this book is on coaching, influencing has equal importance as a soft skill for change practitioners to learn and master. Influencing overlaps and has similarities with coaching but it is important to know what the subtle differences are. These definitions are all offered from the perspective of the change practitioner who may want to coach their stakeholder.

Formal coaching: what it is and what it aims to do

With formal coaching the agenda is the responsibility of the stakeholder being coached, not the change practitioner. This might pose a problem for the change practitioner who feels the need to share their goal or agenda. In which case, this would be a different intervention and not formal coaching. With formal coaching the meetings are structured, contracted and agreed with the stakeholder with goals and outcomes agreed and identified based on a particular development area or problem the stakeholder may have.

Sessions are booked over a period of time and are rarely one-off sessions. Questions asked by the change practitioner will depend on the response given by the stakeholder. There are no set questions or script used by the change practitioner. The focus is on the stakeholder's needs not the change practitioner's needs. Actions are agreed and commitment is gained from the stakeholder.

Informal coaching: what it is and what it aims to do

A general conversation takes place that is not planned, agreed or contracted. This could pose a problem if the stakeholder does not want to be asked questions or is not committed to agreeing to actions by the end of the session. The change practitioner uses a range of questions to engage with the stakeholder with the aim of opening up the conversation to gain insight and understanding. Conversations can happen at any time in any situation and there is a gentle approach to building rapport and understanding. If the stakeholder is willing to engage in the conversation, it can leave them feeling listened to and understood. As with formal coaching, the focus is on stakeholder's needs not change practitioners.

Influencing: what it is and what it aims to do

Influencing is another way of persuading the stakeholder around to the change practitioner's way of thinking. The goal is a win-win negotiation to gain buy-in from the stakeholder where the change practitioner may use a pre-determined set of questions as well as supplementary questions such as open, closed, leading and suggesting to help the conversation flow. The stakeholder is encouraged to think the same way as the change practitioner, which could pose a problem if the stakeholder has not brought in to that idea. The focus is on the change practitioner's needs, not necessarily the stakeholder's needs.

The coaching conversation process

A typical conversation may include many different styles of communication. The important thing for the change practitioner is being mindful of what intervention they are using at any given time and if this is the right intervention for the person and the situation.

Before entering into any conversation, it is useful to remember the REST (Noble, 2021) framework to prepare and guide the conversation:

1 Rapport and being present

2 Empathy

3 Setting the scene

4 Target (stay on track).

Set up a meeting with the stakeholder and agree on the reason why you are both there and what you both want to get from the conversation. Set a goal for the meeting by asking 'What do you want to have achieved by the end of our meeting?' or 'What would be a good outcome for you?'

Listen to the stakeholder and allow them to off-load and speak about what is on their mind or what their concerns are. Useful questions to ask are:

- Is there anything else you would like to say about that?
- What else are you thinking?
- How does this make you feel?

Usually, the more you ask these questions the more you will get to the root of the problem.

If the issue presented by the stakeholder is around influencing skills, then training might be the best solution. However, there is still work that can be achieved through coaching and asking questions.

Coaching techniques for stakeholder engagement conversations

In Chapter 12 of this book, the authors have offered a selection of tried, tested and favourite techniques widely used by coaches and non-coaches alike. The two techniques mentioned below, CIA (Change, Influence, Accept) (Thompson and Thompson, 2008), and Circle of Concern and Influence (Covey, 2020), are relevant as they both focus on change and influence. Chapter 12 offers alternative ways of using the models as well as those offered in this chapter.

Neither of these techniques are complex to use. Testing these techniques on a trusted friend or colleague first will help to build confidence in using them. Both can be adapted by the change practitioner to suit the stakeholder and the situation. The outlines given are a guide only and there are no restrictions to how you apply these with the stakeholder.

Coaching a stakeholder in the C, high influence, low interest: keep satisfied group

This particular stakeholder is resistant to entering into a discussion but agrees to a short 30-minute meeting. The change practitioner recognizes that there is a lot that can be achieved in 30 minutes if the conversation is focussed and does not veer off track, taking responsibility for this. (See point 4 of the REST framework above.)

Suggested technique: CIA – Control, Influence, Accept

This is a widely used, simple and effective model to help stakeholders focus on the situation they are in, what is within their control, their level of influence and what they are willing to accept. Always focus on what is and is not achievable and follow the order of:

- Control (or Change)
- Influence
- Accept.

CIA in practice

The conversation resumes after the change practitioner has set the scene and agreed a good outcome. The importance of the change initiative has been explained to the stakeholder along with the influential role they can play in the process.

Stakeholder: I understand what you are saying and I know the project is of utmost importance. If I had more time I would be more engaged in the process. My current workload will not allow me the headspace to think about this or do anything about it. I have been asked to deliver and manage another project and I have several staff off sick at the moment.

Change practitioner: From what you say, you are going through a busy time at the moment. I can really empathize with your situation. You have mentioned that you would like to be more involved if you can. You know how influential you are in this change initiative. Without you, I am not sure the initiative will get off the ground. I was wondering, can you control or change your current situation?

Stakeholder: Partly. I have no control of the other project or staff being off sick, but I could delegate more, but this will put pressure on those who are still at work and I don't want to do that.

Change practitioner: If you asked them, your team may have the capacity to do more. You might be surprised at their response, particularly if they can get involved in something exciting, such as your other project.

Stakeholder: Good point, I've not asked, but I will.

Change practitioner: What else can you influence to enable you to get more involved in this project?

Stakeholder: If this change initiative is a higher priority than my other project then I can move the timescales to free me up. I can only give so much of my time so I would want that managed and agreed. The team may be able to help too.

Change practitioner: What are you willing to accept about being more involved with the change initiative?

Stakeholder: I am willing to accept that I can't do everything, that some things need more of my time than others and that I have more influence with this change initiative than I first thought. I am willing to accept that I could be very busy over the next couple of months.

The session finished with the stakeholder and change practitioner agreeing on an action plan and managing expectations in terms of the stakeholder's time.

The most important part of this conversation is the connection, rapport and empathy early on in the conversation. If rapport is not built and maintained, then communication can be strained and unsuccessful.

Top tip

Self-coaching questions using CIA:

A useful way for change practitioners to use the CIA model is by coaching themselves before a meeting, particularly with a stakeholder who you are concerned will be resistant in the meeting. Ask yourself these questions:

- What is within my control in this meeting?
- Can I control or change the stakeholder's mindset or behaviours?
- What or whom can I influence to get a good outcome?
- What am I willing to accept if none of this works?

The aim is for the change practitioner to feel more in control of the meeting and gain the outcome they are hoping for.

Coaching a stakeholder in B, low power, high interest, keep informed group

This is the group that is highly motivated but lacks the necessary influence to support the change initiative. The role of the change practitioner in supporting stakeholders in this group is vital. Coaching the stakeholder through any issues they may have will increase the change practitioner influence to make the change initiative a success. They are likely to be on board, hence high interest.

The number of stakeholders in this group could be too many to consider meeting individually. Choose the target group wisely and focus mostly on the people who you know are struggling most with the change.

Assumptions can be made that the stakeholders within the B group could include those who are:

- Junior end-users.
- Not trusted by others to take responsibility for an aspect of the change initiative despite an enthusiasm to do so, possibly due to their level within the organization.
- Not aware of how to influence, where to start and with whom.
- Being blocked by some senior stakeholders.
- Not feeling listened to when they have alternative ideas on the change initiative.
- Not finding time to fully embrace the additional work.

Suggested technique: the Circle of Concern and Influence

This model can be used when the stakeholder is experiencing an overwhelming sense of being out of control. The exercise aims to identify all the things – people, activities and situations relating to the change project that are causing stress or concern for the stakeholder. Through careful questioning, the change practitioner can help reframe and refocus the stakeholder to identify things that are within his or her control.

This simple but effective model explained below shows the difference between when we allow our influence to shrink the concerns and when we allow our concerns to shrink our influence.

Circle of Concern and Influence in practice

Working with the stakeholder, change practitioners will be asking questions and listening out for the energy behind the words used, the body language and generally how the stakeholder looks, feels and sounds when talking about the situation they are in.

Ask the stakeholder to draw a large circle with another circle in the middle of it. Using sticky notes. Ask the stakeholder to:

- Write down each of their stress-causing activities, tasks and situations on separate sticky notes.

- Place these notes in the outer circle.

- Select no more than five (to start with) tasks or situations they know to be things that they have direct and indirect influence over.

- Place these in the inner circle, querying any that are placed in the circle or that are left outside of the inner circle which may need to be moved.

- Prioritize these influences and open a discussion on the blocks and barriers the stakeholder may be using as excuses getting in their way. The aim is to help your stakeholder make a plan of realistic and timely action points.

The change practitioner can continue with the exercise and questions making sure that everything within the inner circle is within the stakeholder's control and influence and is actionable.

The change practitioner can continue to work with the stakeholder asking questions to help them recognize new insights and learning and workable solutions to avoid falling back into the Circle of Concern.

Emergenetics and the behavioural spectrum

Chapter 5 of this book explains how the psychometric tool Emergenetics® can be a useful tool to managing change, with the behavioural spectrum being particularly helpful in this situation.

Returning to the EazyGlaze case study, Jeremy's behavioural preference would suggest he is at the third-third end of the assertiveness behavioural spectrum. He likes to tell others what he thinks, he is not worried about upsetting anyone else and can be viewed as outspoken and, at times, domineering in meetings. The fact that Jeremy has had previous workplace relationship problems would suggest this trait is either a blind spot or he is in denial or is being ignored. If Saskia is on the first-third assertiveness behavioural spectrum, she will find this behaviour uncomfortable and will be likely to avoid getting into an argument as experience has told her that she will not win any battles with Jeremy. Walking away from these difficult situations has been her preferred option but she is now realizing that this is not sustainable. The CEO is expecting Saskia to step into her authority. Saskia knows she needs to dial up her assertiveness preference.

One option is to suggest that Jeremy has a coach (either internal or external) to help him to recognize the consequences of his actions. The coach would help Jeremy to accept the change and to build working relationships with his colleagues. Although this seems a sensible idea, it is unlikely to work. Jeremy seems to be resistant to change and therefore he is unlikely to be receptive to coaching, particularly if he feels this is being 'done to him'. To be coached requires the individual to recognize something that needs to change in themselves (not others) and to be committed to do something differently, for example a behaviour, a mindset or skill. The problem in Jeremy's case is his lack of emotional intelligence or willingness to make the most of his influence at his level within the organization.

Most external coaches will recommend that the manager of the individual with the 'difficulty' is the person to be coached. However, the manager still must recognize the benefits of coaching and be committed to the sessions.

Throughout this book, the authors have encouraged the change practitioner to step into the role of internal coach or to at least use the skills of a coach when meeting with stakeholders. There are times, however, due to the complexity of the situation or the level of employee, when using an external executive coach is the best option.

What this section aims to do is to demonstrate how an external coach might work with Saskia to manage the dynamics between Jeremy and Alan and Jeremy's resistance to change, specifically to the important CRM tool. With Jeremy not engaging with this project, he will create a significant problem for the organization. However, when this has been explained to him, Jeremy has played it down.

CASE STUDY   The coaching session

Saskia agrees that she is the best person to be coached in this situation and looks forward to spending time with a professional who will listen to her concerns without feeling judged or shamed.

The coach listens as Saskia explains her role with managing Jeremy, the history of their working relationship and how she does not feel respected by him.

Saskia thinks Jeremy may have applied for her job at the time but was not successful. Saskia continues to explain how she is feeling overwhelmed with work pressures, the changes in the organization, not all of them she feels for the best, and the fact that she isn't confident enough to stand up to Jeremy when he goes into one of his 'temper tantrums', which seems to her to be a daily occurrence. Saskia continues to talk about how she is fed up with playing mediator between Alan and Jeremy and in some situations she has had to step between them. The more Saskia talks the more she seems to complain about the situation, feeling aggrieved that she does not have enough support, feeling angry about Jeremy and his attitude, and generally blaming Jeremy for how she feels.

The session continues with the coach asking Saskia some pertinent questions to help her see things from a different perspective. The coach asks to share a model with Saskia to help her make sense of what could be affecting the working relationship between herself and Jeremy. The coach shares the Drama Triangle (technique 11, Chapter 12), which is a popular model used by coaches because of its relevance when there is a relationship issue.

The triangle explains three 'toxic' roles at each of the three angles of the triangle, Victim, Persecutor and Rescuer. Saskia resonates most with the role of 'Persecutor'. In this role she sees herself as being unkind about Jeremy, blaming him for things that he is supposed to have done and generally criticizing him, which may be why he does not respect her as a manager. The coach asks her how the role of Rescuer might be relevant in this situation. Saskia continues to talk about how she feels the need to fix the problem and make things better between Jeremy and Alan, even though it is not her responsibility. Saskia recognizes now that her 'stepping in' to help is making things worse. She should let them get on with it. The coach then asks Saskia about the role of Victim. When the behaviours are explained to Saskia, she recognizes that she can at times feel very sorry for herself and feel as if the world is against her (or at least, Jeremy is). She does not like feeling this way and is willing to consider how to step out of the Drama Triangle and into The Empowerment Dynamic (technique 11, Chapter 12). The coach explains the 'antidote' to the Drama Triangle* and together they work through how to recognize when each of the 'toxic' roles is being played out in the triangle and how to adopt more healthy roles in The Empowerment Dynamic.

The session ends with Saskia feeling exhausted but relieved that she has at last found a strategy to work with. The coach gave Saskia feedback on the language patterns she was using and how these impacted on her overall behaviour towards Jeremy and her behaviours as a senior manager.

Saskia's coaching sessions continue for several weeks and she is supported through the management of Jeremy's performance (mostly behavioural) and how to manage the triggers which can send her into 'flight' or 'avoid' mode.

Once familiar with these techniques change practitioners can introduce them into their formal and informal coaching sessions to help stakeholders make sense of relationship dynamics caused by a change project or initiative.

Coaching with ADKAR

Earlier in this chapter ADKAR was explored as a useful tool for change practitioners to check stakeholder engagement throughout a change initiative.

The EazyGlaze case study offers an example of how to use the ADKAR model with Jeremy during a coaching conversation, despite Jeremy's resistance to the conversation.

Awareness

Jeremy is resistant to the new CRM tool. His reactions are likely to be:

- 'It won't work and my team are not interested.'
- 'The current system is working just fine at the moment.'
- 'I wasn't asked for my opinion so why should I agree to it?'

Jeremy may not be aware of the need for a new CRM tool. Discussions took place when he was on leave and when he returned he was informed of its introduction. Any attempt to explain the reasons for the change were met with selective hearing. The change practitioner could utilize their coaching skills by asking Jeremy a few questions to help him think of the reasons and consequences of him rejecting the tool.

- What is the main challenge with the CRM tool for you?
- What is the worst that can happen by adopting the new CRM tool?
- What do your team think about the CRM tool? (Assuming Jeremy has asked them).
- Why do you think your team are resistant to this change?
- In what way might you be influencing their decision?
- What needs to happen for you to be committed to this CRM tool?

Desire

Even though Jeremy is now aware of the need to change, he still needs the desire to participate in supporting the change. Jeremy's responses in his low desire state might be:

- 'I'm not interested in changing.'
- 'What's in it for me?'
- 'I don't have the time or energy for this.'

These reactions again link to resistance to change. Jeremy is not one to accept change readily and so his motivation for change may be due to wanting more control of the situation. Awareness and Desire are closely linked to resistance and so the questions are quite similar but have a different emphasis. The change practitioner could ask the following questions to help Jeremy think of things from a different perspective.

- What would it take for you to be interested in supporting the CRM system?
- What is the worst that would happen if you did support the CRM system?
- What is the best that would happen?
- Is there a fear attached to this? If not fear, then what?
- What is stopping you from moving forward with this?
- What support do you need to be more engaged with this new system?
- What are the consequences of continuing in this way?
- What might your senior colleagues be thinking about this?

Knowledge

A commitment to learning more about the CRM tool will only happen once the barriers of Awareness and Desire have been mitigated. Once Jeremy has a willingness to learn and know more about the system, he can then move towards the other stages of ADKAR with relative ease. Sending Jeremy on training before having the conversations on awareness and desire would be pointless due to his lack of commitment to the CRM system. At this stage, it is best not to tell Jeremy what training he should attend but to ask him what type of training he would like and to check out his learning styles. Would he prefer to read a book, attend a training course or complete online training for example?

Ability

Ability is about putting the knowledge learnt into practice and even after training there could still be a gap between the two. Being able to demonstrate new learning in the workplace is where the real change takes place. If Jeremy has the knowledge but not the ability he might say the following:

- I just don't get it now that I am giving it a go.
- It all seemed logical on the training but in reality it's not so easy.
- This is all taking much longer than I want it to.

To bridge the 'knowledge-to-ability gap', Jeremy would benefit from some 1-2-1 training and/or mentoring from someone who knows the system. This could even be one of his team who has grasped the concepts quicker. The change practitioner could also ask the following questions to find out what would work for Jeremy.

- Is there someone in your team who could provide you with some guidance on this new system?
- To help familiarize yourself with this new system, what other learning interventions would work for you?
- When would you like to be up and running with this new system?
- What support do you need from me?

Reinforcement

The final element of the ADKAR model is reinforcement. The human brain is wired for habit and can easily revert to old habits. Jeremy's response to this new way of working might be:

- This is taking too long.
- We are all finding it frustrating trying to remember what to do.

Jeremy needs to be committed to using the new system and to check that his team are using it too. Jeremy could use his leadership skills to hold coaching conversations with his team to check on their success and any challenges. Working with his team will enable a shared learning experience where those who are more familiar with the system can help others who aren't. The change practitioner could ask Jeremy the following questions.

- What do your team need from you at this stage?
- What questions could you ask your team to ensure that they are using the new system?
- What are the consequences of not reinforcing this learning?
- What support do you need to reinforce the learning and pass it on to your team?

Using ADKAR and scaling questions during 1-2-1 coaching conversations

Scaling questions are used by coaches to give some perspective to a thought, feeling or idea, and to evaluate and measure where on the scale that person is. It also sets parameters when describing things. For example, if the coach were to ask 'How much do you know about this project?' the response could be anything from 'not much' to 'loads'. There is no way of measuring these values. By asking 'On a scale of 1–10, with 1 being nothing and 10 being I'm an expert, how much do you know about this change project?' The response will be more realistic and measurable. Using the number given by the stakeholder (eg 7), the change practitioner can then ask further questions to find out what is stopping the stakeholder from being higher up the scale (eg 8). What are the blocks, barriers and fears? These questions are a useful technique to add to the change practitioner's coaching toolkit.

It is important to calibrate the numbers before you use these questions. So, 10 does not always have to be high. What is important is that the numbers and range are consistent. It is also a good idea to let the stakeholder know that you will be asking these questions and the reason why; this will avoid any resistance or strange responses. Here are some examples:

- Out of 10, where would you place your level of awareness of the need for this change to happen? What would it take to move you up to (for example, 5)? What would you be noticing (seeing, hearing, feeling) when you are at a 5?

- Out of 10, what is your desire to participate and support the change? Imagine if you were at a 10, what would that be like? What would be different about you and those around you?

- Out of 10, how resistant are you to this? What would it take to bring you down the scale to a 3, for example? What is stopping you? (You could be provocative by suggesting, pride, stubbornness, fear.)

- Out of 10, what level of knowledge do you have? What skills do you need to move this up the scale?

- How would you rate your ability to implement the skills and behaviours (out of 10)?

- And what about motivation and energy? What would it take for you to be at the top of the scale? What do you have to gain by not being at the top of the scale?

- What would help you to maintain this level of awareness, desire, knowledge and ability? Where is your level of strength to keep going at the moment (out of 10)? Where would you like to be? (Remember that not everyone wants to be at the very top of the scale.)

Continue using these and other useful questions to help you understand where the stakeholder is and to determine what support they need during the change project.

Facilitated group sessions

To speed up the process, the ADKAR model could be used as a framework with larger group sessions where those attending would be taken through a range of exercises and interventions using ADKAR as a focus. The aim would be to break down barriers to raising awareness and desire, and to look at ways to drive knowledge and ability. Finally, practical steps can be developed to reinforce the change. Scaling questions could be used during these sessions along with other facilitation skills.

Conclusion

The ability to manage and engage stakeholders is crucial in the successful delivery of change. Traditional change tools such as Mendelow's matrix and ADKAR provide the user with a robust framework for internal and external stakeholder management. However, if the change practitioner overlays these tools with activities tailored to the individual's position in the organization, they can develop a more nuanced stakeholder engagement approach to win hearts and minds. These traditional change management tools work well with coaching as techniques and frameworks to help not only the stakeholder make sense of the situation but also aid the change practitioner in their support role.

Chapter 10 explores the subject of making change sustainable and evolving. The use of coaching tools and techniques has an important place in this intervention.

References

Caldwell, R (2003) Change leaders and change managers: Different or complementary?, *Leadership & Organization Development Journal*, 24, pp 285–293

Covey, S (2020) *The 7 Habits of Highly Effective People*, Simon & Schuster, London

Foley, M (2013) Microsoft's new mission statement: No more computer on every desk, https://www.zdnet.com/article/microsofts-new-mission-statement-no-more-computer-on-every-desk/ (archived at https://perma.cc/PWC7-8GRC)

Hiatt, J (2006) *ADKAR: a model for change in business, government and our community*, Learning Centre Publications, Colorado

Hodges, J (2016) *Managing and Leading People Through Organizational Change: The theory and practice of sustaining change through people*, Kogan Page, London

Lawrence, P (2014) *Leading Change: How successful leaders approach change management*, Kogan Page, London

Mendelow, A (1991) *Environmental Scanning: The impact of the stakeholder concept*. Proceedings From the Second International Conference on Information Systems, pp 407–418, Cambridge

Sowden, R (2011) *Managing Successful Programmes*, Stationery Office, London

Thangarathinam, T (2020) How to bridge the gap between vision and execution, www.forbes.com/sites/forbestechcouncil/2020/02/19/how-to-bridge-the-gap-between-vision-and-execution/?sh=755e9d836354 (archived at https://perma.cc/MR6M-ZDK6)

Thompson, N and Thompson, S (2008) *The Critically Reflective Practitioner*, Palgrave Macmillan, Basingstoke and New York

Making change stick

10

Introduction

Let's return to the Hammer and Champy statistic cited in Chapter 1 – 70 per cent of change initiatives fail. So far, we have explored four 'change challenges' that commonly frustrate the delivery of organizational change. It is challenges such as these that often lead practitioners to focus their planning on the period leading up to the project go-live date and overlook the importance of what happens afterwards. This is a common oversight and a serious one – the weeks, months and even years post-implementation are when changes to peoples' ways of working become embedded in an organization for the long term. This therefore becomes our fifth and final challenge – delivering sustained change, or 'making change stick'.

In this chapter we will:

- Identify the reasons why many practitioners overlook the post-implementation period.
- Appreciate the link between sustained change, end-user adoption and benefits.
- Learn about the seven Leadership Sustainability (LS) disciplines.
- Understand how change practitioners can apply these disciplines to any change initiative.

The definition of success

The main reason that the significance of the post go-live period is so frequently ignored is linked to the concept of the 'iron triangle' we explored in Chapter 1 (see Figure 10.1).

Figure 10.1 Iron triangle

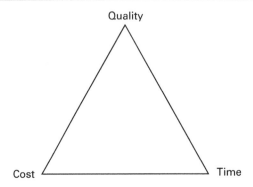

This model has cemented the idea of what makes a project successful, namely if it is delivered:

- on time
- to budget
- according to the agreed quality.

However, this provides the somewhat oversimplified view that a project has been successful if it was delivered on time and this is the root cause of why new ways of working often do not become embedded in an organization.

Let us revisit our colleagues at EazyGlaze, where they launched their new Customer Relationship Management (CRM) system, Sales4U, six months ago. If we apply the parameters of the 'iron triangle', the implementation has been successful:

- The system was rolled out to the Sales team on time.
- The approved budget was not exceeded.
- The functionality conforms to the agreed specification and quality.

In reality, six months post launch, very few members of the Sales team use Sales4U. Fewer than half of the team members have created prospect client records, and there are only a handful of closed sales showing. When the Managing Director queries this with the Head of Sales, he explains that his team is using the same Excel spreadsheets they have relied on for many years. The spreadsheets are saved on their desktops and they do not need to sign into a password-protected application to access them. Since the adoption of Sales4U is so low, the Managing Director, Saskia, is not convinced that the project has been a success because, although it did not go over budget, her investment has been wasted. She is understandably angry and frustrated and she knows she will have a difficult conversation at her next Board meeting.

Figure 10.2   Alternative iron 'square' Amy Tarrant (2021)

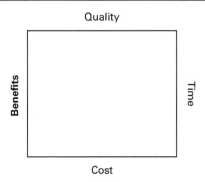

Saskia is not alone as this is a very common scenario. While delivering to time, cost and quality are clearly important metrics for success, there is a key missing component – benefits. We know from Chapter 1 that the driver for investing in a change initiative is to obtain financial and/or non-financial benefits. Therefore, it would arguably make more sense to re-frame success in the context of the 'iron square' (see Figure 10.2).

With this model, a change practitioner can help stakeholders see a more benefits-led view of project success.

The tracking, monitoring and reporting of project benefits is the subject of many project and corporate finance texts, and this book is not aimed at that reader. For our purposes, it is sufficient merely to recognize that delivering the benefits stated in the original business case should be the leading factor when determining whether a project has been successful. Benefits are typically split into two categories:

- Financial, for example a reduction in operating costs or growth to top-line revenue.

- Non-financial, for example enhanced data quality, employee engagement or client retention.

It is important to stress at this stage that it is only possible to measure the extent to which a benefit has been delivered if it was agreed and documented at project initiation stage, together with corresponding acceptance criteria. It is not unrealistic to wait until the project is in flight (or complete) before determining whether benefits have been realized because there will be no baseline for comparison or acceptance.

It is not uncommon for a more forensic approach to a project's expected benefits to reveal that, once offset against the estimated costs, the project is no longer financially viable. In this instance, the project manager should raise it with the project sponsor and Steering Committee, which may lead to a decision to close the project. This should not be viewed as a negative outcome – nobody will thank the project manager or Sponsor for spending months delivering an initiative whose costs outweigh the expected financial benefits. However, some projects only have non-financial benefits, for example increased brand awareness or better data quality, which a sponsor and Steering Committee may feel are attractive enough to stand alone without financial benefits. This is not wrong either – the key is ensuring the benefits are documented and approved in a transparent manner.

Adoption as a benefit driver

Given the above overview of benefits and their importance, we return briefly to EazyGlaze. It has invested in Sales4U but has not realized the benefits because most of the Sales team does not use it.

The key to this dilemma is known in the Change discipline as 'end-user adoption'. The fact that the new CRM has not been adopted by the end-user group it was designed for suggests that EazyGlaze has a problem with adoption.

Throughout our research for this book, almost every change practitioner who responded to our survey cited this as a common frustration, irrespective of the size of the organization or the sector. Many change professionals report a tendency for organizations to rush to close projects and redeploy their teams as quickly as possible post go-live so that they can begin the next project. However, this is highly counter-intuitive and means that firms make the mistake of '… declaring victory too soon' (Hodges and Gill, 2014). By doing this they ignore the importance of supporting the adoption of the new way of working, long after it has been implemented and the project has closed.

Sustainability disciplines

Having acknowledged the correlation between a project's success with benefits and end-user adoption, the next step is to identify a set of tools and techniques to foster and facilitate adoption.

The Seven Leadership Sustainability (LS) disciplines published by Dave Ulrich and Norm Smallwood in 2013 provide a useful framework. They are:

1 Simplicity

2 Time

3 Accountability

4 Resources

5 Tracking

6 Melioration

7 Emotions.

Ulrich and Smallwood originally devised these disciplines as a framework for leaders to make and sustain changes to leadership behaviour. They collated and distilled their research into a set of activities that they believe make the difference between good intentions and effective action. However, the framework applies equally to the sustainment of any activity, whether it is good leadership or the long-term success of a change initiative.

The following section provides Ulrich and Smallwood's original definition, together with the suggested application for the change practitioner.

Simplicity

Ulrich and Smallwood believe it makes most sense for leaders to prioritize activity that would have the greatest impact on key issues. Rather than become overwhelmed and dazzled by long and complex to-do lists, leaders can make a greater impact on their teams if they simplify activity in small and actionable tasks and then prioritize. This may sound like a common-sense approach to life, let alone leadership, but it is surprising how many leaders become so caught up in the size and difficulty of their role that they neglect to deliver even smaller tasks that are impactful for their teams.

A change practitioner can add significant value by adapting this discipline to a project or programme. Often project goals and objectives fail to target the end-user's greatest 'pain points'. However, if stakeholders could agree to segment and prioritize project deliverables in a way that directly addressed genuine business needs, the impact would be greater. Furthermore, if the business sees that its pain points are being reduced or removed, end-user adoption becomes more likely.

Time

This is linked to simplicity. Having simplified and prioritized tasks, it makes most sense for leaders to spend the most time and energy on high priority items for maximum impact.

Similarly, a project's time and budget should be allocated in such a way that mirrors its size and importance to the business. It is highly likely that these will match the business 'pain points' identified above, thus increasing the chances of the benefit being delivered and adopted. It also reduces the likelihood of diverting too much time and attention towards low priority project activity that adds less value to the end-user but uses up resources and goodwill.

Accountability

Ulrich and Smallwood correctly identified the importance of accountability to leadership success. This means accepting responsibility for actions and holding oneself and others accountable for delivering on promises. If leaders consistently state bold visions and objectives that they fail to deliver, this erodes trust and credibility over time, which in turn saps confidence and motivation.

Accountability is arguably the most important of the seven Disciplines in the change context. Research conducted by the authors of this book revealed some worrying trends relating to accountability and project sponsorship:

- The chosen sponsor being from a different business area than the one the project impacts most.
- A sponsor inherits a project they did not initiate, possibly due to someone leaving.
- A total lack of named sponsor at all.

These scenarios pose an enormous risk to a project because if nobody is willing or able to be accountable for a project or programme, then nobody has any 'skin in the game' if it fails.

As we have seen in earlier chapters, for optimum success a project sponsor should be a senior leader within the function most impacted by the new ways of working. This ensures the sponsor has sufficient authority as well as a vested interest in the change being implemented and embedded successfully. A good sponsor will also articulate and continuously 'sell' the vision, own the related business case and take accountability for the benefits realization. Finally, he or she must be able to give the role the appropriate time and focus.

There are various ways in which both the project team and the wider organization can support the role of the sponsor and foster accountability. At a project level, the initiation documentation should state roles and responsibilities very clearly, preferably in a RACI (Responsible, Accountable, Consulted, Informed) way, which is typically located within the Project Initiation Document (PID) or Project Definition Document (PDD). By approving this document, sponsors accept the level of accountability contained within and, crucially, this acceptance is documented and therefore visible to other stakeholders. Change practitioners can also help to reinforce the importance of the role by re-stating it often, both verbally and in written form in regular artefacts such as Steering Committee packs and project update communications.

Beyond the project itself, it is useful if the sponsor's line manager and Human Resources collectively agree to embed the role and its constituent responsibilities in his or her annual objectives. This acts as an additional incentive if it is tied to a year-end bonus scheme. Finally, it is important to embed an understanding that accountability for a project's success does not suddenly come to an end when the project goes live. Forward-thinking organizations understand the longevity of the role in the weeks and months post-implementation and incorporate it into their company procedures. Common ways to do this are, where practical:

- Tying employee bonus and incentive programmes to adoption of the change (this works particularly well for Sales teams).
- Creating a Business Partner role, which includes supporting ongoing adoption.

Resources

According to Ulrich and Smallwood, is that leaders can enlist 'intangible resources' to be successful. In this context, this includes activities such as self-coaching, expert-coaching, peer-coaching and even 'boss-coaching'. A self-aware leader is alive to the benefits of these 'intangible resources' just as much as he or she is aware of having appropriate tangible resources in their team.

Tracking

Lawrence Appley, former president of the American Management Association famously claimed: 'you get what you inspect, not what you expect'. Unless desired leadership behaviours and changes are translated into quantifiable and trackable actions, they are at risk of not being acted upon.

Tracking and monitoring the progress of deliverables are central activities in governance-led project delivery. Reports, scorecards and dashboards are all useful ways to provide transparency and metrics with which to monitor their progress. From a practical perspective, the clarity helps to illustrate the project's health and the risks, issues and dependencies that may jeopardize success. From an emotional perspective, providing stakeholders with transparency is also the best way to acquire and maintain their trust, which is an important ingredient for successful change.

Melioration

This refers to a cycle of continuous improvement that leaders should pursue if they wish to develop and learn from their mistakes. This involves a constant journey of success, failure, reflection and learning from mistakes.

Many readers will be familiar with process improvement projects and business process re-engineering (BPR) which have Continuous Improvement (CI) at the heart. However, melioration can be applied more generally in the context of change, irrespective of the type of project being delivered. A robust governance structure includes an activity known as the post implementation review (PIR), which is an opportunity for the project team and the stakeholders to reflect openly at each stage gate of a project, from initiation to implementation. This includes an evaluation of project documentation, planning, structure, communication, training, quality and testing. It allows stakeholders to provide feedback on the way the project has been managed and is a valuable way for change practitioners to gather the views of stakeholders to feed into future project activity. This is an exercise of reflection and feedback that works well as a blended approach of workshops, anonymous surveys and one-to-one discussions.

The mistake many change teams make is to wait until the end of a project before going through this exercise. While doing this can of course provide valuable insights into the way future projects are run, scheduling a session after each project phase or stage is even more beneficial. This generates a continuous feedback loop into subsequent project phases, but crucially it promotes a culture of melioration with constant learning from success and failure. The regular flow of stakeholder feedback allows project teams to make subtle adjustments to their approach, which in turn increases the chances of the solution being successfully adopted by its intended end-users.

Emotion

Ulrich and Smallwood stated that 'action without passion will not long endure'. A leader needs a strong emotional agenda and not simply an intellectual one, made possible by drawing on their core values and doing work that has meaning for them. This increases the likelihood that the changes they make will have a ripple effect out to the wider team.

In a similar vein, the momentum for change is generated more from the emotional side than the rational or intellectual. Therefore, if change practitioners invest time building the emotional case for change this will have a positive effect throughout the organization. The most obvious way for a project team to do this is to structure project interaction in such a way that stakeholders feel they own the change. End-users are high importance stakeholders and must be fully invested in the emotional case for change. For example, inviting a cross-section of the end-users to act as subject matter experts or change agents provides a useful opportunity for the project team to interact with them, gauge possible resistance and articulate the emotional case for change. This interaction helps teams to feel that change is happening 'with' them and not 'to' them, which is pivotal to higher levels of adoption.

As we have seen, a key component in delivering sustainable change and making it 'stick' lies in the adoption of change. In the next section, we will explore the ways in which coaching tools can be used to drive adoption. We will also re-visit the EazyGlaze team to understand how a change practitioner could support Saskia with some coaching techniques.

Coaching solutions to making change stick

Introduction

It is no coincidence that as part of the 'intangible resources', Ulrich and Smallwood recommend four coaching interventions that can be applied together to drive adoption of new ways of working. As mentioned previously, these interventions are:

- self-coaching
- expert-coaching
- peer-coaching and
- boss-coaching.

The following section aims to demystify each of these coaching types, when to use and not use them and provides example questions to use.

Self-coaching

This is a technique adopted by anyone who has a good understanding of what coaching is, how to ask the right questions to get to the heart of the issue, gain insight and, importantly, move to a workable solution.

How it works: An individual asks themselves coaching style questions instead of being asked by another coach or person.

Useful when: A problem needs solving quickly or there is a need to reframe a thought or feeling. When a coach is not immediately available or when costs prevent the use of a coach.

Not so useful when: Self-coaching might sound easy but it requires the individual to dig deep and ask questions that they might not feel comfortable in asking and, even more so, answering. Verbalizing thoughts and feelings can be both cathartic and embarrassing. What is important is that the responses need to be spoken, not just thought.

Self-coaching questions

- 'What is the/my issue or problem?'
- 'What do I want to have happen?' or 'What is a good outcome for me?'
- 'Why am I finding this difficult to solve?'
- 'What belief and or value is this problem bumping up against?'
- 'If I can't solve this, who might be able to?'
- 'What are the first steps to achieving this?'
- 'What/whom might get in my way?'
- 'What have I learnt from all this?

> **Top tip**
>
> The concept of talking to yourself might seem uncomfortable for some and so it is important to do this in a quiet and private space. Walking, thinking and talking is a great way to try out self-coaching, particularly when there is plenty of space not to be heard by other walkers. Another option is to give a friend or partner the set of questions you want to ask yourself and to ask them to ask you the questions instead. Your friend or partner could be a sounding board as long as they don't feel the need to solve the problem for you. If this happens, let them know that you would like to solve the problem for yourself through the use of incisive questions.

Expert-coaching

This is a coach who has built up many hours of coaching experience with a variety of different clients in different scenarios, at different management levels and with complex problems. An expert coach can sometimes mean someone with technical knowledge and is used to gain advice or expertise from that person. This is not technically coaching and falls under the remit of mentoring but may be useful all the same.

How it works: An expert coach is equipped to deal with most challenges and is not fazed even by the most complex issue brought to the session. They are fully qualified, receive regular coach supervision and adhere to a code of ethical practice as defined by one of the three leading global coaching bodies. The expert coach has experience of applying a wide range of coaching tools.

Useful when: In most situations, an expert and experienced coach is preferable to one who is not.

Not so useful when: The client sees the expert coach as an advisor or mentor and is expecting the answers to be given to them.

Expert-coaching questions

- 'What are you giving up?'
- 'What is your fear in relation to this problem?'
- 'What are you responsible for?'

- 'What do other people notice in you that you are not noticing in yourself?'
- 'What are the consequences of doing nothing?'
- 'What question do you need to ask yourself that you'd rather not have to answer?'

Peer-coaching

This is a process where two or more colleagues work collaboratively to problem solve. Ideally, they would both have a knowledge of coaching and of using a coaching style and approach.

Useful when: There is a need for advice and guidance and possibly mentoring where colleagues share their experiences, expertise and understanding. Action Learning is a process where peers or colleagues meet up periodically to work through issues, share ideas and challenge perceptions in a trusting relationship. Action Learning is a popular form of peer-coaching and mentoring and has proven to be successful in building team cohesion and strong working relationships.

Not so useful when: There is a power dynamic between peers where one person is more dominant, not willing to share information but is more interested in instructing and telling.

Peer-coaching questions

- 'How shall we work on this together?'
- 'What is a good outcome for us?'
- 'What support do we need from each other and from others?'
- 'What would success look and feel like?'
- 'Who do we need to influence?'
- 'Who are our stakeholders in this situation?'
- 'What is the first step to achieving our goal?'

Boss-coaching

This is another name for 'coaching up' or coaching the manager. It is tempting to just accept what the manager asks for without clarifying expectations or challenging assumptions. Therefore, being able to confidently question the manager will help to avoid ambiguity and assumptions being made.

Useful when: An employee has a manager with a person-centred approach and feels able to give feedback to them. The employee wants to respectfully challenge the manager's assumptions by asking them to think differently. The employee is curious and engaged in their job and wants to work collaboratively with their manager. The employee has a good rapport with their manager and has been delegated a piece of work.

Not so useful when: The manager is autocratic and is not open to conversations or discussions of any sort. When the manager is not receptive to being given feedback on that day.

Boss-coaching questions

- 'Could you expand on that please?'
- 'What are your expectations of me?'
- 'What do you need from me to reassure you that I can get this right?'
- 'When would you like to review what I am doing?'
- 'What would you like me to do if I get stuck?'
- 'How do you feel about me offering some alternative ideas and suggestions?'

Top tip

Managing up can feel uncomfortable for some if the manager in question is not responsive to being asked questions. It is easy to assume the worst when in fact, when asking questions in a way that uses the right tone of voice and with the right intentions can work really well. Remember to respect the status and position of the manager and ask questions respectfully. Using language such as 'I was just wondering' or 'I am curious to know' or 'I have a concern about that' shows interest, curiosity and respect.

Making change stick by embedding a coaching culture

One of the most effective and sustainable ways of building lasting change and making change stick is to have both coaching and change realized within the organization's DNA. However, the organization must be truly invested in embedding a coaching culture and not just pay lip service to it.

In practice, a coaching culture means that everyone from the highest level of authority through to first-line managers and non-managers must be fully engaged with using a coaching approach and know how to use these skills with their teams, effortlessly. For non-managers that means knowledge and capability in how to apply a coaching style and approach within everyday conversations, with performance reviews and to support their teams with delegation and problem-solving. Leadership programmes would have the golden thread of coaching woven throughout, particularly when building a capability to lead, develop, engage and motivate the team. Team meetings would be vision and goal-focussed with the Chair encouraging team members to offer ideas and opinions. Facilitation and team coaching skills would be included as part of the learning and development strategy, thus offering leaders and managers the confidence to use these skills regularly.

The next Chapter provides guidance on the importance of developing an internal coaching capability for long-term and sustainable change. The chapter offers essential factors to ensure success, including how to embed coaching within the organization by developing internal coaches, coaching skills for managers and the role of change practitioners in developing themselves as qualified coaches.

Conclusion

The traditional 'iron triangle' project success criteria could lead to a project being delivered on time, on budget and to the required quality, and thereby be judged successful. The triangle ignores the fact that many projects deliver an end product that is not adopted by the target end-user group and this scenario therefore cannot be considered a genuine success.

Arguably, there should be an additional ingredient to the 'iron triangle', incorporating 'Benefits', making it an 'iron square'. This is because if expected project benefits are not delivered (realized), a project cannot be labelled a success. The key driver for the realization of project benefits is the adoption of the project's key deliverables by the target user group they were designed for.

The seven Learning Sustainability (LS) disciplines provide a comprehensive framework for change practitioners to support the delivery of project benefits and end-user adoption, the most important being Accountability, Tracking and Resources. With this toolkit, change practitioners can deliver lasting and sustained change.

References

Appley, L (1969) *Values in Management*, Amacom, Noord-Brabant

Harshak, A, Aguirre, D and Brown, A (2010) Making change happen, and making it stick, Booz & Company, www.strategy-business.com/article/00057 (archived at https://perma.cc/49WC-4A6L)

Thorne, K (2004) *Coaching for Change*, Kogan Page, London

Ulrich, D and Smallwood, N (2013) *Leadership Sustainability: Seven disciplines to achieve the changes great leaders know they must make*, McGraw Hill Professional, London

Building an internal coaching capability

Throughout this book the authors have discussed, evaluated and analysed the challenges organizations face when implementing and embedding change and how, by adopting coaching tools and techniques, change practitioners can significantly increase the chances of the change initiative being a long-term success. We have also reviewed different challenges traditionally associated with organizational change and proposed coaching interventions to complement the existing change toolkit.

Katherine St John-Brooks, in her book *Internal Coaching: The inside story* (2018), hypothesizes that internal coaching is likely to be professionalized over the next 10 years as organizations invest in and increase training, accreditation and CPD.

More and more organizations are embracing the benefits of internal coaching by taking the next step and introducing a permanent approach – developing a pool of internal coaches to build internal coaching capability. In fact this approach is becoming increasingly widespread – according to the CIPD (2022), 90 per cent of organizations use coaching and 63 per cent delivered it internally through line managers supported by trained internal coaches. The International Coaching Federation (ICF) identified in their research paper, 'Building a coaching culture' (2014), that the adoption of coaching skills by managers has now become the norm in most organizations.

When an organization invests in developing and embedding an internal coaching capability the outcome is a specialist in-house skillset and mindset that has myriad benefits for the organization and its employees.

In this chapter we will explore:

- Whether culture plays a role in developing an internal coaching capability.
- What an internal coach is.
- The benefits of developing a pool of internal coaches to support change.
- The practicalities of achieving this aim, for example training and accreditation.
- The common pitfalls and how to avoid them.

A coaching culture: is it necessary?

Much has been written about the significance of a coaching culture. This chapter does not aim to repeat the theory and thoughts from others, but the subject of coaching culture is worth a mention at this stage and how it might influence the ability to develop internal coaching.

Developing an internal coaching capability will be more successful if the organization creates an environment that values learning and growth of its people and has a belief that coaching is a positive development tool rather than used as a tool to 'fix' someone. Success will depend on whether the organization is willing to invest in the right type of training, time and ongoing support, and to allow people to be coached and to coach others in addition to their day job.

What comes first, the coaching culture or developing internal coaching?

This is a difficult question to answer. On one hand, it could be argued that, in the absence of a coaching culture, the development of internal coaching could drive the organization's culture towards one with a coaching ethos. Likewise, if the organization has an ethos of using coaching within all aspects of leadership, change and development, this would help an internal coaching initiative to be accepted and adopted.

It is worth considering what others say on the subject of coaching culture. Peter Hawkins in his book *Creating a Coaching Culture* (2012) states that

A coaching culture exists in an organization when a coaching approach is a key aspect of how the leaders, managers and staff engage and develop all their people and engage their stakeholders, in ways that create increased individual, team and organizational performance and shared value for all.

Developing a coaching culture does not necessarily benefit every organization, despite the research suggesting that organizations that embed a coaching culture have seen a strong and positive impact on business performance. The ICF study found that 65 per cent of employees from companies with strong coaching cultures rated themselves as highly engaged and have boosted financial performance.

Clutterbuck, Megginson and Bajer (2016) continue this discussion by confirming that developing a coaching culture is not an easy task. It demands a significant amount of commitment, effort and resources. They have identified two main factors to help organizations make this decision:

- **Relevance** – the extent to which a coaching culture is expected to support an organization in achieving its primary objectives.

- **Supportive climate** – the organizational context and whether it can support the development of a coaching culture.

Peter Hawkins (2012) stated the importance of developing a clear coaching strategy that aligns with other organizational plans, visions and values.

Creating a strong coaching purpose linked to organizational need can be easily established. Here are just some examples of where internal coaches can have a clear purpose and remit when coaching is aligned to:

- A restructure following, for example, an acquisition or merger to support individuals at all levels in handling these changes and in overcoming resistance to the change.

- A graduate scheme or internship where coaches can support new starters in their career progression. Although this initiative is typically aligned with mentoring, working concurrently with a coach and mentor can provide career guidance, commitment and engagement to the graduate's work. It will also highlight the difference to the graduate between being mentored and being coached.

- 'Bring a problem – find a solution' initiatives where the coach provides ad-hoc, usually one-off coaching sessions for anyone within the organization, at all levels, with a specific workplace problem they want to air and off-load. The coach is the sounding board and listening ear and is not obliged (or recommended) to providing advice or suggestions.

Hawkins' recommendations suggest that the coaching strategy and purpose is just the beginning of the process. Once this has been established and there is a clear understanding of how to align coaching with organizational need, the next step is to establish how coaching skills can be developed within the organization.

What is internal coaching?

To understand what internal coaching is, is to first understand what external coaching is. The skills, experience and competence required to commission an external coach within the organization should have equal importance and relevance when developing and choosing internal coaches. Internal coaching should not just be about saving money. It offers an excellent opportunity to cascade coaching within all levels of the organization and to build and develop interpersonal skills to support others through change.

Internal coaching is the practice of developing and supporting a committed group of coach ambassadors with the skills, knowledge, competence, confidence and credibility to formally coach others within the organization. This coaching role is usually carried out on a part-time basis in addition to the internal coach's employed role. The exception to this is where the organization specifically employs people as full-time internal coaches.

Who is the internal coach?

An internal coach is likely to be employed within the organization in a specific role and with an enthusiasm to support and help others by way of coaching, mentoring or other interventions which require highly trained interpersonal skills. The understanding is that any coaching undertaken is agreed with the internal coaches and line manager and completed alongside their normal paid work. As coaching is seen as a benefit to the organization and to the internal coach. What follows are some key aspects of the role.

The internal coach:

- Will be part of a team of other internal coaches who support each other through and following their training. They form regular co-coaching groups and action learning sets to learn from each other, deepen their coaching skills development and become a strong and cohesive team in their own right.

- Will have completed a formal, rigorous and structured coach development programme, usually delivered within the organization and leading to a qualification at the end. This formal training will build confidence and credibility in coaching others who they may potentially know within the various teams and departments. The potential for ethical dilemmas is ever present, even more so than for external coaches.

- Has the right mindset and skills and understands the need to complete many hours of coach practice, self-development and CPD to maintain the standards required to coach others.

- Is no different in many ways to an external coach other than they are employed within and know more about the organization. This is yet another potential ethical dilemma, the subject of which was discussed in Chapter 4 of this book and is discussed again later in this chapter.

One of the objectives of introducing an internal coach is to emulate the characteristics of an external coach. If organizations do not embed the skill-set and behaviours an external coach would bring, they risk eroding the benefits and not seeing a return on their investment. An example of this is that in the same way an external coach sets up formal and contracted coaching sessions with their clients, an internal coach will do the same with people within the organization, carefully contracting the session to ensure the internal coach is the best person to coach the employee.

To ensure that these characteristics are present, it is crucial that the internal coaching candidates are fully committed to:

- Discovering what coaching is.
- Understanding how it supports the organization.
- Taking an interest in people.
- Developing their own skills in coaching and supporting others.

Managing expectations

As mentioned earlier, unless an employee is specifically employed by the business to carry out a full-time coaching role, internal coaches will balance this coaching role with their existing job. It is difficult to estimate how many hours the internal coach will spend on coaching others and it will largely depend on business needs such as coaching newly appointed graduates, high performers or internal training cohorts.

A survey carried out by Coaching Focus in 2013, specifically for Katharine St John-Brooks found that:

- 41 per cent of internal coaches spent less than 5 hours a month on coaching.
- 35 per cent spent 5–10 hours a month on coaching.
- 32 per cent of internal coaches had one coaching client.

- 23 per cent had 2 coaching clients.
- The average number of the coaching sessions was four × 1-hour sessions for each client.

This research would suggest that there is a broad spectrum of approaches and therefore, whatever the expectation of the coach's time, it should be agreed with the line manager and documented to ensure expectations are managed on all sides and enable line managers to plan team capacity and staffing levels.

The benefits of developing a pool of internal coaches to support change

Benefits for the organization

Although the initial investment in training and the long-term support for internal coaches is often seen as prohibitive, over time the benefits far outweigh the cost:

- It is more cost effective to use internal coaches than hiring external coaches.
- Internal coaches can work with people at all levels.
- Internal coaches have in-depth knowledge of the organization, its culture and people.
- Coaching sessions can be organized and set up quickly and efficiently.
- Internal coaches are excellent change agents as the skillset helps drive positive communication and mindsets.
- The opportunity of cascading coaching throughout the business is increased.
- Improve staff engagement, motivation and performance.

Although there is an advantage to having an understanding of the organization, there are disadvantages too. Knowing too much can be a barrier to impartial coaching. The internal coach may:

- Have a burning need to share what they know that they think is helpful, or indeed, inappropriate, depending on the person they are coaching.

- Feel the need to collude and agree with the change process and the person they are coaching. This is likely to take the internal coach away from what they are there to do.

With practice and the right coaching supervision support, the internal coach can learn how to suspend their knowledge and understanding of the person they are coaching or the organization, to ensure that the coaching remains impartial and stays on track.

Benefits for the internal coach

Apart from the satisfaction of achieving an advanced qualification that supports other management development programmes, internal coaches will learn and develop the multi-faceted skills of coaching and will have a high level of competence and confidence to work with employees at all career levels. It is important to point out at this stage that the skillset internal coaches acquire is not solely designed to be used during times of organizational change. It is a 'business as usual' skill. This may extend to their day job, where the skills can easily be transferred to give the coach the confidence to communicate and influence at all levels.

Coaching skills are relevant when the internal coach is working with stakeholders to:

- Unlock a barrier or limiting belief to accepting organizational change.
- Reframe ideas presented.
- Hold the mirror up and offer useful feedback.
- Reveal blind spots (unaware) and or hidden spots (aware but in denial).
- Overcome resistance to change and supporting people through the process.
- Hold stakeholders to account particularly when actions have not been met.
- Offer insight into change management methodology.
- Offer insight into communication tools and techniques which are not familiar to the senior manager.

Other benefits for the internal coach include:

- Being part of a community of coaches with support from their fellow coach colleagues.
- Feeling valued by the organization.
- Expanding internal and possibly external networks.
- Increasing organizational awareness.
- Understanding internal politics.
- Knowing that they are working for a company committed to a person-centred coaching culture that allows everyone at all levels to feel listened to.

Benefits for employees

The following list is by no means exhaustive and will largely depend on the individual being coached and what they want from coaching. The benefits for employees when they are offered internal coaching will include the opportunity to:

- Speak with someone who is not their line manager.
- Be listened to and have a professional conversation.
- Have a sounding board to work through an idea or challenges.
- Have a specific goal or target to work towards.
- Share an idea or concern in confidence.
- Build confidence with a specific skill or behaviour.
- Off-load with the understanding of working towards an outcome or solution.

One of the key benefits of having an internal coach to call upon is the speed and efficiency with which sessions can be set up. The internal coach will be skilled at guiding the individual through a structured process to a successful solution or outcome. They will encourage the manager to speak openly in the knowledge that the conversation will remain confidential. The trust and rapport between the manager and internal coach is integral to this.

The practicalities of introducing internal coaching

If organizations can embrace the opportunities and benefits of developing internal coaching, the next challenge is how to introduce and embed this initiative.

In this section we provide practical guidance on the engagement, training and support required to make internal coaching a success.

Selecting the right people

Sadly, many businesses do not invest enough time selecting the right people to take on the role of an internal coach. This can sometimes result in a cohort of learners who have been nominated or volunteered by their managers or who are interested solely in gaining a qualification, without the motivation or commitment to complete the programme, or to coach people afterwards. Selecting the right people with the right mindset is essential to the success of developing an internal pool of coaches.

Application process

The starting point is an application process to determine who has the right skillset and/or interest level, using a set of incisive questions to ensure that the applicant is fully aware and committed to the role of internal coach. The effort of completing an application is part of the commitment, although other forms of recruitment in the way of discussions or interviews, could be considered to avoid discriminating against those with a learning difficulty, such as dyslexia.

It is recommended that the questionnaire asks for a statement from the applicant's line manager to check that they understand the commitment of their team member being an internal coach. It is wise to get this agreement signed to avoid problems later; however, it does not guarantee that the manager will not change their mind when the team is under pressure.

Useful questions to consider within the application are:

- What or who has inspired you to become an internal coach?
- What do you hope to gain from this training?
- What are your qualities that make you a good coach?

- How will you manage your time and motivation to coach others when you are busy?
- What coach training have you previously had?
- Where else might you want to use these coaching skills?
- What concerns or questions do you have about the training?
- Describe your commitment to fulfilling the rigours of a coaching qualification.
- What are your reasons for wanting a coaching qualification?
- What do you know about coaching supervision?
- Describe your motivation and interest in having ongoing CPD and coaching supervision.

The selection process would ideally be followed by a shortlisting selection process to bring the cohort down to a reasonable number. A reasonable number will depend on the size of the company, how the qualified coaches will be used post training and if the initiative is part of a coaching strategy and aligns with organization plans, goals and objectives.

Training is an essential part of engaging the right candidates by providing a rigorous, structured and advanced training programme that will stretch their learning and thinking, and will increase their credibility as an internal coach. The programme should also offer ongoing support before, during and after the training.

The following section highlights the options for training and development for an organization aiming to set up a pool of internal coaches.

Training the internal coach

St John-Brooks in her research and according to the Ridler report (Ridler & Co, 2013) found that:

- 54 per cent of participating organizations expected their external coaches to be accredited.
- 37 per cent expected their internal coaches to be accredited.

Either way, the authors' experience suggests that the driver for accreditation often comes from those wanting to be an internal coach. Another driver can come from the programme coordinator when they themselves have had some form of accredited coach training in the past. If the programme coordinator is fully committed to training, they will no doubt see the benefits of gaining a coaching qualification.

A qualification programme can be costly, time consuming and requires a full commitment from the business and the learners. The result is that the internal coaches will be perceived by others with a level of credibility, knowledge and skills, and they will have experienced the rigour of a training process which includes both coaching theory and coaching practice.

To embed a quality internal coaching programme, the organization must invest time, money and commitment. Scrimping on any or all of these three factors is doomed to failure. Let's take a look at each in turn.

Time:

- Has been spent thinking through what is required and finding the right training provider.
- Is given for a programme with adequate training days to cover the theory and the practice.
- Is allocated for enough CPD and supervision days to support the internal coaches during and after training.

Money:

- Enough budget is allocated to find the right provider with the right level of experience and expertise to provide an in-depth training programme to develop internal coaches to the required standard.

Commitment:

- To the overall programme without losing interest or support for internal coach development along the way.
- To ensuring that internal coaches are given permission to provide this additional service alongside their contracted job.
- To ensuring that internal coaches are helped to identify enough people to coach.

Accreditation

Accredited training is by far the most effective route for developing internal coaches. The result is a deeper level of structured learning, observed coaching practice and ongoing coaching supervision to support the learner in how to use these skills most effectively and when any challenges emerge in the coaching relationship.

The training will prepare internal coaches to deal with most situations and will increase confidence and competence. Credibility will be gained over time as the internal coaches gain reputation within their role.

Generally speaking, a Level 5 internationally recognized qualification in coaching provides the right depth and breadth of training and provides the relevant balance of theory and practice. A Level 5 coaching qualification offers a starting point for those who want to improve and increase their internal coaching practice. Level 5 can also be a springboard into achieving a Level 7 coaching qualification should an individual move into a strategic coaching role where they are responsible for embedding coaching within the organization.

Ongoing support

Furthermore, it is important to increase the credibility of the internal coach with a qualification supported with coaching supervision. This CPD will help internal coaches to grow, enhance and transform their coaching practice to the standards and confidence required to coach others within the organization. Coaching supervision has been mentioned earlier in this chapter.

Training syllabus

A training syllabus is an outline and summary of topics covered during a training course. The topics included within the training must meet the needs of the overall programme and also link with the qualification undertaken for that training. When delivering a qualification programme there can sometimes be a challenge in delivering enough content to learn how to coach and ensuring that learners have enough knowledge and understanding for them to complete the assessment criteria. To balance this need, the programme usually requires learners to invest time in self-managed learning, including research and reading outside of the training room. This approach allows the trainer to provide time in helping learners to understand the nuances of coaching and allow enough time for learners to be observed in their coach practice. Appendix E offers more information on the types of coaching accreditation and qualifications available.

The characteristics of an internal coach development programme will typically comprise five or six days of intensive, classroom-led training and can include the following:

- Understanding what coaching is and is not.
- Similarities and differences to mentoring and other 'helping' roles.
- The role of internal coach and comparisons with external coaching.
- Core coaching competencies including active listening, incisive questioning, building rapport, use of silence, reflection and reflective practice, noticing intuition and being goal not problem focussed.
- How values and belief systems can shape the coaching session.
- Who you are is how you coach – the role personalities play in coaching.
- Contracting and setting the scene for successful workplace coaching.
- Coaching structure and goal setting.
- Coaching ethics, boundaries and avoiding ethical dilemmas.
- The coaches role in giving feedback during coaching – how, why, when.
- Managing difficult subjects/situations which emerge during coaching.
- Introducing tools and techniques to enhance your coaching.
- At least 50 per cent of observed practice by the tutor and colleagues to raise confidence in coaching others and practising the core skills.

In addition to these five days of classroom based coaching, as part of their self-managed learning, learners will be required to complete the following:

- 20 hours of evidenced formal coaching with three other people (not friends or family).
- Reflective learning logs to reflect on each of the formal coaching sessions.
- Peer coaching triads to practise coaching on each other and sharing feedback based on the core competencies.
- Coaching supervision within a group and/or one-to-one supervision with a qualified supervisor (often provided by the qualified tutor).
- Tutorials to support ongoing coaching practice and assignment completion.
- Written assignments (between one and three).

Although the subject of organizational change is not typically included within a coach development programme, it is covered in terms of how to coach people through change, specifically when there is resistance. The theory around the change process is not usually seen as necessary, but it can be included as an added value subject outside of the coach development training.

In addition to the training syllabus outlined above, organizations can offer an even greater learning experience for their trainee internal coaches by offering them coaching with an external, experienced executive coach. This additional learning has been proven to greatly enhance the speed at which coaches learn how to coach others based on their own experience.

Avoiding common pitfalls of developing an internal coaching capability

Developing a coaching capability is not without its problems. There are many organizations that ride a wave of enthusiasm for embedding internal coaching. This usually includes a handful of people who recognize the value of coaching but without a clear idea of how these interventions can be woven into the company's DNA. There is often no real sense of purpose, structure or direction that is aligned to organizational strategy, goals and vision. What emerges is a team of enthusiastic newly qualified internal coaches eager to use their new found skills, searching for people to coach despite various marketing strategies to encourage others to be coached. The outcome is that coaching is quickly seen as a fad and can lose credibility. Furthermore, coaching for some is still seen as a remedial ploy to 'fix' them in some way. Without the underpinning understanding of what coaching actually is and the true benefits of coaching for everyone, then developing an internal coaching capability will be a challenge.

In this section we explore how to avoid some of the pitfalls when developing an internal coaching capability and includes:

- Knowing who to coach and who not to coach.
- Coordinating and supporting learners during and after the programme.
- Preparing learners for the training.

- Finding enough people to be coached during training.
- Promoting internal coaching and the promotion of internal coaches.
- Seniority of learners in each cohort.
- Commitment from the top and change of leadership.
- Ethical dilemmas.
- Continual professional development and coaching supervision.
- Evaluating the programme.

Knowing who to coach and who not to coach

It is not recommended for the internal coach to formally coach those who they manage. If the internal coach has gone through a significant coach training programme and is also a manager, there may be temptation for this manager to formally coach their own team members. How terrible would this be? If no harm is done, then does it matter? The answers to these questions really depend on potential conflicting demands, the dynamics between the manager (internal coach) and the team member, and what issues the team member would like to bring to the session. These issues could be related to the manager themselves. Prudence suggests that it is best to offer formal coaching for the team member to another one of the internal coaches.

However, what is recognized is that managers and leaders can adopt informal coaching in the way of a coaching style and approach during performance reviews and general 1-2-1 meetings. Although this is not formal coaching, it is a useful way for managers to introduce a coaching concept and encourage the direct report to think independently, to make decisions and generally to engage with an open and honest conversation with the support from the manager. During these conversations the manager may identify a larger coaching need which may be more appropriate for one of the organization's internal coaches.

Coordinating and supporting learnings during and after the programme

The coaching programme coordinator plays a pivotal role in the success of the internal coaching pool by being the coach ambassador and promotor of coaching within. The coordinator has a vested interest in the success of the programme and ideally spends at least 50 per cent of their time coordinating the programme.

The coordinator is there to provide support for learners outside of the training days and will help them find people to coach to enable them to complete the required number of coaching hours during training.

A frustration for external trainers delivering an internal coaching programme is when there is no dedicated person to drive and deliver the programme from within the organization. This often means that the person originally assigned to set up the training programme is no longer available to answer queries from either the learners or from the trainer. The consequence is that when the cohort meets up with the trainer, valuable time is spent managing queries that could have been dealt with previously by the programme coordinator. The underlying message is the lack of commitment from the organization.

Post-training support involves helping to coordinate the matching and coaching process as a whole and the ongoing CPD and coaching supervision. The coordinator will encourage the internal coaches to meet up as a coaching collegiate to support each other with their continual professional coach development. The most appropriate champion for this role would usually work within learning and development and/or HR.

Preparing learners for the training

Offering an induction session between the selection process and the launch of the programme will give successful applicants the opportunity to discover and discuss:

- The programme details, content and outcomes.
- The number of coach practice hours required to complete the programme.
- The assignments and timescales.
- Questions on the process and the practical aspects of the training.
- How to be removed from the coach programme if it is not for them.

Finding enough people to be coached during training

Most, if not all, coaching programmes require learners to complete a minimum number of formal coaching practice hours which is recorded in a learning log. This coach practice is in addition to the training days, is usually a minimum of 20 hours and has to be completed before the end of the coach training programme.

Learners are advised to find people to coach who:

- They don't line manage.
- Is not a friend or family member.
- Is someone they don't know well.

Finding enough people to be coached in a small organization can be a problem but is easily mitigated. The programme coordinator, working ideally alongside senior management, would be responsible for promoting the internal coach programme by requesting people to come forward to be coached, possibly by including it in their objectives to address a particular development need. Problems can also be avoided by having the programme aligned with an organizational initiative including:

- Coaching interns and apprentices.
- Coaching people through a management development programme.
- Coaching people through a recent restructure or change initiative.

Seniority of learners in each cohort

Consider the seniority of those attending the qualification programme and if their level of seniority might hinder the confidence of others in the cohort. This can work both ways, with the more senior person being uncomfortable with opening up or sharing information with the rest of the cohort who may be more junior. Equally, team members starting out in their careers may feel uncomfortable taking training with more senior people.

One proposed solution to avoid this problem would be offering a separate training session for different levels of seniority. With a smaller senior leadership group the external trainer can tailor the training to the needs of the group while delivering a consistent training programme and maintaining the integrity and requirements of the qualification.

Commitment from the top and change of leadership

Unfortunately, even with a clear coaching strategy, clearly aligned organizational objectives, coach training and developing an internal coaching capability can often fail when there is a change of leadership. This is a challenge for any organization and is rarely something that can be controlled but it can be managed with the right mindset from the internal coaches.

CASE STUDY

A fast expanding third sector organization, with a commitment from the executive management team invested heavily in embedding a coaching culture. Twelve committed individuals were taken through a rigorous training programme with the aim of developing a further 12 coaches the following year.

Coaching for Managers courses were delivered at the same time to equip managers and leaders in how to use coaching with their teams.

The organization wrote a clear coaching strategy that aligned with their strategic mission, vision and values. Various internal communication campaigns promoted internal coaching, including a professionally produced video that interviewed key coaching ambassadors and leaders within the organization to express the purpose and benefits of coaching.

The first cohort of 12 delegates made an enthusiastic start and all was going well until a financial crisis hit the organization.

Three years later the organization is no longer committed to coaching and the qualified coaches are left with little or no support to coach others.

A change in senior leadership then saw a rapid programme of redundancies and restructures. The internal coaching pool was reduced to seven people with a clear message from the top that coaching was no longer a priority.

In reality, this period of organizational change would have been a perfect opportunity for internal coaches to have supported their colleagues through the change and uncertainty. This was made even more difficult with the arrival of Covid-19 and more pressing priorities got in the way of coaching.

Since the change in leadership, the pool of qualified internal coaches has met up regularly to form an Action Learning Group to identify ways in which they can promote themselves as internal coaches and as an ongoing internal coaching support. They are also working with an external coach supervisor for their CPD.

The message with this scenario is that although senior leadership does not support coaching in this instance, this does not prevent coaching from going ahead. This case study demonstrates that with the right mindset the internal coaches can continue with their coaching practice and CPD by being proactive in making internal coaching work.

Ethical dilemmas

Ethical dilemmas are explored in Chapter 4 of this book. The challenge for an internal coach is that there is no way of knowing what issues, discussions or problems could be unwittingly brought into the session.

To avoid this dilemma, ensure the training programme spends enough time on discussing the potential ethical dilemmas and issues around boundaries that may emerge. Time should be set aside to work through scenarios, case studies and strategies. Provide coaching supervision to support internal coaches when dilemmas and challenges arise.

Continual professional development and coaching supervision

One of the biggest mistakes organizations make is to avoid, ignore or fail to consider CPD important enough for their pool of internal coaches.

Coaching supervision for internal coaches will increase the confidence and competence of internal coaches. It provides support, guidance and an opportunity to reflect on their role and responsibility as an internal coach, the skills they are using and any challenges such as ethical dilemmas or boundary issues they may encounter when coaching individuals within the organization.

All significant and quality coach training programmes include coaching supervision as part of the training package and programme. It is recommended that organizations go further by offering post-training coaching supervision to continually promote and build coaching competence and confidence.

Evaluating the programme

Evaluation is an ongoing process and needs to start before any coaching takes place. It has been well documented by coach experts such as Hawkins and Clutterbuck et al that calculating a return on investment for coaching in monetary terms is almost impossible. Peter Hawkins in his book *Creating a Coaching Culture* (2012) states that '... the term "return on investment" is now being included in coaching strategies' and that 'some of this upsurge is driven by the concerns, or possible anxiety of coaches and coaching managers who have to defend their expenditure, in times of austerity and financial scrutiny'.

What is evident from the research into evaluating internal coaching is that results are difficult to measure in monetary terms. The return on investment is often measured in qualitative terms, by the overall employee engagement, reduced absentee rates, staff retention, sickness levels and customer satisfaction surveys.

Hybrid working and coaching

We are living in a very different world to where we were in the spring of 2020. Along with the obvious challenges this has caused for organizations, it has also brought about some benefits. In terms of coaching, working from home has created a need to undertake all meetings, including coaching, using video conferencing. The sudden increase in new video conferencing technology made this possible, almost overnight.

As an independent coach and trainer Sue Noble had her concerns in the early days about how this change from face-to-face coaching to virtual would work in practice. What she found was that with some careful adaptations and clever use of the interactive video platform facilities, her training and coaching had no negative impact. Adapting to change enabled the author and her clients to continue successfully with video calls, so much so that even now that a return to meeting in person is acceptable, the author is going to continue with a hybrid way of working. The author found that shorter, more intensive video coaching suits some clients far better than the usual two hour face-to-face sessions.

The message here is that by adapting to change good things can emerge from what would otherwise been thought of as impossible. In the same way that businesses have had to adapt to the hybrid way of working, internal coaching can easily be managed and completed virtually. Meeting up does not have to be in the office. Nature walking and coaching has increased in popularity and can greatly enhance coaching. This has been experienced by the author when using a vineyard as a walking route on one of her coaching sessions. The vines acted as milestones and because the goals were represented by something visual as well as the physical action of walking to each milestone, the coaching had more impact for this particular client.

Here are some useful tips to remember when setting up online coaching with the stakeholder.

It is essential that both the internal coach and stakeholder:

- Use video as well as audio to greatly enhance the interactive experience.
- Are using a static PC or laptop with a camera set on top of the computer. This will enable you to look at each other rather than be turned away from each other.
- Are in a private room with no distractions and definitely no one else in the room, not even a family member. This creates a barrier to honest and open communication and can be distracting. This includes people wandering in and out of the room from time to time and sitting in the room with ear phones on.
- Carry out careful contracting, highlighting the confidentiality clauses and agreeing what the stakeholder wants to get from the coaching session and from you as the internal coach.
- Give feedback to each other at the end of the coaching session to check out your experiences from both the internal coach and stakeholder's perspective.

Conclusion

This chapter highlights the significant benefit of introducing an internal coaching capability for the organization, coaches and coachees alike. However, it is also clear that developing internal coaching takes time, money, commitment and energy to be successful. An advanced qualification programme will support internal coaches in building confidence to coach people through challenging situations, build competence in the multifaceted skills required to coach others and build credibility as an internal coach. However, the support and commitment of the organization is crucial to the capability's long-term success.

As researched by experts in the field, a coaching strategy is recommended to help the organization decide what is best for their needs with some useful questions to ask in terms of the purpose and expected outcome of the internal coaching initiative.

Although internal coaching does not remove the need for external coaching expertise, it can greatly enhance the speed and efficiency at which coaching can be delivered to all levels and all people within the organization.

References

Coaching Focus (2013) www.coaching-focus.com (archived at https://perma.cc/ G6ZK-GTTV)

CIPD (2022) www.cipd.co.uk (archived at https://perma.cc/7M8Y-D37C)

Clutterbuck, D, Megginson, D and Bajer, A (2016) *Building and Sustaining a Coaching Culture*, CIPD, London

Hawkins, P (2012) *Creating a Coaching Culture*, Open University Press – McGraw-Hill, Berkshire

International Coaching Federation (2014) Building a coaching culture [Online] https://coachingfederation.org/research/building-a-coaching-culture (archived at https://perma.cc/354S-LPC7)

Musselwhite, C and Plouffe, T (2010) Four ways to know whether you are ready for change, *Harvard Business Review*, https://hbr.org/2010/06/four-ways-to-know-whether-you (archived at https://perma.cc/HNV9-MJB7)

Ridler & Co (2013) The Ridler report, www.ridlerandco.com (archived at https:// perma.cc/HVD5-4J7F)

St John-Brooks, K (2018) *Internal Coaching: The inside story*, Routledge, New York

Techniques to coach people through change   12

Introduction

In Chapters 6–10, the authors have offered a range of practical coaching tools and techniques to support change practitioners in overcoming the challenges of organizational change.

This chapter sets out a variety of coaching techniques to support people through change. Although these techniques are typically used by experienced coaches and facilitators, with practice and confidence change practitioners who may or may not be qualified or experienced coaches can learn how to apply them.

These practical coaching tools, and questions can be used within 1-2-1 coaching conversations, some of which are adaptable and suitable for use in a team or group coaching session.

Managing resistance when asking questions

Not everyone likes being asked questions. Some people feel interrogated or they are not ready to do the thinking behind the answers to the questions. Questions should always be asked from a place of curiosity, not judgement or criticism. If your mindset is one of judgement, your tone of voice will let you down. Make sure questions are open which encourages the stakeholder to talk more about what is on their mind and be careful not to jump in to offer advice or give suggestions unless the stakeholder has specifically asked for it or if they are struggling with the answer.

Here are some tips should you encounter resistance when asking questions during a coaching conversation.

When someone says 'I don't know' very quickly after hearing the question:

- Remain silent, focussed and interested in the individual. (When done naturally and carefully this can help the individual to say more.)

Ask one or more of these questions to help move the conversation forward without the need to give advice:

- Do you need more time to think about the question?
- And what if you did know the answer?
- What is your perception of the answer?
- Is there another question I can ask you instead?
- What might someone else say the answer is?
- What stops you from knowing the answer?
- What's the best question I can ask you right now?

When someone goes off on a tangent when asked a specific question:

- Could I just bring you back to the original question, please?
- The question I asked was....
- Could we go back to your original goal and the purpose of being here?
- I am noticing that when I ask you a question, your responses tend to go off on a tangent.

When someone crosses their arms and is silent:

- Is everything OK? I noticed that you crossed your arms when I asked that question.
- Was there something about that question that did not sit comfortably with you?
- What is on your mind at the moment?

As highlighted in Chapter 7, resistance to change can be expected and the questions and techniques offered within this chapter are there to help the change practitioner work with the stakeholder to identify where the resistance is coming from, what they need in order to accept the change and how to avoid the coaching conversation from ending on a bad note.

When the stakeholder is showing signs of resistance to the coaching conversation the questions and techniques offered may not always work as expected, but they can help the change practitioner to remain calm when faced with resistance and to clarify what is concerning the stakeholder at that given moment.

Levels of challenge and complexity for each technique

The following techniques are placed in order of complexity. The authors have included a summary matrix of all the tools and their potential uses in the appendix.

Level of complexity explained

- **Level 1: Easy.** Can be used by anyone who has an understanding of open and closed questions and communicating with others.
- **Level 2: Intermediate.** Can be used by anyone who has some experience of coaching, mentoring or in a role that requires structured questioning. These may take some practice to refine. Practising these techniques on colleagues and or others first would help to build confidence and understanding of the technique.
- **Level 3: Advanced.** Would most likely be used by someone with experience of coaching and or counselling and with confidence to work with individuals at a deeper level of questioning and support.

Where do these techniques originate from?

Some of these tools and techniques are easily referenced to an originator but many have been used and adapted over the years and the original version or owner has been lost in time or not documented. Each technique has been referenced where it has been possible to trace back to the originator. Each original visual model used where the originator is known, has been given strict permission to use and publish the model.

Who can use these techniques?

These techniques have been included with the change practitioner in mind and can be used by anyone managing organizational and personal change. The term 'stakeholder' in this instance refers to the individual the change practitioner is working with.

Preparing for your conversations

Before starting any coaching conversation or using these techniques, consider the REST framework as set out in Chapter 4 of this book: 'Best practice coaching methods for change practitioners.' As a reminder, REST stands for:

- Rapport and being present
- Empathy
- Setting the scene
- Target (stay on track).

These guiding principles will help those using these techniques to stay focussed on the goal or outcome of the conversation, particularly if there are any concerns about how the individual may react to any of the questions asked. Setting the scene and agreeing or contracting the session is useful to gain an understanding of expectations.

Technique 1: a walk in the park

Level 1: technique explained

A very simple and visual exercise to use with a stakeholder to help navigate a goal they may be struggling to achieve as part of a change initiative. The headings are Want, Doing, Self-Evaluation, Options and Commitment. The originator is unknown.

Figure 12.1 A walk in the park

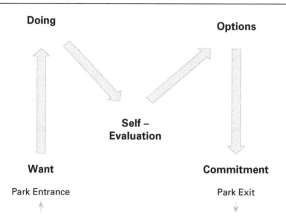

Useful when?

The stakeholder likes to have the visual focus of a model or framework. Some people struggle with eye-to-eye contact when being asked questions in a formal setting and this exercise offers a structured approach to coaching with clear steps along the way. It also enables the coach to formulate their questions in a meaningful way. Some people react well to metaphors with the park being a journey and having resting points in the process.

Technique in action

Remember that as change practitioner you are the guardian of the journey. Starting at the bottom left (figure 12.1), of the page enter the park and ask questions that relate to the stopping-off points as you go around the park. The model focuses on what the client wants as an outcome, what they are doing at the moment (open this out to what is going well and not so well, etc). After more questions, there is a bench to stop and reflect where the client is now and what new insight they have before moving on to options and finally commitment and action. A useful question to ask before finishing the conversation is, 'What are you taking away from the park today?' 'What have you learnt most on your walk?'

Adaptations

If the coach forgets to bring the model then it is easy to ask the stakeholder to draw the model while in the session using the same stop-off points. This would work well when coaching someone outside, particularly if there was a real park you could both walk around. There is plenty of evidence to suggest that coaching outdoors has huge benefits and allows people to expand their thought process instead of being confined to a room.

What could go wrong?

Very little.

Technique 2: C-I-A model – Control, Influence, Accept

Level 1: technique explained

This is a widely used, simple and effective model used by coaches to help people focus on the situation they are in and identify what is within their control, their level of influence and what they are willing to accept. Acceptance is the first step to change. This model has parallels with Stephen Covey's Circle of Concern and Influence concept (technique 3 below). The originators, Neil Thompson (an HR specialist) and Sue Thompson (a social work lecturer) have given the authors their kind permission to use this technique.

Useful when?

This has particular relevance in a change situation where the stakeholder can feel stuck and frustrated with the change they are faced with. Asking a few simple but powerful questions can help someone to reframe the situation, look at ways to move forward and find a solution that works for them. The coach practitioner would use this model as part of a wider coaching conversation and not as a stand-alone technique.

Technique in action

Always use the model in the order of Control, Influence, Accept, focusing on what is and is not achievable. Ask the stakeholder the following and other relevant questions as you move through the model.

Control or change

- Is this a situation or decision that you have direct control over or something you can change? No? Move to Influence.
- Yes? How will you exercise that control and what outcome do you want to achieve?

Influence

- If you have no control over this situation, can you influence it? No? Move to Accept.
- Yes? What parts of this problem or situation can you influence and how would you make this happen?

Accept

- If you are unable to control or influence this situation then what are you willing to accept?
- What else are you willing to accept?
- If you are not willing to accept, what can you adapt?
- If you are not willing to accept, what are the consequences?

What could go wrong?

Very little if the stakeholder is open to being asked questions and to reconsider the situation they are in.

Technique 3: Circle of Concern and Circle of Influence

Level 1: technique explained

This popular model originates from Stephen Covey's *The 7 Habits of Highly Effective People* (1989). His book distinguishes between proactive people who focus on what they can do and influence, and reactive people who focus their energy on things outside of their control. The authors have described how to use this technique as it has so much relevance to organizational change.

The model is based very simply on two circles. The outer circle is:

- **Circle of Concern.** Things of everyday situations, problems and concerns over which the individual may or may not have any control over.

The inner circle is the smaller,

- **Circle of Influence.** This includes things that the individual has control over.

Useful when?

This model can be used during a change initiative or when the stakeholder is experiencing an overwhelming sense of feeling out of control. The change practitioner will be listening for the energy behind the words used by the stakeholder, the body language and generally how the stakeholder is looking, feeling and sounding when talking about the situation they are in.

Technique in action

The role of the change practitioner is to facilitate a discussion to help the stakeholder understand all the things that are of concern to them that are causing them stress and anxiety and those things that are within their control and that they can focus their attention on.

An example of this technique is also described in detail in Chapter 9 where it is used to support a stakeholder who is interested in a change initiative but has little or no influence over the results.

What next?

This model is ideally used as part of a coaching conversation and not as a stand-alone exercise. The change practitioner would continue to work with the stakeholder asking questions to help them recognize new insight and learning and workable solutions to avoid falling back into the Circle of Concern.

What could go wrong?

Very little if the client is willing to open up and be honest about their stressful situation.

Technique 4: time line

Level 1: technique explained:

This original model was called *Time Line Therapy*, created by NLP practitioner Tad James (James and Woodsmall, 2017). Over time, this approach has been adapted by coaches to use as a quick and effective, physical way to guide someone through a set of milestones to where they want to be in the future.

Useful when?

In most situations, the stakeholder will have a goal they want to achieve, so this technique can be used in most, if not all, situations. It is particularly useful when coaching someone who:

- Learns by doing and being active.
- Has a particular skill or mindset they want to improve on, for example gaining more confidence in transitioning from a middle to a senior manager.
- Has a preference for visualizing what something will look like, sound like and feel like.
- Wants to build confidence in a particular skill.
- Is stuck in terms of change.

Technique in action

Ideally, the coach practitioner would use a length of string or rope to demonstrate the length of time and have a room large enough to lay the rope down. Identify what the stakeholder would like as an ideal outcome or a specific goal, for example to build confidence. Encourage the stakeholder to be as expressive as they can.

Ask the stakeholder to:

1 Agree which end of the rope is 1 (now) and which end is 10 (future – ideal outcome).

2 Stand on the rope where they are now in terms of their level of confidence and to describe what they are noticing about themselves at the moment.

3 Describe what they can hear, what they can see, what it feels like being here.

4 Explore some limiting beliefs and look at where this belief comes from. For example, 'What choices are you making in terms of the way you are thinking?'

5 Explore strengths and what they are doing well.

6 Walk up to a point where they would like to be and what timescale this is (ie six months).

7 Describe as fully as possible, what they are seeing, hearing, feeling.

Useful questions to ask:

- What is it like to be here and to have these skills?
- Where is your comfort zone at this moment?

Ask your stakeholder to return to where they are now and take them on a gradual journey with milestones, steadily moving up the rope and describing each stage of the journey and process.

Useful questions to ask:

- What are you experiencing at each milestone?
- How will you gradually improve and increase your skills?
- Where might the blocks and barriers be to your success (internal or external)?

Return to a coaching conversation and talk about new insights and learning.

Adaptations

If the room size is too small then it is possible to do this exercise using a piece of paper on a desk, asking the stakeholder to draw a line and then talk them through their vision in the same way. However, this approach is not quite so powerful.

Using this exercise virtually needs a bit more creative thinking and thought but is not impossible. The stakeholder can still stand and walk up and down the line. Both screens will probably need adjusting so that you can still see each other.

Using this exercise outside works well, particularly when using trees, lamp posts, cars or anything else that can be used as check-points and milestones.

What could go wrong?

Very little. As long as the client is clear as to the purpose of this exercise. People with a physical disability may find this exercise challenging. Check what would work for them and how they would like to use the model.

Technique 5: AIR your feedback

Level 1: technique explained

This is a popular and simple model using the acronym AID or AIR. The model is typically used by managers to give feedback to their team members but can equally be used by change practitioners if there is important information to convey to a stakeholder. The originator is unknown and has been adapted by the author from the original AID feedback model (D = desired outcome).

- **Action:** The problem or issue that is causing concern.
- **Impact:** The impact this problem is having (either personally or with others).
- **Request:** An outcome or solution worded as a request, not a command or demand.

Useful when?

This feedback technique can be used by change practitioners to give feedback to stakeholders in a very succinct, structured and clear way, particularly if the problem is directly impacting on the change practitioner or the change project.

Technique in action

The change practitioner can use this technique either as part of a coaching conversation or as a direct request to the stakeholder for a meeting to discuss something on their mind. Focusing on a goal or outcome for the session will help the change practitioner stay on track. The following is an example of how this technique might be used by a change practitioner in conversation with a stakeholder who is demonstrating a lack of engagement with the change practitioner or with the project:

- Consider what needs to be said and who needs to hear the information.
- Write down a short and clear script of what to say using the acronym AIR.
- Arrange a meeting with the individual and explain that they would like a constructive meeting to discuss something of importance.
- When in the meeting explain to the stakeholder that they will have a chance to offer their thoughts once you, as change practitioner, have explained your concerns.

Action

- I overheard a conversation you had with Sam this week where it would seem that my position as change practitioner is not understood or appreciated by yourself.

Impact

- I am concerned about how this might have come across to those you are speaking with and the impact on the overall change project, which is at a crucial stage at the moment. I admit to being frustrated by this and how it might be viewed by other senior people. You are in an influential position and your opinion matters to others.

Request

- I would really appreciate if you could explain to me what you think my role is in this project, how it is relevant to the change and how we might work collaboratively.

What next?

Ideally, the stakeholder will be willing to continue the coaching conversation, particularly if they have a good rapport with the change practitioner.

What could go wrong?

That largely depends on the reaction from the stakeholder and how they respond to the feedback and request. The outcome of this conversation may also be influenced if either the change practitioner or stakeholder chooses to compete (argue until they get their own way) or avoid (ignore or walk away from the conversation). Neither style is helpful and an ideal style is to work collaboratively to find a solution to the problem. Although this is a Level 1 technique in terms of how to use it, the resulting resistance could take it to a Level 2 or 3. Be prepared for this.

Words of wisdom

The change practitioner will help themselves by not over justifying their own position. Always focus on an ideal goal or outcome and avoid getting into an argument as this rarely ends well. If necessary, suggest another meeting another time, particularly if the conversation gets heated.

Technique 6: Neurological or Logical Levels

Level 2: technique explained

The Neurological Levels are an adaptation of Gregory Bateson's Logical Levels and was first produced by Robert Dilts in his book *Changing Belief Systems with NLP* (1990). The levels provide a helpful structure for evaluating what is happening in any given situation where there is resistance or a feeling of being stuck. The six levels are:

- Purpose
- Identity
- Beliefs and Values
- Capabilities
- Behaviours
- Environment.

These six levels all have significance but generally speaking Dilts proposed the principle that change occurs most naturally at the highest levels around Beliefs, Values, Identity and Purpose.

The change practitioner may also use this model either moving up and down the levels or in a more systemic way where the headings of each of the levels are placed in a circle and the stakeholder is invited to choose which of the levels has most relevance or significance for them. The change practitioner can facilitate the conversation by guiding the stakeholder through the process and see what emerges.

Useful when?

Change practitioners can use this model to explore at which level the stakeholder connects with during a conversation. Some levels may have more significance than others. The change practitioner must not place their own interpretation on each of the levels. For example, the environment level for some people can mean their work situation, where they are sitting or it may have a wider meaning in terms of the organization and its culture.

Technique in action

There are so many ways to use this model that to suggest specific questions feels counter-intuitive. However, for those who are new to coaching these questions are useful for guidance. Remember that if someone identifies a level where they are stuck, then guide them through the other levels as well to see if there are any 'blinds spots' or 'hidden' areas.

Possible questions to ask using Logical Levels

Purpose

- In terms of this issue or problem, what is your sense of purpose?
- What would give you a sense of purpose?
- How might the change affect your feelings about being part of the wider organization?
- What else would help you to have a sense of purpose?

Identity

- What would help you to gain a sense of identity?
- What does this change say about you?
- What sense of self do you have?
- How might you lose or gain your sense of self?
- How might your identity give you a sense of purpose?

Beliefs and values

- What beliefs or values do you have that drive this feeling of being stuck or challenged?
- What else is challenging your beliefs and values?
- What belief do you have in the process?
- What belief do you have about yourself?
- How might you regain a sense of belief in the process that does not impact on your values?
- What do these beliefs and values say about who you are and your identity?

Capabilities

- How is this change process impacting on your skills?
- What else do you need to regain these skills?
- What would it take for you to move from your comfort zone to your stretch zone?
- What beliefs do you have about your ability to learn these new skills?

Behaviours

- How is this change impacting on your behaviours?
- What are you noticing about yourself that you are not happy with?
- What positive behaviours would you like to adopt?
- What is stopping you?
- What is triggering your behaviours?
- And your positive behaviours, how would you describe these?

Environment

- Where do you feel most stuck?
- How is your environment impacting on your feeling of being stuck and challenged?
- What is within your control in terms of this?
- What would be your ideal environment to work in?

Things to listen for

When asking these questions, if the stakeholder replies with a very quick 'I don't know', this could mean a number of things:

- I don't know and I don't want to talk about it. It's too painful to talk about it (hidden spot).
- I don't know and I need more time to think about the question.
- I don't know but I am curious to know more.
- I don't know but I have a strong perception of the answer.

Here are some useful questions to ask when faced with a quick 'I don't know' response:

- And what if you did know, what would that be like?
- If you knew the answer, what would it be?
- What might your best friend say the answer is?
- What are you thinking but not saying?
- What is your greatest concern about knowing the answer right now?

Experienced coaches are aware of the barriers their clients can hold up when a question is too painful or raw for them. As a change practitioner you can learn these skills by listening out for the quick 'I don't know' responses and be curious to know what is preventing the stakeholder from knowing. Being curious will help the stakeholder to open up and be less resistant and will avoid the change practitioner from jumping in with advice or suggestions.

What next?

Once the exercise has been completed the change practitioner can resume the coaching conversation checking for new insights and learning, and where the individual is now in terms of the proposed change and what further support they need.

What could go wrong?

Very little unless the stakeholder is resistant to being asked questions. Most people resonate with at least one of the levels and so this could open up other aspects of where they are stuck in the change process.

Technique 7: the change cycle

Level 2: technique explained

In his book *Leadership Coaching* (2007) Graham Lee explores the use of a change cycle and demonstrates the pattern of feelings that people typically go through when they experience change. This model is useful for understanding and identifying the characteristics of change, understanding the conscious and unconscious patterns of behaviours we experience and acknowledging the emotions people go through when change happens.

In figure 12.2 the model highlights the vertical and horizontal axis. The vertical axis represents a person's emotional state, ranging from positive feelings to difficult feelings. The horizontal axis represents time and, because experience of change is pertinent to each person, this cycle is dependent on the individual and the impact the change has on them. As previously mentioned in Chapter 7, there are five stages to this model.

- uninformed optimism
- unconscious resistance
- conscious realism
- conscious optimism
- conscious integration of changes.

The challenge for change practitioners and the organization is that people can't be made to move or accept change if they are not ready. Showing this model to the stakeholder can help them identify what their unconscious and conscious feelings are. Revealing unconscious feelings and emotions can only be achieved through the individual having a conscious realization of what is happening and the impact on them. Otherwise these thoughts and feelings remain a 'blind spot'. The other way to bring these thoughts, feelings and

Figure 12.2 The change cycle

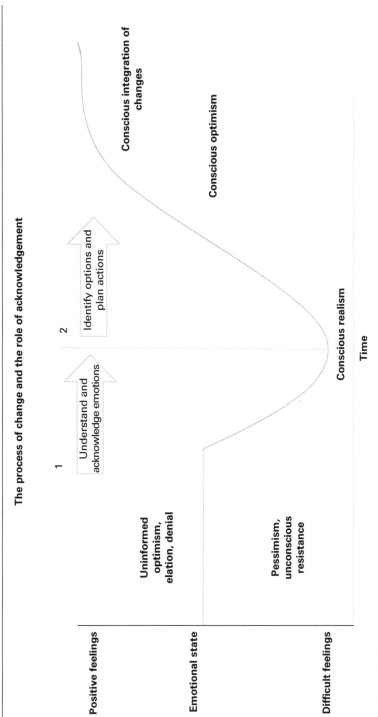

The process of change and the role of acknowledgement

Positive feelings

Uninformed
optimism,
elation, denial

1

Understand and
acknowledge emotions

2

Identify options and
plan actions

Conscious integration of
changes

Conscious optimism

Emotional state

Pessimism,
unconscious
resistance

Conscious realism

Time

Difficult feelings

SOURCE Lee, 2007

emotions to the surface and therefore into conscious awareness is through the change practitioner asking relevant questions to help that realization to emerge. The important part of the change and coaching process is to know how to help someone shift from the left-hand to the right-hand curve of the change cycle.

Not everyone starts at the beginning of the change cycle. Some people may be consciously aware and optimistic from the start, in which case the change practitioner will ask questions offered under 'conscious optimism', evaluating the strategies for how the stakeholder will avoid returning to pessimism and resistance.

Useful when?

This technique is useful in any situation where there is organizational, interpersonal and/or personal change. The change practitioner can work with the stakeholder to help them understand their emotional state at various times during the change process and help bring them into conscious awareness of any underlying feelings and tensions that may create pessimism or resistance.

Technique in action

The success of this technique relies on the change practitioner opening up the conversation and asking questions to help the stakeholder to think of the situation from different perspectives and acknowledging emotions to help them accept and plan for the change ahead.

To explain the model it is useful to consider a typical situation where someone is likely to experience resistance to change, for example being asked to do a different job following a restructure. The following questions could be asked at each stage of the change cycle to help the stakeholder integrate the changes through choice.

Uninformed optimism

The individual starts their new job with optimism and generally has positive feelings based on relatively little information they have received about the new role. The individual is protected from the full force of difficult feelings due to either shock or unconscious denial. Acknowledging emotions at this stage is important otherwise there is less chance of the individual feeling able or willing to move to the right side of the cycle.

- How are you feeling right now? And what are you thinking?
- You sound positive about the changes about to happen. Are there any underlying concerns that you might have?
- Could there be a 'blind spot' with your thinking?
- If you were playing 'devil's advocate' or you asked a critical friend, what might yours or their counter argument be?
- What might your critical friend be noticing that you are not?
- Who do you ask in order for you to be fully aware of all the changes, consequences and options available to you?
- In six months' time and once you are in your new job, what would you like to be thinking, feeling and hearing?
- What might happen if the job does not turn out as you had hoped?
- What might cause you to move from optimism to pessimism?

Unconscious resistance

The individual has been in the new job long enough to realize that the role has its problems and it was not quite the job they signed up for. Feelings of pessimism and disillusionment are common and may be an unconscious resistance to change. The individual is feeling less positive than at the outset but the unconscious aspects of the experience means that they are still protected from the full reality of the change.

- What do you know now that you didn't know before?
- If you could turn back the clock, what advice would you give yourself?
- How are you feeling right now? And what are you thinking?
- What are the difficult feelings you would like to off-load at the moment?
- What are your greatest concerns?
- I am concerned that you are still experiencing some unconscious resistance. Is there a difficult question you need to ask yourself?
- What is stopping you from doing this?

Conscious realism

Something happens, a thought process or possibly a coaching conversation, which moves the individual to being aware of the reality of the situation and the challenges of the new role. This is when most people feel stuck and unable to move forward. In order to move forward from these difficult feelings it is important to have a practical and realistic understanding of what they must do to achieve their new goals. A shift in mindset from negative to positive is likely for change to happen.

- You are now experiencing conscious realism, what happened for that to happen?
- How are you feeling? What are you thinking right now?
- How deep do these emotions go?
- What is triggering these emotions?
- Where would you like to be in terms of the change and how you are feeling?
- What is stopping you from moving forward?
- What is your mindset or attitude at the moment?
- What is the worst and best that can happen if you did move forward?
- What advice would you give to a trusted best friend in a similar situation?
- What is the first step to you reaching conscious optimism? And then what happens?

Conscious optimism

A conscious appreciation of the task and challenges ahead help the individual to become consciously optimistic, trying new solutions and feeling more positive.

- What does it feel like being here instead of where you were?
- What was the shift that made this happen?
- What is your mindset now?
- How will you remain in conscious optimism and avoid going back to pessimism?
- Describe your emotions now compared to where you were.
- Are you fully aware of what needs to happen for you to move to the next stage?

Conscious integration of changes

This is the stage where people are feeling most positive and energized, having thought about the change in more detail, understanding the reasons for the change and what it means for them. There is an awareness and realization that goals can be and will be achieved.

- What has happened for you to be willing to integrate the changes?
- How does that feel right now?
- What is the shift that made this happen?
- What's in it for you?
- What are your goals going forward?
- What support do you need?
- Who will you turn to if you feel like you are shifting back down the curve?
- What words of acknowledgement and appreciation would you like to give yourself?

What next?

The important part of the change and coaching process is to know how to help someone shift from the left-hand to the right-hand curve of the change cycle. Taking a closer look at the change cycle, there are two possible interventions:

1 Understand and acknowledge emotions.

2 Identify options and plan actions.

A coaching conversation will help the stakeholder understand the nuances of these two interventions and how they can make the shift to conscious integration of changes.

Intervention 1: If emotions are made conscious and are acknowledged, stakeholders can move easily through the change cycle. Acknowledgement and understanding allows the individual to be open about the feelings they are experiencing and to move to conscious optimism and conscious integration of the changes, through the identification of options and action planning. If the emotions associated with unconscious resistance to change have not been addressed, such interventions are likely to fail. However, change practitioners should be cautious about rushing this part of the process.

Intervention 2: As mentioned above, this intervention can only succeed if the understanding and acknowledgement of emotions has been established first. These insights will help the stakeholder to consider and plan options and actions to enable them to accept the change. Not rushing either of these interventions is essential for success.

Further reflection will take place outside of the meeting and so it is best not to rush the stakeholder into committing to the change if they are not ready. Continue with the coaching conversation and check for new insights, thoughts, feelings and also actions to move forward, if the individual is ready. This may take time but the conversation will hopefully have led them to think and reflect about the current situation, their emotions, where they want to be and how they will get there.

What could go wrong?

The stakeholder could be resistant to being asked questions. If so, it is best to ask them what the reason is for their resistance (in a curious not judgemental tone). They may not be aware of their resistance and this could open up a useful conversation.

It can be assumed that most people understand and can relate to the language within each of the five stages of the change cycle. People will often appreciate having an open and trusting conversation on the impact the change is having on them. If the change practitioner has a good rapport with the stakeholder, the conversation and level of trust are likely to work well.

Be prepared for a display of emotions during the conversation. Give the stakeholder space and time to continue with the discussion. If the stakeholder gets upset during the conversation and the change practitioner is feeling uncomfortable, it is not advisable to stop the session. Instead, check if the stakeholder is willing to continue. Take a deep breath and continue with the conversation, supporting them with the support they need to move forward.

Technique 8: Bridges' transition model

Level 2: technique explained

Bridges' transition model (2017) is an alternative model to the change cycle and is equally valuable in helping organizations and individuals understand and more effectively manage and work through the personal and human side of change. The model originates from William and Susan Bridges and is explored in *Managing Transitions: Making the most of change* (2017). Their model suggests that people experience three stages of change and they do so at their own pace depending on how comfortable they are with these changes. A copy of the original model can be obtained via the internet or from www.wmbridges.com and can be used for non-commercial purposes.

The three stages are:

- Endings, losing, letting go (resistance and denial)
- The Neutral Zone (confusing, uncertainty)
- New Beginnings (energy and optimism).

Useful when?

This technique is useful in any situation where there is organizational, inter-personal and/or personal change. The change practitioner can work with the stakeholder to help them understand what they are experiencing during each phase of the change process and help bring them into conscious aware-ness of any underlying feelings and tensions which may create a resistance to the change. Understanding what is being lost or left behind is an integral part of this transition model.

Technique in action

Obtain a copy of Bridges' transition model and guide the stakeholder through each of the three stages. The following questions are examples of how to support individuals at each stage, remembering that some people may not feel they are losing but gaining. Adapt the questions accordingly.

Endings, losing and letting go

The first phase of transition begins when people identify what they are losing and learn how to manage these losses. For this reason the Bridges' transition model has Endings as the start of the transition process. As part of this pro-cess people determine what they will lose and leave behind because of the change. This may include relationships, team members, systems or locations or even habits.

- What are the changes you are experiencing?
- What is actually going to change? (Be as specific as possible.)

- What are you potentially losing, letting go or giving away due to this change?
- How is this impacting on you?
- How are you feeling? What are you thinking about this change?
- What is the worst and the best thing that might happen because of the change?
- What assumptions are you making?
- Are your assumptions true?
- What would help you to rationalize the losses?
- What are you willing to accept?
- How will you know when you are ready to move forward?
- What support do you need from me?

The Neutral Zone

The second stage of transition, the Neutral Zone, refers to what happens after letting go. People go through an in-between stage when the old has gone and the new is not yet fully operational. This is when realignment and readjustment takes place. It is the very core of the transition process. This is the time between the old reality and sense of identity and the new reality. People are creating new processes and learning what their new roles will be. They are in flux and may feel confusion and distress. The Neutral Zone is the seedbed for new beginnings.

- Is there a metaphor for how you are feeling and thinking now that you are through the Endings stage and in the Neutral Zone?
- What are you feeling and thinking right now?
- What are you experiencing in this zone? (Usually confusion, uncertainty, numbness.)
- What would help you to feel less confused, uncertain and numb? (Or use whatever words they use.)
- How can you make this phase as bearable as possible before you move into New Beginnings?
- How long do you want this to take?
- Who can support you through this phase?
- What could you do which will help this transition?

The New Beginnings

Beginnings involve new understandings, values and attitudes. Beginnings are marked by a release of energy in a new direction – they are an expression of a fresh identity. Well-managed transitions allow people to establish new roles with an understanding of their purpose, the part they play and how to contribute and participate most effectively. As a result, they feel reoriented and renewed.

- Is there a metaphor for how you are feeling and thinking now that you have reached New Beginnings?
- What are you feeling and thinking right now?
- What are you experiencing in this zone? (Usually contentment, renewed energy.)
- How will you maintain this new energy?
- What happens now?
- Looking back at when you started this journey, what words of advice would you like to give yourself back then?

What next?

As with all transition models, further reflection will take place outside of the meeting and so it is best not to rush the stakeholder into committing to the change if they are not ready. Continue with the coaching conversation and check for new insights, thoughts, feelings and also actions to move forward, if the individual is ready. This may take time but the conversation will hopefully have led them to think and reflect about the current situation, their emotions, where they want to be and how they will get there.

What could go wrong?

Be careful not to argue with what you hear. Change is subjective and different people experience different things. Don't be surprised if people overreact to the change. The reaction is likely to be due to the transition rather than the change itself.

Technique 9: Johari Window – communication and feedback tool

Level 2: technique explained

This is a well-used and popular model to help individuals and teams understand the importance of open and honest communication, to build trust and be open to feedback from others to reduce 'blind spots'. Johari Window was developed by psychologists, Joseph Luft and Harrington Ingram in the 1950s and like many of the more traditional psychological techniques, it is still as relevant today as it was then.

A copy can easily be found on the internet (www.businessballs.com/self-awareness/johari-window-model-and-free-diagrams).

The model has four windows or arenas. Each of the four windows describes what people choose to disclose to others, what they choose to hide from others, what they are not aware of and what has not yet happened.

Each window explained

Open arena: This is what is known to self and known to others. This is generally information that people feel safe in disclosing and sharing, and which helps others to know the individual better. The more information shared with others, the more others will know about the individual and generally speaking the more trusted they are. However, professionally it is not always appropriate to share too much information and so this can also create problems.

Hidden arena: This is what is known to self but not known to others. Information is hidden for fear of judgement and shame or for reasons of privacy. Over time, people may decide to disclose more information and this then widens the 'open arena'. Some people are naturally introspective and this can, rightly or wrongly, create a lack of trust towards that person.

Blind spot: This is information not known to self but is known to others. This is information that others choose not to share for fear of upsetting the person with the blind spot or which may create an uncomfortable situation. However, if this area is kept 'blind' then the individual will never know what others are thinking, feeling or the impact of behaviours. This is where individuals can ask others for feedback to highlight the impact of their behaviour and is vitally important to avoid and reduce the blind spot. Likewise, giving feedback to others where there may be a 'blind spot' is important. By giving or receiving feedback, the person has a choice to either accept or deny it. How can the person (or the team) be aware of what the issue is unless they are made aware of the problem it is causing? Is this really a blind spot for them or are they just ignoring the facts? Ignoring the facts would suggest this is in the Hidden arena.

Unknown arena: These are things that are unknown to self and unknown to others and which have not yet happened. Over time, when situations occur, they will either enter into the Open or Hidden arena. Or they may occur but are not made aware to the individual and so will enter the blind spot.

Useful when?

This is useful when working with stakeholders or teams to help them understand how communication can help or hinder a change initiative. Identifying the pros and cons of disclosing information and understanding blind spots to behaviours and habits that may impact on change.

Technique in action

Obtain a copy of the model from the internet and show the model to the stakeholder when in a coaching conversation. Or simply draw the model as follows:

- In the top left box write the words *Open Arena*.
- In the top right box write the words *Blind Spot*.
- In the bottom left box write the words *Hidden Arena*.
- In the bottom right box write the words *Unknown Arena*.

This technique is more likely to be used as part of a wider coaching conversation or as part of a team coaching session. The three situations in which the change practitioner can use this technique are:

Self-coaching

Take some time to reflect on the model and each of the windows. The change practitioner can then reflect on their role and their responsibility to the organization and stakeholders. Useful questions to ask concerning the change practitioner role are:

- What information am I open and honest with?
- Is the information I disclose relevant and helpful for myself and others?

- Is there anything which, in hindsight, I wish I had not disclosed? And does it matter?
- If I were to ask X, what would they say about me? Is that a blind spot or am I aware of this and possibly in denial? Because?
- What is the worst thing X could say about me that, if I am honest, might be true? How would I feel about this?
- What do I choose to keep hidden and is this helpful for my role?
- What am I willing to change about myself to get a better outcome in the situation?

Stakeholder coaching

If the change practitioner has a good rapport with the stakeholder during a coaching conversation, they could give the stakeholder feedback on what is being noticed about a particular behaviour or habit. For example, 'Are you aware that you can come over as being direct in your language at times?' This would elicit either an awareness of a 'blind spot' or an awareness and admission of behaviour that is in denial. The model can be adapted to the person and the situation and not all of the windows need to be discussed, although usually, as soon as one window is discussed then the other windows come into conscious awareness. At times these questions can be perceived as being direct and 'provocative'. This is useful as these questions will raise awareness in the stakeholder and enable an understanding of the potential impact of their actions. If the change practitioner has a good rapport with the stakeholder and there is a clear contract at the start of the conversation, then these questions are more likely to be received as positive and with good intent. Try asking these questions from a place of curiosity, not judgment.

Useful questions to ask are:

- I am wondering if the information you are sharing with others is appropriate and ethical?
- By sharing this information, what are you hoping for?
- Is what you are doing a blind spot? If not, then what are you possibly not admitting to?
- What important information might you be choosing to keep hidden from others?
- I am curious to know what would happen if others were aware of this information?
- Could there be a trust issue here?

As part of this conversation and to show commitment to Johari's Window principles, the change practitioner could then ask the stakeholder for feedback on a behaviour or habit the stakeholder would like feedback on.

Team coaching

When working with a team, this model will help them recognize how the team's behaviour and actions are impacting on other teams and stakeholders. These questions would be asked in generic terms as a collaborative team intervention and would not necessarily be directed at individuals within the team. However, an additional and useful exercise could be introduced where team members pair up and are asked to coach each other on the model. This would include giving feedback to each other and checking if the feedback is a 'blind spot' or if it is in the hidden arena. Pairs could be swapped around and the exercise continues until everyone has met with each of their colleagues, giving and receiving feedback.

What next?

Following on from the Johari Window exercises the change practitioner would continue with the coaching conversation or team intervention and work towards action, outcomes and new insights.

What could go wrong?

Very little, particularly if the change practitioner has a good rapport with the stakeholder and team. An ideal outcome would be for the individual or team to enter into a conversation where positive change is actioned as a result of recognizing unhelpful behaviours.

Technique 10: Disney strategy for team and group coaching

Level 3: technique explained

Originally designed by Walt Disney as a creative process, the model was adapted and described in detail by Robert Dilts in his book *Tools for*

Dreamers (Dilts and Epstein, 1991) and *Strategies of Genius* (1994). Walt Disney was described in meetings as having three different personas: the dreamer, the realist and the critic. However, no one knew which one they would be getting until the meeting happened. The Disney method is described as a complex creativity strategy in which a team or group uses three specific thinking styles to turn a problem into an action. This model does not have to be complex. What matters is the way the exercise is set up, contracted and facilitated.

Useful when?

There are many barriers to the success of a change situation. This model can be used to analyse a problem, generate and evaluate ideas, and construct and critique a plan of action. This model has particular relevance when working with teams or groups to harness creative thinking around a problem or idea. This can trigger new thinking and actions. However, it could also be adapted to work with individuals.

Technique in action

The group or team is invited to look at a current and real problem from three different perspectives:

- **The dreamer** – vision, purpose, benefits, want, imagination, magic wand.
- **The realist** – logical action plan, making the dream real.
- **The critic** – judgements, barriers, critique, weak points, practicalities, relevance.

Each of the stages needs to be taken in the order of dreamer, realist, critic. This is because the idea needs to be formulated before a plan of action can take place and then the pros and cons to implementing the idea considered.

Possible questions to ask at each stage

The dreamer:

- What do we want?
- What is the purpose?
- What are the benefits?
- What will we see, feel and hear when we've got it?

- What is the solution?
- What are the options?
- What are the benefits of applying this solution?

The realist:

- How can we apply this idea in reality?
- What is the action plan to apply the ideas?
- What needs to happen to implement our ideas?
- What is the timeline?
- How do we evaluate this idea?
- Who is involved?

The critic:

- Why are we doing this?
- What could go wrong?
- What is missing?
- Why can't we apply our idea?
- What are the weaknesses in our plan?
- What is getting in the way of our idea?
- How realistic is this in the timeframe?
- What is necessary?

What next?

If working with a group or team, ideally there would be different rooms or a large enough room for groups to spread out and spend time in each stage. The aim is for the team or group to reach a solid creative idea with an action plan.

What could go wrong?

This depends on the team dynamics and how mature the team or group is when working together. There may be a disagreement of ideas that will need to be facilitated and managed by the change practitioner. In these situations it is useful to give feedback to the group or team on what you are observing:

- There seems to be a disagreement between you – are you OK with that?
- What is stopping you from coming to a consensus?

Technique 11: the Drama Triangle

Level 3: technique explained

The Drama Triangle is attributed to psychotherapist Dr Stephen Karpman and was originally designed in the 1960s. Although the model is typically used within therapy, the business world has picked up and used the model to help them make sense of the toxic relationship dynamics within organizations.

The model suggests three habitual psychological roles that people often take in difficult situations particularly when there is a breakdown in relationships. The model refers to the person who:

- Thinks and feels as if they are the Victim (Vulnerable).

- Pressures, coerces and blames the victim, and assumes the role of Persecutor (Powerful).

- Feels the need to intervene and help the situation and assumes the role of Rescuer (Responsible).

The model is always displayed as an inverted V with the role of Victim at the bottom of the V being pushed down by the Persecutor and the Rescuer. These roles are often subconscious causing the 'drama' to continue for a long time unless the three different 'actors' in the 'drama' are made aware of the roles. When this happens people either actively move outside of the 'drama' or they use the roles as a 'game play'. Stephen Karpman stated that once you become aware of the drama you have the choice and responsibility to move away from the 'drama'.

Figure 12.3   Karpman Drama Triangle

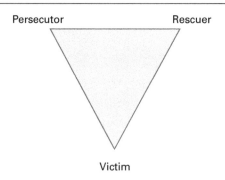

SOURCE Karpman, 2014

The Victim is closely aligned to the Persecutor. The Victim will blame the Persecutor for 'making' them feel the way they do. Paradoxically, when the Victim blames the Persecutor, the Victim is being a Persecutor themselves. The Victim will assume they are not responsible and feel helpless or power-less about the situation they are in. The Victim will be looking for a Rescuer to sort the problem out or to take the problem away.

The Persecutor can be a person, a situation or an event. This is the person who the Victim feels is causing them to feel the way they do. The Persecutor can display many negative behaviours including intimidation, aggression, manipulation, criticism and/or control.

The Rescuer is often perceived as a helpful role. In reality, the Rescuer is as toxic as Persecutor and Victim. The Rescuer is often either invited into the 'drama' or invites themselves in when they notice someone is not feeling or sounding OK about a situation. The Rescuer feels let down if they are not allowed to help the Victim. This does not empower the Victim to help them-selves. The Rescuer thinks they are helping by taking responsibility for the Victim, but the reverse is often the case.

The Rescuer will take on the Victim's problems and when the result is not what the Victim was hoping or expecting, the Victim can then turn on the Rescuer. The Rescuer then feels like the Victim with the Victim assuming the role of Persecutor. These roles are shifting all the time and each of these roles being acted out at any one time by the same person or within a relationship of two or more people.

Useful when?

This is useful in any change situation where negative behaviours and language is being noticed by others or by the change practitioner. These behaviours can and often do have a negative impact on the change initiative and create a barrier to the change process. Sharing this model will help the change practi-tioner support the stakeholder in making sense of where they are at and what is going on at a subconscious level. The ultimate aim is to have a conversa-tion which raises awareness in the stakeholder and the change initiative is a success.

Technique in action

This technique is unlikely to be used as a stand-alone model and is useful as part of a wider coaching conversation. The three situations in which the change practitioner can use the Drama Triangle technique are:

Self-coaching

If the change practitioner is perceiving themselves in one or more of these roles then they can identify which role(s) they are in and what has led them to be there. In terms of Persecutor, is it a person, situation or event which has led the change practitioner to have these feelings? Other questions to consider:

- What am I feeling right now?
- Where do I see myself in this model?
- Who is at fault here?
- What are 'they' doing that is causing me discomfort?
- What responsibility am I willing to take?
- What support do I need to move me out of this 'drama'?
- Who am I rescuing and why do I feel the need to do this?
- What is my responsibility in terms of this situation?
- What next?

These questions are relevant depending on where the change practitioner perceives themselves within the 'drama'. More questions will flow naturally once the change practitioner starts asking themselves questions. A more useful exercise is for the change practitioner to ask a trusted friend or colleague to 'coach' them using the questions.

Stakeholder coaching

The change practitioner could be in a conversation with a stakeholder and may notice the stakeholder using Victim type language around blame and a feeling of helplessness and being 'stuck' in the situation. The change practitioner can then ask the client if they would be willing to work through a model to help the stakeholder make sense of what is going on for them. If the model is not to hand then the change practitioner can ask the stakeholder to draw an inverted V on a piece of paper (adding a line on top of the V) and to write 'Victim' at the bottom of the V, 'Persecutor' top left and 'Rescuer' top right.

Without any more explanation of the model at this point, the change practitioner can ask the stakeholder where they feel they are with the current situation. They can allow the client to talk freely about what is going on for them and what thoughts and feelings they have about the change and/ or situation. Be willing to explain each of the roles if needed.

Guide the stakeholder through a conversation to enable them to recognize each of these toxic relationships and which one they relate to most. If the stakeholder relates with Victim then questions to help them take more responsibility for themselves in this situation will help the stakeholder to move forward, instead of being stuck in the 'blame game'. The change practitioner could ask similar questions to those given in 'self-coaching' by replacing 'I' with 'you'.

Team facilitation

This is a little more complex and requires careful contracts and agreements set up with the team at the start of, and throughout, the session.

The model could be introduced if the coach practitioner, as part of a team facilitation session, is noticing a heated discussion taking place and/or is hearing Victim and or Persecutor type language within the team. The change practitioner needs to be careful not to feel the need to 'Rescue' the team by intervening to calm thing down.

The role of the change practitioner in these situations is to remain calm, to observe the team dynamics, and to give feedback to the team on what is being noticed from the change practitioner's perspective.

At this point, the change practitioner could introduce the Drama Triangle to explain in generic terms what can happen during change and uncertainty. The aim is that the team are not *told* where they are at on the Drama Triangle but become aware of what is going on for themselves and how this impacts on the wider team.

This type of facilitation requires patience, confidence and experience on the part of the change practitioner to manage potential reactions and behaviours. If the team are in a mature place then this model can help guide a further conversation around what support is needed to get the team to where they need to be.

What next?

The Empowerment Dynamic® (TED)* is a useful model to use alongside the Drama Triangle (DT). TED* is the positive antidote to DT and can help the team (or stakeholder) move away from the problem to options and possibilities.

What could go wrong?

It is not advisable to suggest to someone that they are a Victim. This is coming from your own perception and not theirs. 'Victim' is often seen as a negative and it is more helpful for the stakeholder to come to their own conclusions, although there are some useful questions you can use to help raise awareness including:

- How would you notice a Victim role from their language and behaviours?
- Have you ever perceived yourself previously in this role?
- What might it feel like to be in the Victim role?

Use similar questions to raise awareness of the other two roles, Persecutor and Rescuer. If the client is not ready to talk about this model or there is a trust issue with the change practitioner or organization, then there may be resistance, a strong denial or acceptance. In this situation, the change practitioner should continue the conversation without using the Drama Triangle.

Technique 12: The Empowerment Dynamic

Level 3: Technique explained:

TED* was developed by David Emerald in the 1990s as a result of his own experience of working through the Drama Triangle with his therapist. Emerald wanted to provide positive alternatives to the toxic roles by reframing and seeing things from a more enabling position, described in his leadership fable, The Power of TED* (Emerald, 2016). TED* is known as 'the antidote' to the Drama Triangle and works best alongside the Drama Triangle. Each of the toxic roles has been reframed to more positive roles:

- Victim becomes Creator.
- Persecutor becomes Challenger.
- Rescuer becomes Coach.

The Creator focuses on the desired outcome. The Creator is rational and thoughtful and takes responsibility for the situation and for themselves.

The Challenger is the 'critical friend', the mentor, truth-teller and provocateur. The Challenger does not blame others and holds the Creator to account for their actions without criticism or shame. They provoke/evoke learning and growth and display compassion because such change is not always easy.

Figure 12.4   *The Empowerment Dynamic (TED*)

The **Coach** is curious, supportive and calm. They hold the Creator in positive regard. The Coach asks questions to help the Creator take responsibility, develop a vision and action plan.

Useful when?

The change practitioner is aiming to work with stakeholders and/or teams to move away from negative to more positive mindsets that are likely to have a more sustainable impact on the change initiative. This can raise awareness of habits and behaviours that may not be apparent by the stakeholder or team. It is also an antidote to the toxic Drama Triangle roles.

Technique in action

This technique is best used and makes more sense when used alongside the Drama Triangle as part of a wider coaching conversation. When using this model it is important to be aware of which of the toxic roles is being played out in the Drama Triangle, either personally or when working with others and making the shift from the toxic roles to the healthy TED* roles. Change practitioners can use this when:

Self-coaching:

If the change practitioner recognizes themselves as Victim, they can make the shift to Creator by:

- Changing the way they view themselves – the Creator is a positive role that takes responsibility for self.

- Being conscious of the roles they play and perceive themselves with others, for example is the change practitioner seen as the one who likes to blame others and complain?

- Noticing when they are complaining and asking the questions 'so, what do I want to have happen?'

- Staying focussed on the desired outcome and not on the problem.

- Deciding what they want and asking what needs to happen to get there.

If the change practitioner recognizes themselves as Persecutor, they can make a shift to Challenger by:

- Changing the way they view themselves. Challenger is a critical friend and is provocative in style but with a learning intent rather than needing to 'look good'. This is not about blaming others but being on their side with the aim of helping others to move forward.

- Changing the mode of communication. Less telling and commands and more suggesting and showing interest in others.

- Being aware of the purpose and skills of the Challenger instead of Persecutor.

- Being conscious of the roles the change practitioner plays and how they perceive themselves when with others, for example is the change practitioner seen as argumentative? How can they change this behaviour to one of supportive challenge?

- Remembering that no one has the control to change anyone else, only themselves.

- Encouraging feedback from others on how they, the change practitioner, is perceived by others. Is this a blind spot? or hidden because of shame, denial or embarrassment?

If the change practitioner recognizes themselves as Rescuer, they can make the shift to Coach by:

- Believing that those they perceive as Victim are capable of solving their own problems.

- Identifying the underlying need to rescue and solve other's problems. Awareness of self leads to choices and responsibility.

- Asking more questions to help others find their own solutions.

- Having a positive regard for the Creator: this includes not taking over.

- Believing that others are responsible for their own life choices.
- Not feeling responsible for others when it's not appropriate.
- Supporting the Creator to find their desired outcomes.

Stakeholder coaching

If the change practitioner is working with a stakeholder and has used the Drama Triangle, the flow of the conversation can easily turn to the alternative TED* model. If the TED* model is not to hand the change practitioner can ask the stakeholder to draw a triangle. Ask the client to write down Creator at the top of the triangle, Challenger bottom left and Coach, bottom right. The change practitioner may need to explain each of the roles but first allow the stakeholder to interpret them themselves. Guide the conversation by asking the client questions to help them reframe where they are now to where they want to be. If the client perceives themselves as the Persecutor then ask questions that relate to them being a Challenger. The questions set out for self-coaching could be a useful start, by replacing 'I' with 'you'.

Other useful questions to consider:

- What do you really want to achieve?
- What is stopping you from moving forward with this?
- What are you willing to accept and not accept?
- What would you be noticing about yourself as Creator and or Challenger?
- What language would you be using if you were Challenger? How would that sound to the other person?
- How different is this to Persecutor?
- What would your experience of moving from Persecutor to Challenger be like for you?
- What options do you have in this situation?
- What happens next?
- What have you learnt from this?

Team facilitation

Although TED* is potentially less complex than the Drama Triangle (DT), when working with a team, the change practitioner would still need to be patient, confident and experienced enough to work with the team dynamics and to field questions and concerns. If the Drama Triangle has been introduced the change practitioner can then introduce TED* as an alternative and ask the team what needs to happen for each of the toxic roles to be reframed to healthy TED* roles. This intervention is likely to create a more uplifting and positive conversation which can then lead on to actions and ways forward for the team.

What next?

The change practitioner continues with the coaching conversation. There may be some discussion around the role of the Challenger and how to avoid sounding like the Persecutor, particularly if the Challenger is the 'provocateur'. The change practitioner can explain that it is all in the 'intent' of the message and the tone of voice. If the Challenger is coming from a place of positive regard for the Creator then the tone of voice is likely to sound curious, not critical. This would be a good opportunity for the change practitioner to set up a quick exercise to test this out in pairs or small groups.

- Ask everyone to pair up – Person A and Person B.
- Person A to listen to Person B talk about a challenge at work.
- Person A to respond to B in the Persecutor role (critical, controlling, undermining, sarcastic) and see the reaction.
- Person A to then respond to B in Challenger role (interested, critical friend, provocative, adviser) and notice the change.
- Debrief in pairs and swap over so that A is now B and vice versa.

Open up a discussion asking the following questions:

- What was it like being talked to by the Persecutor and Challenger?
- What was it like being the Persecutor and Challenger?
- What was different?
- How did the two different roles sound?
- What language was used for each role?

Debrief the exercise and continue with testing out the Drama Triangle and TED* roles.

When stakeholder coaching, this same exercise can be set up as a role play with each other.

What could go wrong?

If the stakeholder or team does not want to move on from discussions around the Drama Triangle then using TED* could be a challenge.

Technique 13: Perceptual Positions

Level 3 – Technique explained:

The concept of Perceptual Positions was originally formulated by John Grinder and Judith DeLozir in *Turtles All the Way Down* (1987). Robert Dilts expanded and referenced this model in many of his books, the earliest being *Changing Belief Systems with NLP* (1990). This is a popular model with coaches to support their clients in raising social awareness and empathy. Coaches generally use this model when there is a breakdown in relationships and where the client is unable or unwilling to see things from another person's perspective.

There are three positions:

- First position is the individual you are working with (the stakeholder).
- Second position is the person with whom the stakeholder has an issue.
- Third position is the fly on the wall, the impartial observer.

Useful when?

During organizational change, relationships often break down and what was originally a minor irritation can soon turn into a conflict or disagreement between two or more people. Each person wants to be right and wants to be heard and understood. This exercise can help change practitioners guide the stakeholder into a new or alternative way of thinking and to see the situation from a different perspective. This exercise would be used as part of a wider coaching conversation and not as a stand-alone exercise.

Technique in action

Set the scene. Explain that there is a purpose to this exercise and that coaching is all about stepping into a stretch zone. Encourage and support by saying, 'just give it a go'. The stakeholder is likely to thank the change practitioner once they have completed the exercise as there is so much to gain from it. Interestingly, the change practitioner can also learn a lot from this exercise as things are often said in this exchange which the stakeholder may not say in a conversation.

Position 1 – self: The change practitioner asks the stakeholder to sit opposite another chair and to imagine that the person they have an issue with is sitting in that chair (eg Freda). The stakeholder is asked to talk to Freda as if she is sitting in the chair and to express their thoughts, feelings, experiences and problems with Freda. The change practitioner encourages the stakeholder to add more to what they want to say and to be honest. While this is happening the change practitioner is standing out of the stakeholder's sight and listens to what is being said.

The change practitioner asks the stakeholder to stand up and to shake themselves out of Position 1 and walk around the room until they are ready to take up position 2.

Position 2 – other person: When the stakeholder is ready they are asked to sit in the Position 2 chair, where Freda was sitting. The stakeholder is asked to imagine they are now Freda. The change practitioner works closely with the stakeholder to make sure they are ready to take the second chair and see themselves as Freda. The stakeholder is asked to talk like Freda, act like Freda and be Freda as far as possible. The change practitioner asks the stakeholder to respond to what they have just heard, as Freda. The change practitioner stays out of the way while the client is talking. The change practitioner listens carefully to what is being said and observes the stakeholder's body language, encouraging them to say as much as they can in response.

The change practitioner asks the client to stand up again and shake themselves out and change their state by walking around the room.

Position 3: The change practitioner asks the stakeholder to stand in a place in the room where they can detach themselves from these two people. This is usually carried out standing up. In this third position, the stakeholder is now the 'fly on the wall' and the impartial observer. What has the fly noticed about how these two people are interacting? What advice would the fly give to each of these people to resolve the matter?

When ready, the change practitioner asks the stakeholder to sit down in the Position 1 chair and to ask what new insight they have into this problem. This is where the magic happens. The client can usually, suddenly see things from the other person's perspective (in this case, Freda) and then work through what they can do to work towards a solution.

Adaptations

If there is not enough room or chairs, this exercise can be carried out just by asking the stakeholder to think from each of these different perspectives whilst they are sitting in the same chair. It is not quite so powerful and it is often difficult to see things from another person's point of view if they are sitting and talking from Position 1, but it can be a quick way to get the same points across and to help with empathy and understanding.

Example questions:

- What would you like to say to this person if they were in the room?
- How do you think they would respond to this?
- How would you respond?
- If you were them, what would you be thinking about you?
- What assumptions are you making about this person?
- How can you check that your assumptions are true, or not?

Other 'provocative' question might include:

- So, there seems to be a disagreement here and you both think you are right?
- Given that you can't control the other person, what are you willing to change or accept for this to be a good outcome for you?
- Imagine there was a fly on the wall listening to all of this, what would the fly be thinking of you both right now?
- What advice do you think the fly would give to you both?
- What new insights do you have now?

What could go wrong?

The stakeholder needs to trust the change practitioner and the process. The stakeholder needs to know that there is good intent behind being taken outside of their comfort zone. They may not at first understand the purpose of the exercise and could feel embarrassed talking to an empty chair and then being asked to respond as if they, the stakeholder, was this other person. Stay with it! It is a very worthwhile exercise.

Conclusion

This chapter offers readers a variety of tried and tested tools and techniques to support the coaching process. For some people, being coached can feel uncomfortable and challenging particularly when asked questions for the first time. These tools and techniques offer the chance to enhance the coaching conversation, to take the emphasis away from the change practitioner and to engage the stakeholder or client to think in a different way with the help of a visual model or technique.

References

Bridges, W (2017) *Managing Transitions: Making the most of change*, Nicholas Brealey, London, Boston

Covey, S (2020) *The 7 Habits of Highly Effective People*, Simon & Schuster, London

Dilts R (1990) *Changing Belief Systems with NLP*, Meta Publications, Capitola, CA

Dilts, R (1995) *Strategies of Genius Vol I*, Dilts Strategy Group, California

Dilts, R and Epstein, T (1991) *Tools for Dreamers: Strategies for creativity and the structure of innovation*, Meta Publications, Capitola, CA

Emerald, D (2016) *The Power of TED* – *The Empowerment Dynamic*, Polaris Publishing, Bainbridge Island

Grinder J and DeLozir J, (1987) *Turtles All the Way Down*, Grinder DeLozier Associates. USA

James, T and Woodsmall, W (2017) *Time Line Therapy and the Basis of Personality*, Crown House Publishing, UK and USA

Karpman, S (1960) *A Game Free Life*, Drama Triangle Publications, San Francisco

Lee, G (2007) *Leadership Coaching: From personal insight to organisational performance*, CIPD, London

Luft, J (1969) Of Human Interaction: The Johari model, Palo Alto, California

Thompson, N and Thompson, S (2008) *The Critically Reflective Practitioner*, Palgrave Macmillan, Basingstoke and New York

APPENDIX A: STAGES OF EMERGE

How and why to use them

To fully embrace using EMERGE as a coaching model it's important to understand not only what each stage aims to do but also why it is important to address each of the stages. The model is not intended to be used in a strict regimented way but to think about which stage is most appropriate to focus on once the conversation gets underway.

However, experience shows that to optimize a coaching conversation it is best to start with **Expectations** and end with **Evaluate**. During the conversation it is acceptable to move around the model until the conversation comes to a natural end or time has run out.

Using EMERGE during a coaching conversation

Table A1 demonstrates how the EMERGE model can work during a coaching conversation between a change practitioner and a manager within the organization. There are two examples: the first is a positive conversation and the second starts off as being negative but the change practitioner, by keeping calm and on track, manages to turn the conversation around.

The change practitioner is not a trained coach and is using a coaching style and approach to help the manager to recognize the importance of a restructure for their team. The change practitioner has used the previously outlined REST Framework to plan and prepare herself for the session and is now using EMERGE to help structure the session.

We pick up the conversation at the Expectations stage after the contracting has taken place. The manager understands the importance of the meeting, has some concerns about the team and is ready to engage in the meeting. (This is an abridged version of the conversation.)

Table A1 EMERGE what and why

Stage	What it aims to do	Why it's important
Expectations	Contracting, agreeing the session, setting the scene. What are our roles and responsibilities? Goals: What are the overall goals? (long term) and goal for the session (short term).	Contracting and agreeing the session ensures the expectations are spoken and agreed and allows the option of referring back if the conversation goes off track. Goals: Without a clear idea of where the individual wants to get to it is difficult to know what the best questions are to help to get them there. Asking what the individual wants to get by the end of the session will help you to steer the conversation to a successful outcome.
Motivation & energy	What is driving the want and need to change? Is this an intrinsic or extrinsic motivation? On a scale of 10 (10 = high) what is the level of motivation to change the current situation? What is energizing the client to want to do something different? What may affect the energy to change?	As humans we are driven by emotions that drive our motivation. If there is no 'appetite' to change then it's unlikely to happen. Finding an internal motivation is more sustainable and is likely to encourage the individual to change. Once the motivation has been established, the energy to achieve the desired outcome is the next step. What are the individual's skills and strengths that will ensure there is enough drive and energy to ensure success?
Explore	What has already been achieved about this issue or goal? What has worked well? And not so well? What are the blocks and barriers to success?	It is important to understand if and what the individual has done already to achieve their goal. This stage can take time to gain clarity and what might have got in the way (self or others) to prevent the goal being achieved.

(continued)

Table A1 (Continued)

Stage	What it aims to do	Why it's important
Review and reflect	Following exploration, what else could be done to reach the goal? What new insights have you gained thus far?	Reviewing and reflecting is an essential part of any communication and change process. It is essential that the individual reflects on what new insights can be learnt at this stage before they look at options.
Generate	Ideas for options and choices. What feels right? What are the pros and cons? What would happen if you did or didn't do anything?	Generating options is essential to help the individual to understand their choices and the pros and cons to these choices. At this stage you may need to return to Explore or even Motivation and Energy. For some people the goal can also change at the Generate stage.
Evaluate	Actions and way forward. Summarize the session from the client's perspective and new insights that have emerged during session. Give feedback and ask for feedback.	Even with a short session you should not end the session until you have evaluated and summarized the session and agreed what actions the individual is going to take once they have left the meeting and/or if you have a future meeting.

Conversations using EMERGE – positive response

Expectations: goal

Change Practitioner (CP): In terms of our conversation today about the restructure and your team, what would be a good outcome for you today?

Manager (M): I'd like to talk through some of my concerns about the proposed restructure and how this may affect me and my team.

CP: What are your main concerns about the restructure?

M: That the decision has been rushed through, my team will be separated and some people will lose their jobs.

CP: And what about you, what are your concerns about how this leaves you?

M: I am concerned about my own job too. I don't agree with the decisions made and it doesn't make sense to me.

CP: I sense that you are quite resistant to the changes. How might this affect your ability to make the right decisions for the organization and your team?

M: I am a bit fed up with it all and the team keep asking me questions which I can't answer. I'm finding myself joining in with the negative talk which I know is not helpful.

CP: Sadly, the restructure needs to go ahead for financial reasons and I do appreciate your concerns. It's not a good time for people at the moment. If you had a choice, what would be a good outcome for you in terms of the restructure?

M: I would be happier knowing some more information which I can tell the team. I would be happier knowing that my team's jobs were protected.

Motivation and energy

CP: The things you mentioned were external motivations. What would be an internal motivation for you?

M: If I could feel good about the whole process which I know is not always practical or possible but some sense of doing a good job for my team would be a motivator for me.

CP: How much energy do you have to work with me on this to help you to get the ideal outcome, as far as possible, for you and your team?

M: I am very energized if I know I have the support from you and senior managers to help make this all work. I need to know I am not doing this on my own.

Explore

CP: These are difficult times at the moment. What have you done already to support yourself and your team?

M: I have been meeting with my team regularly to check in with them and their well-being. I have been speaking with my peers about how they are managing the changes and generally keeping as positive as I can in the circumstances.

CP: I am pleased to hear that you have been meeting with your team and you know that I am always here as a listening ear. What has been going well and what have your challenges been?

M: The challenges have been what we have already talked about and the uncertainty of the future.

Review and reflect

CP: Shall we reflect on where you are at and review what new insights you have?

M: To summarize, it's a tough time at the moment. Morale is low. I am doing as much as I can to keep motivation going. I know that you are there for support as well as my manager. New insights? Well, I guess we are all in this together and I could speak with my peers to offer them support as well.

Generate ideas

CP: OK, so, given the stage we are at now, what options do you have to maintain a good level of morale in your team and to ensure the deadlines will be met as discussed?

M: I could set up a team outing to have a bit of fun. I could meet up with Josh in Finance to go through the figures as I've avoided this up to now. I could set up another meeting with you in a four weeks to talk through my progress. That will encourage me to keep to the timescales.

Evaluate

CP: That all sounds positive and possible. Shall we set some dates against these ideas? What will you do first and then what?

M: Meeting with Josh, week 1 of July; Team outing, week 3 of July; Meeting with you, week 4 of July.

CP: That's great. So, what has been helpful about this meeting? Do you have any new insights?

M: Thank you for suggesting the meeting, it's been good to talk things through. I just had a lot of thoughts going around my head before. What I realize now is that I am not alone in how I feel and I could do with speaking with my peers more to be a support to them.

Conversations like these give people the chance to off-load and think out loud with someone who is a good listener and can help formulate views from a different perspective.

Not all conversations are so positive and the following example shows how the conversation may have happened with a more resistant person and how the change practitioner may have handled the difficult conversation.

Conversation using EMERGE – negative response

Expectations – goal

CP: In terms of our conversation today about the restructure and your team, what would be a good outcome for you today?

M: I have no idea. I can't see the point of this meeting and I'm busy.

CP: I appreciate you finding the time to meet. This meeting is to help me understand how I can support you with the restructure. What are your main concerns about the decision?

M: I don't agree with the decision. We have been working well up until now. Why change what isn't broken? The decision has been rushed through and some people will lose their jobs. How does that make me look?

CP: And what else? What are your other concerns about how this leaves you?

M: Well naturally I am concerned about my own job too. I don't want the team to hate me. I bet they think it's my fault. It doesn't make sense to me.

CP: From what you say you seem quite resistant to the changes. How might this affect your ability to make the right decisions for the organization and your team?

M: I am a bit fed up with it all and the team keep asking me questions which I can't answer. I'm finding myself joining in with the negative talk, well, wouldn't you?

CP: Sadly, the restructure needs to go ahead for financial reasons and I do appreciate your concerns. It's not a good time for people at the moment. Thinking realistically about the options, if you had a choice, what would be a good outcome for you in terms of the restructure?

M: For it to all go away. For us to go back to how it was. I know you are going to say this is not possible. I don't know, maybe that you give us more time to think about the changes and give people more time to decide what to do.

Motivation and energy

CP: What would motivate you to work with our team on making this restructure successful?

M: Nothing. I am not motivated at all to want to make this work. There is no point in trying to make me either.

CP: It sounds like your energy is low at the moment and you are not energized to make this work at the moment. Do you need more time?

M: Yes, I do need more time but I don't know how much time. It will take a lot for me to agree to this.

Explore

This stage would be difficult to manage due to the low motivation of the individual. Questions are likely to get a negative response. The change practitioner may decide to leave this until another time.

Review and reflect

CP: You can always contact me if you have any questions or concerns. I am hoping that meeting up like this has been helpful if only for you to off-load and express your concerns. Is there anything which has been going well since you heard the news?

M: The team is working well except for Sam who is very negative. That's about it.

Generate ideas

CP: OK, so, given the stage we are at now, what options can you think of which will help you to move forward mentally and physically with ideas and suggestions?

M: I don't know. I need more time to think. I am feeling fed up at the moment so this is not good timing.

Review and reflect

CP: So, you need more time but how helpful is this mindset for you and your team? Is the team seeing you in this mood?

M: I'm OK back in the office. I don't let them see me this way. I don't often get the chance to off-load outside of the office and I don't like taking my troubles home.

Motivate

CP: OK, that is understandable and I am happy to be a listening ear. Is there anything which might motivate you to move from resistance to acceptance?

M: Now that I have calmed down a bit, I guess what would motivate me is to have some time off work to rest as I am exhausted. I am sure that I will return after a few days a bit more refreshed and the time off will give me a chance to think about things.

Generate

CP: What options do you have in terms of that?

M: I will speak with my manager and I will ask the rest of the team if they would like to schedule any time off once I am back.

Evaluate

CP: That's great. So, what has been helpful about this meeting? Do you have any new insights?

M: I am sorry I was a bit negative to start. I do feel a bit wound up about it all. It has helped to talk with you, thank you.

The above is an example of how the EMERGE model can be used flexibly and systemically and allows the change practitioner to move back and forth within the model to enable an outcome which ends positively: **Expectations > Motivation > Explore > Review and Reflect > Generate > Review and Reflect > Motivate > Generate > Evaluate.**

APPENDIX B: A FRAMEWORK FOR COACHING CONVERSATIONS

Guiding principles, core values and essential skills

The following core values and essential skills have been adapted from the three leading membership organizations dedicated to coaching and mentoring (EMCC, AC, ICF). These form the basis of the core values that enable a conversation to be on an adult-to-adult basis and will reduce the chances of resistance or defensiveness. Table B1 explains what each of the competencies means in practice.

Table B1 Certification for coaches

Rapport and being present	Relationship engagement. Being truly in the space with positive regard for the person you are with. Awareness of self and your thoughts, feelings and actions. Being fully in the room with no other distractions. Sitting in a way that demonstrates rapport and an interest in the other person. Openness and willingness to find interest and be curious. Get to know the person better.
Empathy	Step into their world. See things from their perspective. Understand as far as you can how things must be for them. Empathize, don't sympathize. Acknowledge what is going on for them. Don't try to rescue or make things better.
Set the scene	This is a two-way agreement as to the purpose of the meeting, what you both want to get from the meeting and what you are both responsible for. This is essential if you have someone who is resistant to having the meeting and may not engage in the conversation. The meeting can only go ahead if there is a dialogue and acceptance of the meeting.

(continued)

Table B1   (Continued)

Stay on track	It is easy to get 'hooked' into a conversation you didn't intend on having. Strong opinions and judgements may cloud your thoughts and what you have to say. Suspending judgements and opinions will help you to stay on track.
Listen with interest and intent	Are you listening or just waiting to speak? What else is going on in your head as you are listening to the other person? How many questions are you thinking of before the person has finished speaking? Really listen to what they are saying – picking up on the words spoken, the tone of voice and the emotional message behind the words. Listen to what is not being said as much as what is said.
Summarize what you have heard	A good way to show that you are listening is to summarize the conversation in short extracts. This gives you a chance to gain understanding and clarity, and is a good opportunity for the person you are with to clarify if you have understood the message. Once you have summarized this then often leads on to an incisive question.
Question incisively and curiously	Ask questions from a place of curiosity not judgement. Consider what response you are wanting from your question. Ask questions that move the person to a goal or ideal outcome. Don't dwell on problems or blame.
Silence is your friend	Relax and pace your meeting so that it does not feel like an interrogation. Silence is used to help with reflection and the thought process. Take a deep breath and count to three before asking the next question. Give the person you are with a chance to think about your question before you ask another.
Advise with caution	An eagerness of giving advice and suggestions is not as helpful as it is intended. Ask questions first to gain understanding and to test the thinking of the client. The best person to come up with ideas is the person with the problem or issue. Only give advice when they are truly stuck.

APPENDIX C: TECHNIQUES TO COACH PEOPLE THROUGH CHANGE MATRIX

Level 1

Table C1 Level 1

T = Technique L = Level of technique	T1 L1	T2 L1	T3 L1	T4 L1	T5 L1
	A Walk in the Park	CIA Control Influence Accept	Circle of Concern and Influence	Time Line	AIR your Feedback
Setting clear goals	✓				
Feeling stuck and frustrated		✓	✓		
Feeling out of control		✓	✓		
Building confidence	✓			✓	
Developing a skill or mindset				✓	
Visualizing the future				✓	
Relationship issues					
Raising awareness and empathy					✓

(continued)

Table C1   (Continued)

T = Technique L = Level of technique	T1 L1	T2 L1	T3 L1	T4 L1	T5 L1
	A Walk in the Park	CIA Control Influence Accept	Circle of Concern and Influence	Time Line	AIR your Feedback
Giving difficult feedback and raising a concern					✓
Resistance to change					
Resistance to being coached					
Turn a problem into action					
Overcoming barriers to change					
Creative ideas for change					
Moving forward					
Communication blind spots					

Level 2

Table C2   Level 2

T = Technique L = Level of technique	T7 L2	T8 L2	T9 L2	T10 L2
	Logical Levels	The Change Cycle	Bridges' Transition Model	Johari Window
Setting clear goals				
Feeling stuck and frustrated	✓	✓	✓	
Feeling out of control	✓	✓		
Building confidence				
Developing a skill or mindset	✓	✓		
Visualizing the future	✓			
Relationship issues				
Raising awareness and empathy				
Giving difficult feedback and raising a concern				✓
Resistance to change	✓	✓	✓	✓
Resistance to being coached				
Turn a problem into action		✓		
Overcoming barriers to change		✓	✓	✓
Creative ideas for change				
Moving forward		✓	✓	
Communication blind spots				✓

Level 3

Table C3   Level 3

T = Technique L = Level of technique	T11 L3 The Disney Method	T12 L3 The Drama Triangle	T13 L3 The Empowerment Dynamic	T14 L3 Perceptual Positions
Setting clear goals	✓			
Feeling stuck and frustrated		✓		✓
Feeling out of control		✓	✓	
Building confidence			✓	
Developing a skill or mindset		✓	✓	
Visualizing the future			✓	
Relationship issues		✓	✓	✓
Raising awareness and empathy		✓		✓
Giving difficult feedback and raising a concern				
Resistance to change		✓		
Resistance to being coached				
Turn a problem into action	✓			✓
Overcoming barriers to change	✓	✓	✓	✓
Creative ideas for change	✓			✓
Moving forward			✓	✓
Communication blind spots				

APPENDIX D: CHANGE CERTIFICATION

Discipline	Certification	Levels	Issuing body
Change Management	Agile Change Agent	Practitioner	APMG International™
	CHAMPS2® Business Change	Certificate	
	Certified Local Change Agent	Certificate	
	Accredited Change Manager	Foundation Specialist Master	APMG International™ in partnership with Change Management Institute
	Change Analyst	Foundation Plus	APMG International™
	Prosci®	• Virtual Change Management Certification Model • Enterprise Change Management Boot Camp • Integrating Agile & Change Management • Leading your team through change • Taking charge of change • Advanced immersion workshop • Experienced practitioner programme	Prosci®

(continued)

(Continued)

Discipline	Certification	Levels	Issuing body
Portfolio management	P3M3®	Foundation Practitioner	AXELOS
	MoP®	Foundation Practitioner	
Project Management	PRINCE2®	Foundation Practitioner	AXELOS
	PRINCE2 Agile®	Foundation Practitioner	
	Agile Project Management (AgilePM®)	Foundation Practitioner	APMG International™
	AgileSHIFT®	Certificate	
	Agile Business Consortium Scrum Master	Foundation	
	Managing Benefits™	Foundation Practitioner	
Project & programme management	British Computer Society	Essentials Foundation Practitioner	BCS
Programme Management	Managing Successful Programmes (MSP®)	Foundation Practitioner Advanced Practitioner	AXELOS
	Agile Programme Management (AgilePgM®)	Foundation	APMG International™
	Integrated Program Performance Management (IPPM™)	Foundation	

Discipline	Certification	Levels	Issuing body
Process Analysis	Lean Six Sigma	Yellow belt Orange belt Green belt Black belt	APMG International™
Business Analysis	Certified Agile Business Analyst Professional (CABAP)	Certificate	APMG International™
	AgileBA®	Foundation Practitioner	
	Agile Business Analysis In A Scrum Environment	Foundation	
	British Computer Society	Certificate Practitioner Professional Consultant Expert Diploma	BCS
PMO	P3O® Project Office	Foundation Practitioner	AXELOS

Note – course offerings change frequently. Please check with the issuing body for the most up-to-date certification.

www.apmg-international.com/services/accreditation

www.change-management-institute.com/accreditation

www.axelos.com/certifications

www.prosci.com/solutions/training-programs

www.bcs.org/certifications/ba

APPENDIX E: COACHING CERTIFICATION

Choosing the right coaching and mentoring qualification course can be daunting as there is a vast selection of providers who offer different things. What we aim to do in this section is to demystify the academic terminology and offer guidance on the pros and cons of each 'certification' to inform the best choice.

Only the most relevant and most popular options have been offered although an internet search will reveal more choice. Research carefully and find out what exactly is on offer and what the final certification or accreditation is.

Beware of 'wolves in sheep's clothing'

When considering whether to undertake a qualification or not, be sure to know what you are entering into. Some training providers are not fully approved to deliver full qualifications but are approved to deliver 'endorsed' programmes. You may see an ILM 'approved' coaching and mentoring course but this is unlikely to be or have the same credibility as a full qualification.

In the case of ILM make sure that the training provider has a logo which states 'ILM Approved Centre' and not 'ILM Recognised provider'. If the training provided does not state a particular qualification level (for example levels 2 to 7) then it is unlikely to be a full qualification.

In the case of CMI, if the training is called a 'development programme', this is unlikely to be a full qualification. Only choose a qualification which clearly states the right level of qualification commensurate with your level of job.

Understanding the different levels

As part of the Regulated Qualification Framework (RQF), all qualifications are divided in to 8 levels of complexity or difficulty. Each of the 8 levels will have a selection of units with each unit having a credit value (where one credit represents 10 hours of learning time). There are three different sizes of qualification within each of the levels:

- Award (1 to 12 credits)
- Certificate (13 to 36 credits)
- Diploma (37 credits or more).

What does this mean for Change Professionals?

Anyone within a change management role or profession and looking to increase their professional development with a coaching qualification would be wise to choose either a Level 5 or Level 7 (there is currently no level 6). Level 5 offers a practical and experiential learning experience where the full skills of coaching individuals and teams are learnt in a rigorous and structured way. Level 7 is aimed at those who will be embedding coaching and mentoring within the organisation. Level 7 learners will be more experienced in coaching or may be using coaching regularly within their day to day role. Level 7 is less practical and more strategic in its approach.

The difference between a Qualification, Certification and Accreditation

Qualification…is an academic examination or an official completion of a course from a recognised awarding body which is regulated by Ofqual, the authority which regulates and accredits British examination boards offering qualifications. Ofqual sets the rules and guidance on qualifications which all awarding organisations have to follow. Two such awarding organisations are Institute of Leadership and Management (ILM) and Chartered Management Institute (CMI). Both ILM and CMI provide management and leadership, coaching and mentoring qualifications which are recognised within the business world and include management coaching and mentoring as part of their suite of qualifications. In July 2022 CMI began offering a Level 5 Professional Coach qualification.

Accreditation…is an official approval given by an organization stating that the learner has achieved a required standard. Accreditations are not full qualifications and are offered out as a recognition of standards for achieving a programme of learning from professional standards membership organizations. Globally, there are three of these organisations dedicated to coaching and mentoring:

- International Coaching Federation (ICF)
- Association for Coaching (AC)
- European Mentoring and Coaching Council (EMCC).

These three professional standards organizations have a common aim of raising the standards of professional coaching and mentoring. Learners can then update and upgrade their professional development by completing an Accreditation through one of these three leading coaching and mentoring membership organisations. Each has developed a competency framework for coaching and mentoring and has a Global Code of Ethics which coaching professionals can choose to adhere to. As neither coaching or mentoring is a regulated profession (in the way that Psychotherapy is) then there is no official requirement to complete either a qualification or an accreditation. However, most coaching practitioners with their own coaching practice are likely to be both qualified and be a member of one of these membership bodies. Most coaching practitioners will also have their own coaching supervisor and or be part of a coaching supervision group.

Who delivers qualifications and accreditations?

A search on the internet will reveal the numerous independent providers, universities and colleges who provide full qualifications programmes through ILM and CMI. All training providers are registered, approved and verified by the awarding body and will be monitored yearly in terms of their standards and application of the qualification to ensure standards are maintained and adhere to the strict rules of the Ofqual regulations. A list of recognised and approved providers can be found on each of the awarding body websites.

In terms of accredited programmes, these are likely to be delivered by independent providers who have been through a rigorous process to have their coaching and mentoring training programmes accredited with either EMCC, AC or ICF. A list of registered and approved training providers can be found on each of the affiliated coaching organisation website.

The following tables offers an overview of the levels of coaching and mentoring qualification programmes and who they are aimed at.

Awarding Body	Levels	Qualification achieved	Aimed at
CMI	5 Award Certificate Diploma	Management coaching and mentoring	Middle and senior managers aiming to use coaching on a day to day basis or as an internal coach. A practical programme with opportunity for coaching practice and supervision.
CMI	7 Award Certificate Diploma	Leadership coaching and mentoring	Senior and executive managers and anyone with a responsibility of embedding coaching and mentoring within the organisation. A strategic qualification with no requirement to coach others.
ILM	5 Certificate Diploma	Management coaching	Middle and senior managers aiming to use coaching on a day to day basis or as an internal coach. A practical programme with opportunity for coaching practice and supervision
ILM	7 Certificate Diploma	Executive coaching	Primarily aimed at external coach practitioners but can also be undertaken by internal coaches and senior managers. Coaching practice at an executive level is expected to pass this qualification.

EMCC, AC and ICF, coaching and mentoring training programmes will differ in terms of content, structure and the assessment process. There is more flexibility with accredited programmes for the training provider to design a course which is not restricted by the requirements of the awarding body such as with ILM and CMI. All providers who deliver coach and mentoring accredited training will have had their programme verified and approved by the professional standards body they have chosen.

International Coaching Federation - www.coachfederation.org

European Mentoring and Coaching Council - www.emccuk.org

Association for coaching - www.associationforcoaching.com/page/membersearch

INDEX

Note: Page numbers in *italics* refer to figures